T0330179

Industrial Relations in the New Europe

Industrial Relations in the New Europe

Enlargement, Integration and Reform

Edited by

Peter Leisink

Professor of Public Management and Organization Studies, Utrecht University, the Netherlands

Bram Steijn

Professor of Human Resource Management in the Public Sector, Erasmus University Rotterdam, the Netherlands

Ulke Veersma

Senior Lecturer in International HRM, University of Greenwich Business School, London, United Kingdom

Edward Elgar
Cheltenham, UK • Northampton, MA, USA

Published by
Edward Elgar Publishing Limited
Glensanda House
Montpellier Parade
Cheltenham
Glos GL50 1UA
UK

Edward Elgar Publishing, Inc.
William Pratt House
9 Dewey Court
Northampton
Massachusetts 01060
USA

A catalogue record for this book
is available from the British Library

Library of Congress Cataloguing in Publication Data

Industrial relations in the new Europe : enlargement, integration, and reform / edited by Peter Leisink, Bram Steijn, and Ulke Veersma.
    p. cm.
  Includes bibliographical references and index.
1. Industrial relations—European Union countries. I. Leisink, Peter, 1952– II. Steijn, Abraham Jan, 1959– III. Veersma, Ulke.
  HD8376.5.I546 2007
  331.094-dc22

                              2006033810

ISBN 978 1 84542 614 9
Printed and bound by MPG Books Ltd, Bodmin, Cornwall

Contents

Figures

Tables

Contributors

Paul Dennison is Principal Lecturer Business Analysis at the University of Greenwich Business School, London, UK.

Heiner Dribbusch is a researcher at the Wirtschafts- and Sozialwissenschaftliches Institut (WSI) of the Hans Böckler Foundation, Düsseldorf, Germany.

David Farnham is Emeritus Professor of Employment Relations at the Portsmouth University Business School and Visiting Professor at the University of Greenwich Business School, London, UK.

Sergio Gonzalez Begega is PhD Research Fellow at the Department of Applied Economics, University of Oviedo, Spain.

Sylvia Horton is Principal Lecturer in Public Sector Studies, School of Social and Historical Studies, University of Portsmouth, UK.

Holm-Detlev Köhler is Professor of Sociology at the Department of Applied Economics, University of Oviedo, Spain.

Peter Leisink is Professor of Public Management and Organization Studies at the Utrecht School of Governance, Utrecht University, the Netherlands.

Miguel Martínez Lucio is Professor at the Bradford School of Management, University of Bradford, UK.

Olivier Mériaux is researcher at the Institute of Political Studies, Grenoble, France.

László Neumann works at the National Employment Office Research Unit, Budapest, Hungary.

Christophe Pelgrims is researcher at the Public Management Institute of the Catholic University Leuven, Belgium.

Thorsten Schulten is researcher at the Wirtschafts- and Sozialwissenschaftliches Institut (WSI) of the Hans Böckler Foundation, Düsseldorf, Germany.

Miroslav Stanojevic is Professor of Industrial Relations in the Faculty of Social Sciences, University of Llubljana, Slovenia.

Trui Steen is Assistant Professor at the Department of Public Administration, Leiden University, The Netherlands.

Bram Steijn is Professor at the Department of Public Management, Erasmus University, Rotterdam, the Netherlands.

Mark Stuart is Professor of Employment Relations at the Leeds University Business School, Leeds, UK.

Nick Thijs is researcher at the Public Management Institute of the Catholic University Leuven, Belgium.

Erin van der Maas works at the Department of Industrial Relations, London School of Economics, London, UK.

Daniel Vaughan-Whitehead has worked for the International Labour Office since 1991, first in Budapest and currently in Geneva. From 1999 to 2003 he worked at the European Commission where he was in charge of social dialogue in the EU enlargement process.

Ulke Veersma is Senior Lecturer International HRM at the University of Greenwich Business School, London, UK.

Urban Vehovar is Assistant Professor of Sociology of Education, University of Primorska, Slovenia.

Kees Vos was senior adviser at the Ministry of Social Affairs and Employment, the Hague, the Netherlands.

Geoff White is Professor at the University of Greenwich Business School, London, UK.

Preface

The IREC network was set up on Richard Hyman's initiative following the first Industrial Relations in Europe Conference (IREC) at the University of Warwick in 1989. Since then, the IREC network has provided a platform for the exchange of ideas and critical debates on work and employment from a European perspective.

The Utrecht School of Governance based at Utrecht University had the pleasure to host the 2004 IREC. The School's interest in governance issues provided an obvious focus when choosing the conference theme: 'Governance issues in shifting European industrial and employment relations'. However, it was not just the Utrecht School of Governance's interest that inspired the conference theme: in 2001, the European Commission had published a White Paper on 'European Governance' recognizing that social dialogue forms part of the democratic governance of Europe and that social dialogue is crucial in responding adequately to the challenges of economic and social reform and of enlargement. Indeed, the enlargement of the European Union, as of 1 May 2004, led to the accession of ten new Member States, with eight of these originating from Central and Eastern Europe. With this enlargement, the diversity within the European Union increased significantly, particularly in terms of employment conditions and social dialogue arrangements. The enlargement spurred European political interest in governance and in the so-called Open Method of Co-ordination as a means to deal with this increase in diversity. A parallel surge in research interest in governance issues can be observed. As a result, IREC 2004 at the Utrecht School of Governance welcomed more than a hundred researchers from 20 different countries, including many from the new Central and Eastern European Member States. Several of the chapters included in this publication, 'Industrial Relations in the New Europe: Enlargement, Integration and Reform', have been developed from presentations at the conference workshops, and others have been specially commissioned.

The success of the conference and the preparation of this book have been made possible by the active support of a great number of enthusiastic supporters, of whom we would like to especially thank Kees Vos and Wim Kool of the Netherlands Participation Institute and David Foden of the European Foundation in Dublin who helped in providing financial support enabling researchers from Central and Eastern European Member States to participate in the conference, and the Utrecht School of Governance for providing financial and administrative support for the conference. Bas de Wit did a great job running the conference secretariat. Edward Elgar supported the conference by indicating their early interest in publishing a collection of papers dedicated to 'Industrial Relations in the New Europe: Enlargement, Integration and Reform', and this has been followed by advice and assistance from Matthew Pittman and other assistants at Edward Elgar Publishing. Giles Stacey provided an English language oversight to the texts produced by non-native speakers, Eva Knies ensured the texts conformed to Edward Elgar's house style and Jos Thoben prepared the camera ready copy. We would like to thank all of them for their assistance.

Our main debt of gratitude is to all the contributors to this book, who were willing to rewrite their earlier papers in response to our editorial comments and suggestions. We would like to think that this collection makes a contribution to understanding how the process of European integration impacts on industrial relations at several levels, and how various actors attempt to influence the processes of integration and reform. If the collection succeeds in this, it is thanks to the individual contributors' understanding of their domain and their competence in taking on a European perspective. We hope that our editorial work has helped to bring out the overall conclusion that the impact of the European integration process is diverse and depends to some extent on supranational and national actors, and that their strategic actions can help to establish a European Social Model with which European citizens will wish to identify.

Peter Leisink   Utrecht School of Governance, Utrecht University
Bram Steijn   Department of Public Administration,
                       Erasmus University Rotterdam
Ulke Veersma   University of Greenwich Business School

1. Industrial Relations in the New Europe: Introduction

Peter Leisink, Bram Steijn and Ulke Veersma

INTRODUCTION

Over the past decade, the process of European integration has been accompanied by the emergence of what is now referred to as the European Social Model (ESM). This concept is used to refer to a number of social policy arrangements, including social security and social dialogue institutions, which are believed to be characteristics that distinguish the European from the American business model (Adnett and Hardy 2005; Vaughan-Whitehead 2003). This is not to deny that there are other interpretations of the integration process which see it as 'negative integration' (Scharpf 1999), meaning that the thrust of legislation has been to weaken those national forms of regulation which are regarded as obstacles to economic integration and the free market. Although no empirical support exists for the anticipated 'race to the bottom', the diversity among Member States and the constraints originating from EU rules on economic integration and competition laws are major reasons to doubt the viability of common European social policies (Scharpf 2002). Fears have been voiced, for instance by Vaughan-Whitehead (2003), that the social model will not be sustainable, one reason being that enlargement has increased the diversity among the EU Member States significantly, another that many of the new Member States have enacted neo-liberal policies in a radical way – under the often unrecognized influence of international financial institutions (Dimitrova and Petkov 2005) – and these add to the neo-liberal orientation which some of the EU-15 Member States are also pursuing to varying degrees.

The formal accession on 1 May 2004 of countries in Central and Eastern Europe (CEE) to the European Union (EU), and the prospect of further enlargement including Turkey, coupled with domestic changes such as longer working hours and increasing barriers to early retirement, which have been perceived as implications of the process of European integration, were reasons for citizens in France and the Netherlands to reject the European

Constitution in 2005. There is a certain irony to this rejection since the Constitution included an explicit listing of social rights which would have become binding upon ratification of the Constitution, whereas the previous Charter of Fundamental Rights was non-binding (Adnett and Hardy 2005, p. 199). Nevertheless, the image of the 'Polish plumber' – and the truck driver, the worker in the construction industry and others all taking the jobs of French and Dutch workers, and whose ready availability is believed to lead to domestic unemployment and worsening employment conditions – has proven very powerful. Trade unions have for the same reasons protested against the 'Bolkestein Services Directive', and have insisted that Polish and other CEE workers are only welcome as migrant workers if their employment conditions comply with the collective agreements of the host country. However, even though this may help to protect social standards in West-European Member States, the greater problem of building industrial relations' capabilities in CEE Member States is not tackled.

Earlier critical evaluations of the process of European integration, the expected effects of eastward enlargement in terms of increasing diversity between Member States and the consequent doubts about the viability of common European social policies, as well as recent protests against the threats posed by increasing flexibility in existing regulatory arrangements and the privatization and liberalization of public services, are the reasons why this publication concentrates on the following question: how does the process of European integration impact on industrial relations at various levels, and who are the main actors in this process? This introductory chapter will elaborate on the reasons for concentrating on this major question and the central concepts we use to deal with it. We will also introduce the chapters that follow and the way they approach this important question.

THE FRAMEWORK

We use the term 'Europeanization process' following Marginson and Sisson (2004) who distinguish between Europeanization as a steady state (following the creation of the EU) and as an ongoing process. The term 'process' helps to emphasize the historical, ongoing character of Europeanization and this is appropriate for this book's subject matter.

The idea that enlargement impacts on, and will continue to impact on, industrial relations in Europe is well founded. For instance, Vaughan-Whitehead (2003) presented evidence which showed that following enlargement the diversity in all dimensions of the European Social Model would increase considerably. He argued that the transposition of the *acquis communautaire* will remain on a formal level in a number of areas, with poor compliance in practice due to the weak administrative capacity of governments. Gradev (2005) adds, from the standpoint of the acceding countries, that the EU itself has not given clear guidance to the CEE Countries in the area of building a social dimension, which he attributes rightly to the growing debate about the prevalence of economic competitiveness and its compatibility with the goal of social cohesion. Further, the lack of a tradition of social dialogue at sectoral and enterprise levels in most CEE Member States is expected to undermine their participation in social dialogue at the EU level, and this may, according to Gradev (2005) and Vaughan-Whitehead (2003, pp. 264-265), contribute to halting the social dialogue at the EU level where recent developments have given a greater role to social dialogue in preparing social policies (Adnett and Hardy 2005).

Our interest in the impact of European integration in the enlargement phase on industrial relations in Europe must take account of the observation (made by Martin and Ross 2004; Visser 2005, among others) that Member States have less room for macroeconomic manoeuvre as a consequence of the further economic integration following the launch of Economic and Monetary Union (EMU) in 1999, and that adaptation to macroeconomic changes will therefore be more orientated towards increasing labour market flexibility and reducing expenditure on social protection benefits.

Our focus is on industrial relations, concerning the framework within which conditions of employment are established and social dialogue with regard to social and economic policies takes place. The process of Europeanization impacts on various levels of industrial relations. At the supranational level, institutions have been created such as social dialogue committees and European works councils which offer platforms for opinions on public and corporate policies (see Keller and Platzer 2003). The European integration process impacts on national level industrial relations in many direct and indirect ways, ranging from specific regulations such as the Directive 'establishing a general framework for informing and consulting employees in the European community' (2002/14/EC) to the constraints on economic and social policies which flow from EMU.

In preparing for EU membership, the candidate countries were required to transpose the *acquis communautaire*, including regulations and directives concerning various aspects of the European Social Model, such as social dialogue, tripartite and bipartite information exchange and consultation, collective bargaining and legal provisions concerning employment conditions and social protection. Vaughan-Whitehead (2003), Dimitrova and Vilrokx (2005) and others, who have studied the transposition of the *acquis* into domestic law and its practical implementation, have pointed out that there are major shortcomings with regard to compliance, and that these will impact on the European Social Model in practice and its further development. This reflects our interest: the development of industrial relations and social dialogue at several levels (EU level, national level of Member States, public sector) under the influence of the enlargement process and the ensuing diversity as regards elements of the European Social Model.

Industrial Relations at the EU Level

Political views on regulating the market and on social protection have always differed among the Member States constituting the European Union. However, the founders of the European Community did share certain views that drew on their corporatist or social democratic welfare state traditions, and these inspired the initial development of European social policy (Adnett and Hardy 2005, pp. 33-34; Marginson and Sisson 2004, pp. 84-85). Industrial relations were among the early topics of interest, but differences in opinions were significant, reflected in the 1980s' failure of the Vredeling Directive, which proposed compulsory worker representation in multinational companies.

Over the years, and notably since the Delors' presidency, the European social dimension has developed, and especially the social dialogue at the EU level. Delors stimulated interprofessional social dialogue, and its active advisory role over the years has paved the way for new social dialogue rights. These consist of the social partners' right to be consulted on the possible direction of the social policy initiatives of the European Commission and of the social partners' right – instead of Commission-led action – to prepare their own agreements, which they can then submit for conversion into directives (Falkner 2003). Other forms of social dialogue at the EU level have grown, including the sectoral social dialogue and the dialogue over macroeconomic policy between social partners, the European Commission, the European Central Bank and the economic and finance ministers of the Member States. However, social dialogue at the EU level has problematic areas, such as the absence of social dialogue in some industrial sectors where employer associations are non-existent or are unwilling to set up social dialogue, and the impossibility of concluding legally-binding collective agreements at the supranational level (Keller 2003; Leisink 2003).

The concept of the European Social Model (ESM) is relatively recent and the common views and principles which it represents include, according to the conclusions of the Nice Summit in 2000, the importance of social dialogue, systems that offer a high level of social protection, and services of general interest covering activities vital for social cohesion. The European social dimension is 'a mix of EU framework and national systems' (Marginson and Sisson 2004, p. 37) and recognizing this multilevel character helps to understand the assumption that the increased diversity, as a consequence of enlargement, will cause the development of European social policy to stagnate if not worsen. Increasing diversity will create enormous pressures for co-ordination. Given the reduced likelihood of framework agreements being forthcoming from the social dialogue at the European level, and of unanimity or majority opinions among Member States who continue to hold a determinant role in social policy, the future of the European Social Model is at best 'uncertain' (Vaughan-Whitehead 2003).

Industrial Relations in Member States

Industrial relations differ among Member States, but the majority are used to an organized multi-level practice of collective bargaining on a centralized level (cross-sectoral or sectoral) and at company, or plant, level. The UK has been an exception with its dominance of company-level collective bargaining (Traxler 2003). In contrast to most EU-15 countries, in the CEE Member States (apart from Slovenia) collective bargaining at sectoral level is almost non-existent, and although formal regulations for free collective bargaining are in place, there is little opportunity in practice due to restrictive governmental income policies and little institutionalization of trade union recognition and the signing of collective agreements in newly-created private enterprises (Dimitrova and Vilrokx 2005; Vaughan-Whitehead 2003).

The absence of industrial relations practices, that are prevalent in most of the EU-15 Member States, in the CEE Member States may be a factor in attracting enterprises to the latter, which regard such industrial relations practices as restraints on their flexibility. Even if this is the case, a far more important factor in enterprises relocating production from EU-15 to CEE Member States is their low level of wages and the low standards in areas relating to working time and health and safety (Vaughan-Whitehead 2003, pp. 409-410). Given that wages in CEE Member States will take a long time to catch up, it is likely that enterprises will continue to relocate production, that CEE workers will want to migrate to EU-15 Member States and that direct and indirect pressures on industrial relations institutions as well as on employment conditions and social provision in EU-15 Member States will be strong. Although national industrial relations institutions are relatively stable (Traxler 2003), there are indications of potentially erosive effects. Examples include debates in the Netherlands about the partial abolition of the extension of collective agreements – with the government refusing to declare generally binding elements that are considered to contravene the government's policy on enhancing the national economy's competitive position – and the French government's proposed bill that would have allowed employers to dismiss workers under the age of 26 during the first two years of their employment.

It is popularly assumed that the CEE Member States will profit from membership in various aspects of their employment and social policy. Indeed, one might easily imagine that it is almost impossible for workers in the CEE Countries not to benefit from European integration, given the dramatic deterioration in their wages and social protection that occurred during the 1990s transition from state socialism to market economies. However, Dimitrova and Petkov (2005, pp. 31-38) argue that the prospect of EU accession gave a powerful impetus for painful reforms and, with the notable exception of Slovenia, the majority of the population in many CEE countries have failed to return to the living standards seen prior to 1989. Vaughan-Whitehead (2003, p. 82) describes instances where CEE governments have introduced amendments to their labour codes – under the justification of transposing the Community *acquis* – that remove or reduce the existing social standards and enact instead labour provisions much less favourable to workers. He also argues (2003, pp. 409-410) that the positive effects of foreign direct investments have been limited, because these have not been accompanied with higher standards in terms of industrial relations and working conditions.

These developments raise concerns about the impact of enlargement on industrial relations in both old and new Member States. If there were expectations of a harmonization or further 'Europeanization' of industrial relations – understood to mean the development of a coherent, horizontally and vertically interconnected 'European' system of industrial relations (Keller and Platzer 2003, p. 172) – such prospects must be regarded as remote if at all realistic. As regards the Europeanization of substantive aspects of employment conditions, an argument against such an eventuality is the increase in the interest shown by EU policymakers in 'soft' law or the Open Method of Co-ordination (OMC), in response to the growing diversity in the EU, which gives Member States greater autonomy in implementing directives, framework agreements and in designing National Action Plans (see the special issue of the *European Journal of Industrial Relations* on Governance and European Industrial Relations, 11 (3)). While Adnett and Hardy (2005) believe that the OMC could be a means to promote social dialogue, and that soft law approaches could be an effective mechanism for promoting social development by eliminating the dysfunctional effects of hard law, one can equally see the logic in Scharpf's (2002) argument that, given the 'asymmetrical' conditions in European legislation on economic integration and a free market, it is hard to see the OMC as an instrument for Member States to promote further regulation in the social field.

Public Sector Industrial Relations

In our view, paying specific attention to industrial relations in the public sector is highly relevant. Several recent books have dealt exclusively with public-sector industrial relations (Bach et al. 1999; Dell'Aringa et al. 2001; and Brock and Lipsky 2003) emphasizing the fact that separate attention to the public sector is warranted. This is especially the case given that public-sector employment relationships have recently been under severe strain.

To explain this, something must first be said about the traditional differences between public- and private-sector organizations. According to Farnham and Horton (1996; see also Boyne, Poole and Jenkins 1999), four characteristics of public-sector organizations are highly relevant with respect to HRM practices in discerning them from private organizations: 1) a paternalistic style of government, which can be illustrated by the relatively high attention given to health, safety and welfare issues; 2) standardized employment practices, which for all public-sector workers imply job security and lifelong employment; 3) collectivized industrial relations, with a strong role for the trade unions (supported by relatively high levels of union membership); and 4) public organizations aspire to be 'model employers', setting standards for private organizations to follow. Although these characteristics were identified with respect to UK public-sector organizations, they are also valid for most European countries, and define the typical playing field for public-sector employers and unions. The situation was of course different within the former communist countries, but conditions there are not within the limited subject matter of this book.

Since the 1980s, governments in almost all OECD countries have been planning and implementing various types of public management reforms. Pollitt and Bouckaert (2004, p. 16) see these reforms as 'deliberate structures and processes of public sector organisations with the objective of getting them (in some sense) to perform better'. A new way of looking at managing the public sector (the so-called 'New Public Management' or NPM – Hood 1991) was an important driving factor behind these reforms, a basic assumption being that the public sector, in order to become more effective and efficient, needed to introduce management methods that have proved their worth in the private sector; and thus that the public sector must become more like the private sector.

This is not the place to discuss these reforms extensively, it suffices here to summarize some of the main conclusions by Pollitt and Bouckaert (2004) who discern three main distinct strategies followed by countries in reforming their administrations. Firstly there were countries that followed a 'maintenance' strategy and tried to implement only relatively small changes that would make the system better – Germany, especially in the 1980s, exemplifies this strategy. Then there were the 'modernizers', including most European countries, who saw a need for more fundamental changes in the way the administrative system was organized. Most radical of all are the 'marketizers', who opted to introduce widespread market mechanisms within the organization of the public sector – within Europe, the UK is the prime example.

Although the picture is complex, it is clear that public management reform is to be found everywhere in Europe, although the timing of its introduction, extent, scope and pace differs considerably among countries. Clearly, the Europeanization process itself is not the only driving factor behind these public sector reforms as these have also been introduced in non-EU countries such as the USA, Australia, New Zealand and Japan. In this respect, the OECD (2005) has played an important role in diffusing ideas about public sector reform around the world. Nevertheless, on a general level, the Europeanization process has encouraged the reform processes. Its role was noted by Hemerijck and Ferrara (2004, p. 248) who pointed out that 'since the 1980s European monetary integration has been a driving force behind domestic welfare reform across the European Union'. In this respect, Bach et al. (1999, p. 18) refer to the process of macroeconomic integration (e.g. the Maastricht Treaty) which has been an important factor contributing to a 'greater similarity in the structure and outcome of public service employment regulation within Europe'. In order to meet the EMU criteria, many countries had to carry out cost-cutting programmes which certainly impinged on public-sector industrial relations. For instance, Bordogna (2003, p. 27) notes that in Italy a law was passed in 1993 that reformed the organizational principles of public administration. This law – weakening the special status of most public employees – was to an extent approved because of the pressure to meet the Maastricht EMU criteria. Mossé and Tchobanian (1999, p. 161) come to a similar conclusion with respect to France, stating that 'European integration is forcing the French public sector to change dramatically, jeopardising the "French exceptionalism" of the public service'. Although we will not discuss it in this book, similar changes have occurred in CEE Countries as part of their accession trajectory towards EU membership.

It is clear that these reforms have had considerable effects on personnel systems and workers, although generally this was not the main aim of the reform itself. A recent OECD study (2005) describes some of the main trends in this respect: 1) in most countries, public employment has been reduced (mostly through privatization of services); 2) civil service systems are changing, such as by limiting or abolishing lifelong tenure; 3) HRM responsibilities have been decentralized and managerial flexibility has been increased; and 4) employment contracts, accountability and pay are individualized (for instance by the introduction of performance-related pay).

According to Bach et al. (1999, p. 19), there appears to be growing convergence in the practices of public- and private-sector systems of employment, although differences between countries remain considerable (see also Bordogna 2003, p. 63). Like Pollitt and Bouckaert, Bordogna (2003, p. 61) discerns three groups of countries with respect to the content and pace of reform of public-sector industrial relations. Some countries (Britain, New Zealand and Australia – the 'modernizers' in Pollitt and Bouckaert) have followed a reform path that resembles the NPM formula. In some other countries, the traditional system of employment relations has only changed to a limited extent and in a very incremental way. These are the 'maintainers' of Pollitt and Bouckaert, and in terms of reforming public-sector industrial relations within Europe, France and Germany belong to this group. A third group of countries (including Italy, Denmark and Sweden according to Bordogna) have seen privatization, contractualization, individualization of pay and an adversarial attitude towards unions as the main developments and fit somewhere between the above two extremes. Our analysis aims to shed further light on the effect that Europeanization has had on these country-specific differences.

EUROPEAN INTEGRATION IN CONDITIONS OF AMBIGUITY

The process of European integration accompanies changes in modes of governance, in institutions, including industrial relations, and in substantive aspects of employment conditions and social protection. The European Social Model is part of an ongoing process of European integration, the direction of which is subject to never-ending interventions by various actors at different levels, and which itself impacts on and intervenes in processes at national, sectoral and company levels.

The relevance of the roles of various social actors in the impact that EU regulatory policies have on national level domestic policies and institutions is analysed by Knill and Lehmkuhl (2002) in relation to three types of Europeanization mechanisms. Firstly, European policymaking can be prescriptive and demand that Member States adopt specific measures in order to comply with EU requirements. This mechanism of Europeanization, i.e. by institutional compliance, can be observed for instance in the case of directives on health and safety and the European Works Council. Knill and Lehmkuhl argue that even here the role of domestic actors must be included in the analysis of the impact of EU policy. Although fundamental changes in domestic arrangements may be demanded, dominant social actors at the national level with significant powers and resources can still develop regulatory changes that deviate significantly from the original EU objectives in order to ensure that their interests prevail.

With the other two Europeanization mechanisms – Europeanization by changing domestic opportunity structures and Europeanization by framing domestic beliefs – the need to consider the national interest constellation and the powers which domestic actors have, is even greater if one is to explain the varying impact of European policies. One example of Europeanization by changing domestic opportunity structures analysed by Knill and Lehmkuhl (2002) is the EU transport liberalization policy which gives wider options to consumers (such as companies wanting goods transported) while outlawing domestic tariff regimes as a means of protecting the market position of national haulage companies. Knill and Lehmkuhl show that the distribution of powers and resources between opposing actor coalitions determines whether Europe-induced changes in domestic opportunity structures are likely to trigger reform, and especially so if the distribution of power is relatively even. The direction of change will not necessarily conform to European objectives, and will only do so, Knill and Lehmkuhl (2002, p. 261) argue, if the actors which are strengthened by the changes in domestic opportunity structures support these objectives. The role of domestic actors in moderating the impact of EU policies is even greater in the approach of Europeanization by framing domestic beliefs and expectations. This form of Europeanization will only stimulate domestic reform in line with EU objectives if there is already a broad consensus for reform that is sympathetic to EU ideas or if the dominant players in the reform process are receptive to EU ideas (Knill and Lehmkuhl 2002, pp. 262-263).

The relevance of this analysis of the impact of Europeanization is that it demonstrates that the impact is not only dependent on the institutional characteristics of EU regulatory policies, but also on the domestic constellation of actors with their beliefs and powers, particularly with the softer forms of Europeanization, but even in the case of Europeanization by institutional compliance.

Another issue which requires critical reflection is whether it really is 'European integration', rather than other processes such as globalization or the transition to a post-Fordist production concept, that induces changes in industrial relations processes and their outcomes. Indeed, in Adnett and Hardy's analysis (2005, pp. 24-26), the roots of the European social model are seen as originating in the period of economic growth following the Second World War, which was based on Fordist technology and solidaristic wage bargaining, welfare programmes and labour market regulation. However, the established industrial relations institutions and labour market and welfare arrangements failed to match the turbulent changes caused by the emergence of flexible specializations and growing global competition, and came to be seen as the causes of growing and chronic unemployment and slow employment growth in service sectors. The labour market policies of deregulation and the introduction of flexibility were a response to these economic and technological changes, just as the current policies (active labour market policies, reduced social security benefits, lifelong learning) are a response to the present conditions of globalization and the emergence of knowledge-based economies. In this context, Adnett and Hardy (2005, p. 25) argue that 'the establishment of EMU has intensified the concern that an EU social policy based upon levelling-up may be inconsistent with increased economic integration and continuing international competitiveness'. Thus, while the changes in social policies may be attributed to European integration – or (lack of) targeted action by the European Commission – the process of European integration itself reflects and is constituted by wider economic and technological changes. Gaining an understanding of these changes is helped when, on occasions, strategic actors express themselves clearly, as in 2004 when large German multinational enterprises (Siemens, DaimlerChrysler) demanded that their workers work longer hours without extra pay under the threat of relocating production. Bosch in France did the same, which was followed in 2005 by the French government's policy to replace the 35-hour working week legislation with 'flexible' arrangements.

The ambiguity of the European integration process, and of the conditions and actors involved in and impacted upon by European integration, justifies the second part of the main question of this book: 'who are the main actors in this process?' The scope of the question will be restricted by concentrating on the impact of the European integration process on industrial relations at various levels.

OUTLINE OF THIS BOOK

Part I of this book includes a number of chapters that study the impact of the European integration process by focusing on the national industrial relations systems and the main actors at that level in EU Member States. Part II concentrates on public-sector industrial relations and their changing characteristics driven by the public management reform ideas that currently hold sway in Europe.

PART I: THE IMPACT OF THE EUROPEANIZATION PROCESS ON INDUSTRIAL RELATIONS

Earlier studies on the effects of the process of European integration create a framework of expectations which guides the present analysis. Some studies concern the effects of the present phase of European integration in terms of the relocation of production to CEE Member States, and in the implementation of the *acquis*. These events can be regarded as the more or less direct effects of the enlargement process. Other effects are more indirect and can be expected to manifest themselves in the longer term. These include stagnation in the development of social policy and the declining interest in social dialogue at the EU level as a consequence of the increased diversity within Member States' values and practices (Falkner 2003, pp. 24-26). Another set of indirect effects concerns the expected pressure on industrial relations institutions and labour standards in EU-15 Member States, driven by both enlargement and the increasing competition as a result of EMU (Economic and Monetary Union) and SGP (Stability and Growth Pact) conditions. When studying the impact of European integration on industrial relations, it is helpful to make this distinction between direct and indirect effects, but it is also necessary to recognize that a clear demarcation of, and control over, cause and effect is impossible given the complex and dynamic character of the object of study.

Vos's contribution deals with the question whether Europeanization implies a convergence towards a single European social model. He notes that the development of social policy at the European level has been very gradual and concludes that, despite continuing differences, increasing convergence can be observed in national models. There are two developments that reinforce the trend towards convergence. First, there is policy learning, with the Open Method of Co-ordination instigating policy convergence in Member States through the introduction of common policy objectives and the exchange of best practices. Second, there is the Lisbon process of modernizing social systems which, under the current situation of stagnating economic growth, is accompanied by increasing income inequalities and levels of poverty. Under these conditions, the notion of an EU social model may come to serve increasingly as an instrument that promotes downward convergence.

Vaughan-Whitehead presents an up-to-date empirical overview of working and employment conditions in the new Member States. The trend is towards increasing flexibility in labour contracts and a high average number of working hours, but these conditions tend to be converging towards the situation in the EU-15. On the other hand, the situation in the new Member

States is also characterized by very poor wages and health and safety conditions at work. The prospects of new Member States catching up with the standards in the European social model are not good, according to Vaughan-Whitehead, because of three factors: persistent threat of unemployment which causes workers to accept poor working and employment conditions, the presence of a large informal economy and the absence of social dialogue, in particular the lack of collective bargaining in small and medium enterprises, and collective agreements at sectoral level. Therefore, without solidarity from the EU's structural funds, economic development in the new Member States will be at the cost of the basic elements of social protection.

Neumann addresses the question as to whether the application of the *acquis communautaire* in Hungary's industrial relations practices actually amounts to an incremental convergence towards common minimum standards. His analysis of the transposition of the 'Transfer of Undertaking' and 'Working Time' directives provides a qualified answer: there is convergence but only in terms of formally adhering to codified laws. However, the material effect is nullified because many employers – particularly small and medium-sized companies – circumvent their obligations. They can do so because workers fear losing their jobs and the control of unions is influenced by the Hungarian system of industrial relations in which sectoral agreements are rare and unimportant. Thus, the employers' needs for flexibility dominate the workers' needs for security, helped by the government's approach to competitiveness. Neumann concludes that these developments do not hold out much hope of a Europeanization of industrial relations, which is becoming increasingly reliant on soft law methods, unless they are accompanied by the promotion of support for institutions and capabilities to conduct meaningful collective negotiations.

Stanojevic and Vehovar argue that Slovenia's transition to a market economy has been a gradual process which, based on historically conditioned institutions, has resulted in the development of inclusive industrial relations in accordance with those found in co-ordinated market economies. This sets Slovenia apart from other post-communist countries which followed a 'shock therapy' approach and created liberal market economies. In Slovenia, trade unions assisted in establishing the Economic and Social Council which has been active in producing social pacts since 1994, resulting in collective agreements at the central level that cover almost the entire labour force. The authors demonstrate that Slovenia's employment relations show some signs of rigidity but that there is also labour force flexibility, contributing to a high-road quality-oriented approach to production. However, competitive pressures have grown both during and after Slovenia's accession to the EU,

Industrial Relations in the New Europe

and increasing efficiency will require changes in corporate governance structures and in the currently unsustainable levels of social equity. The authors believe that the unions will be able to accommodate these pressures and that the preservation of union power is a precondition for the continuation of Slovenia's high-road development.

Köhler and Gonzalez Begega attempt to assess the impact of EU enlargement on Spain. They draw on the maximalist perspective, which sees the tremendous increase in differences in socioeconomic performance and in industrial relations institutions allowing transnational companies to engage in benchmarking, social dumping and the relocation of production, and the minimalist perspective, which fails to see a general relocation dynamic and considers social dumping unlikely. Köhler and Gonzalez Begega believe that while the German economy, whose MNCs are leading foreign direct investment in the new Member States, will probably benefit from enlargement, Spain, as a peripheral EU Member State, will suffer negative consequences because of cutbacks in EU cohesion funding received and because Spanish MNCs will not benefit from enlargement as they have always been oriented towards Latin America rather than Eastern Europe. Mediterranean Member States are, in general, likely to suffer negative consequences from MNCs carrying out competitive benchmarking, and this expectation has induced interest from Spanish trade unions in the European Works Council (EWC) as a platform for transnational cooperation to counteract MNCs' relocation strategies. The authors suggest that this interest in participating in EWCs could also lead to Spanish unions taking more interest in participative practices in domestic industrial relations and greater engagement with European trade union policies.

Stuart and Martinez Lucio describe the remaking of UK employment relations in recent years through partnership-based approaches. They argue that the modernization of UK employment relations has been a part of the New Labour government's agenda since 1997 and addresses the interests of domestic industrial relations actors. Firm-based partnership practices emerged to an extent in anticipation of European Directives (regarding European Works Councils and Information and Consultation), and were thus framed by the values contained in the European Social Model but contextualized by national actors and domestic political and economic environments. The authors make a case for analysing partnership models in terms of the various levels at which workers' voices are institutionalized, the issues over which this voice can be exercised and the traditions of involving industrial relations actors in social and economic policymaking. Drawing on these aspects, Stuart and Martinez Lucio suggest that an Anglo-Saxon, managerialist model of partnership is emerging, one that is different from the continental European approach in that it elicits cooperation on the basis of business interests which mediate the social aspects of work and relate these to the firm's prospects.

Van der Maas looks at the range of UK trade union policy answers to European integration and the 'discourse' on European integration. Unions are caught in a dilemma, between reacting to the threat of liberalized markets without harmonized employment conditions and striving for international cooperation and the building of a social Europe. The policies of the four trade unions studied reflect an adoption of in-between positions. Unison, Britain's largest union representing a considerable number of public employees, highlights the neo-liberal core of the EMU, with the convergence criteria limiting the sovereignty of the national state and endangering the jobs of its members if Britain were to join the single currency. The policy of the GPMU, the Graphical Print and Media Union, has changed from being anti-common-market to becoming a pro-EU trade union. This is mainly due to a pragmatic and positive view taken by the union's leaders. The GMB – a general union with a regionalized structure – has a strong European outlook that supports the development of a social dimension to the EU. The EU is viewed as better able than the nation state to defend and even promote a European Social Model. The TGWU, a trade union with a large presence in the manufacturing sectors, has been somewhat adaptive towards the EU. This trade union views European integration largely as a threat to employment and to national autonomous political and monetary control.

PART II: THE IMPACT OF PUBLIC SECTOR REFORM ON PUBLIC-SECTOR INDUSTRIAL RELATIONS

Returning to what are seen as the four distinctive characteristics of public-sector employment – paternalistic, standardized, collectivized and model standards – one wonders whether these traditional characteristics still exist. A *prima facie* answer is 'no' since 'paternalistic policies' and 'model employers' do not seem to fit with the view that public employers are becoming more like private ones. Moreover, the trends towards decentralization and individualization, described by the OECD, do not seem to fit with the traditional public-sector characteristics of collectivization and standardization. So what do these reform trends mean for public-sector employers and unions? What do they mean for the industrial relation system within the public sector? What is the effect of the Europeanization process on all of this?

These are the questions that we want to address in this book, and especially answer in the concluding chapter. To help answer these, the book includes chapters that consider four different countries (UK, France, Belgium and Germany). The UK and Germany can be seen as representing the two extremes: using Pollitt and Bouckaert's characterization, the UK has followed a marketization strategy in public management reform, and Germany – at least until recently – a maintaining strategy. Bach et al. (1999, p. 14) and Bordogna (2003) also describe these two countries as diametrically opposed with respect to recent reforms. Belgium and France are examples of the larger core of countries that are generally seen as having followed a modernization strategy over a relatively long time – although Bordogna (2003) sees France as leaning towards the 'maintainers' camp in terms of public-sector employment reform. Based on the descriptions of what has happened in these countries, the following questions will be addressed in our concluding chapter:

1. To what extent are the traditional characteristics of public-sector employment still visible?
2. What has been the effect of public sector reforms in Europe on the position of employers and unions within the industrial relations system?
3. What are the differences among the countries studied?
4. What does this tell us about the future of industrial relations in the public sector, such as whether industrial relations in the public and private sectors will grow more alike?

In their contribution, Dribbusch and Schulten discuss the development of public-sector industrial relations in Germany. As outlined earlier, Germany has followed a 'maintaining strategy' with respect to public management reform for a considerable period. According to the authors, this is now changing: New Public Management reforms are beginning to affect the German public sector, and in turn collective bargaining – they see a fundamental structural change within the German public sector. As a result, the former stability of German public-sector industrial relations has disappeared. They not only note a decline in the size of the public sector, mainly as a result of privatizations, but also decentralization processes which have reinforced processes of fragmentation both within the employers' and the employees' sides. The unions are especially affected by this with part of their former power base (public blue-collar workers) having left the public sector as a result of privatizations. Dribbusch and Schulten see a clear shift in power away from the unions.

According to Mériaux, things have happened differently in France. Clearly, New Public Management reforms have had an impact despite France being often seen as a country with strong resistance to such reforms. Traditionally, civil servants have had a special position (or 'status') in the

French system. In this respect, public-sector employees in France have a distinctly advantageous position compared to their private-sector counterparts. According to some, this system is a major hindrance if one wants to achieve a more 'modern', efficient and flexible civil service within France. Mériaux, however, disagrees and sees this point of view as focusing too much on 'judicial' arguments. His main point is that 'status by itself is not an obstacle to reform; it is much more the way in which it has been used by the civil service's "social partners" that has reinforced its potential for rigidity'. Mériaux's main argument is that substantial change within the present employment system is possible if social partners and managers would realize this and act accordingly.

Pelgrims, Steen and Thijs, in their chapter, consider the Belgium, or more specifically the Flemish, situation. Clearly, public management reform has followed a different trajectory in Belgium to those in Germany and France. In the terms of Pollitt and Bouckaert (2004), Belgium has been a 'modernizer' with respect to reforms. However, the Flemish reform project is far from finished, and the authors describe in detail a large reform project started in 1999. More specifically, the chapter focuses on the direct and indirect participation of workers within this large project. The authors note that public-sector unions in Belgium have a particularly strong position, not only due to the high levels of membership but also and especially due to the special characteristics of the system of industrial relations. This system is heavily centralized and has detailed regulations compelling the government to establish formal negotiations and consultations with the trade unions on any reforms they plan. Although Belgian unions have limited influence on the reform agenda itself, they are a force to be reckoned with in the implementation phase. The authors conclude that involving unions during the preparation phase of reforms would probably contribute to a smoother implementation phase.

The chapter by White, Dennison, Farnham and Horton turns the attention to the UK. The UK is an important case in a book like this, since public management reform has been on the agenda there for a long time. In terms of Pollitt and Bouckaert (2004), the UK can be seen as a 'marketizer', with the Thatcher-initiated policies having eroded the power of the unions in general. The chapter describes what has happened since the New Labour government was elected in 1997. Clearly, according to the authors, things have changed, which the authors partly attribute to the fact that the current government has signed the EU employment directives. The main focus in the chapter is on whether the employees' voices are heard, and more specifically the question as to whether differences exist in this respect between the public and the private sectors, a question which of course relates to the issue of whether UK public employers aspire to be 'good' employers. A detailed empirical analysis of this issue leads the authors to conclude that 'employee voice practices appear to be more strongly entrenched in the UK public services than in the private sector'. Further, according to them, this has assisted the ongoing process of public sector reform in the UK: 'partnership' seems to be the magic word for now.

REFERENCES

Adnett, N. and S. Hardy (2005), *The European Social Model: Modernisation or Evolution?*, Cheltenham, UK and Northampton, MA, USA: Edward Elgar.
Bach, S. (1999), 'Europe: Changing public service employment relations', in S. Bach, L. Bordogna, G. Della Rocca and D. Winchester (eds), *Public service Employment Relations in Europe: Transformation, Modernization or Inertia?*, London and New York: Routledge, pp. 1-21.
Bordogna, L. (2003), 'The Reform of Public Sector Employment Relations in Industrialized Democracies', in J. Brock and D.B. Lipsky (eds), *Going Public: The Role of Labor-Management Relations in Delivering Quality Government Services*, Industrial Relations Research Association: University of Illinois, pp. 23-67.
Boyne, G., M. Poole and G. Jenkins (1999), 'Human Resource Management in the Public and Private Sectors: An Empirical Comparison', *Public Administration*, **77** (2), 407-420.
Brock, J. and D.B. Lipsky (eds) (2003), *Going Public: The Role of Labor-Management Relations in Delivering Quality Government Services*, Industrial Relations Research Association: University of Illinois.
Dell'Aringa, C., G. Della Rocca and B. Keller (eds) (2001), *Strategic Choices in Reforming Public Service Employment: An International Handbook*, Houndmills: Palgrave Macmillan.
Dimitrova, D. and K. Petkov (2005), 'Comparative Overview: Changing Profiles, Action and Outcomes for Organized Labour in Central and Eastern Europe', in D. Dimitrova and J. Vilrokx (eds), *Trade Union Strategies in Central and Eastern Europe*, Geneva: International Labour Office, pp. 15-62.
Dimitrova, D. and J. Vilrokx (eds) (2005), *Trade Union Strategies in Central and Eastern Europe: Towards Decent Work*, Geneva: International Labour Office.
Falkner, G. (2003), 'The interprofessional social dialogue at European level; past and future', in B. Keller and H.W. Platzer (eds), *Industrial Relations and European Integration*, Aldershot: Ashgate, pp. 11-29.
Farnham, D. and S. Horton (1996), *Managing People in the Public services*, Basingstoke and London: MacMillan.
Gradev, G. (2005), 'Social Dialogue and Trade Unions in Enlarging Europe: Losers among Winners?', in D. Dimitrova and J. Vilrokx (eds), *Trade Union Strategies in Central and Eastern Europe*, Geneva: International Labour Office, pp. 229-263.
Hemerijck, A. and M. Ferrara (2004), 'Welfare Reform in the shadow of the EMU', in A. Martin and G. Ross, *Euros and the Europeans: Monetary Integration and the European Model of Society*, Cambridge: Cambridge University Press, pp. 248-277.
Hood, C. (1991), 'A public management for all seasons?', *Public Administration*, **19** (1), 3-19.

Keller, B. (2003), 'Social dialogues at sectoral level; the neglected ingredient of European industrial relations', in B. Keller and H.W. Platzer (eds), *Industrial Relations and European Integration*, Aldershot: Ashgate, pp. 30-57.

Keller, B. and H.W. Platzer (2003), 'Conclusions and perspectives; European integration and trans- and supranational industrial relations', in B. Keller and H.W. Platzer (eds), *Industrial Relations and European Integration*, Aldershot: Ashgate, pp. 161-178.

Knill, C. and D. Lehmkuhl (2002), 'The national impact of European Union regulatory policy: Three Europeanization mechanisms', *European Journal of Political Research*, **41**, 255-280.

Leisink, P. (2003), 'The European sectoral social dialogue and the graphical industry', *European Journal of Industrial Relations*, **8** (1), 101-117.

Marginson, P. and K. Sisson (2004), *European Integration and Industrial Relations*, Houndmills: Palgrave Macmillan.

Martin, A. and G. Ross (eds) (2004), *Euros and European: Monetary integration and the European Model of Society*, Cambridge: Cambridge University Press.

Mossé, P. and R. Tchobanian (1999), 'France: the restructuring of employment relations in the public services', in S. Bach, L. Bordogna, G. Della Rocca and D. Winchester (eds), *Public service Employment Relations in Europe: Transformation, Modernization or Inertia?*, London and New York: Routledge, pp. 130-163.

OECD (2005), *Modernising Government: The way forward*, Paris: OECD.

Pollitt, C. and G. Bouckaert (2004), *Public Management Reform; An International Comparison*, Oxford: Oxford University Press, second edition.

Scharpf, F. (1999), *Governing in Europe: Effective and Democratic?*, Oxford: Oxford University Press.

Scharpf, F. (2002), 'The European Social Model: Coping with the challenges of diversity', *Journal of Common Market Studies*, **40**, 645-670.

Traxler, F. (2003), 'European Monetary Union and collective bargaining', in B. Keller and H.W. Platzer (eds), *Industrial Relations and European Integration*, Aldershot: Ashgate, pp. 85-111.

Vaughan-Whitehead, D. (2003), *EU Enlargement versus Social Europe? The uncertain future of the European Social Model*, Cheltenham, UK and Northampton, MA, USA: Edward Elgar.

Visser, J. (2005), 'Beneath the surface of stability: new and old modes of governance in European industrial relations', *European Journal of Industrial Relations*, **11** (3), 287-306.

PART I

The Impact of European Integration on
Industrial Relations in Member States

2. European Convergence and the EU Social Model

Kees Vos

INTRODUCTION

The process of European integration had from the start primarily an economic dimension, with the main aim of the establishment of a common market. During the 1950s and 1960s economic integration was the main policy objective, while keeping social policy firmly national. As far as harmonization of national social legislation took place, it had mainly to do with the fear of unfair competition. Discrepancies of workers' safety and health protection and of payment of women had been identified as factors that could distort competition between Member States (Chassard 2002). Community social action was restricted to the co-ordination of social security schemes in order to ensure the rights of migrant workers.

Since the 1980s more emphasis has been given to the development of a social dimension and the development of a social policy at European level. Although many policy initiatives with regard to the social dimension developed in the 1980s, it was a very gradual development.

During the 1990s, changes in the Treaty and new policy developments implied more fundamental changes in European policymaking. It is almost needless to say that the social dimension did not take precedence over the economic dimension. On the other hand, it is also clear that the notion of a European social model has gained more substance since then and the need to develop and implement such a model has been a topic for debate. The first question to be answered in this chapter is whether Europeanization of industrial relations, as it has become now a substantial element of European policies, implies a convergence of national systems or models. The next question is if this would imply a convergence towards one European social model. To answer these questions the chapter is structured as follows.

It starts with a short discussion about the role and content of different typologies and models, developed to analyse different systems within Europe. These models underline by their nature the diversity inside the Union itself. Different methods of classification are developed in the ongoing debate on divergence or convergence of national models. The paper then explores the most relevant elements of the concept convergence – as dealt with in the third section. This leads to the preliminary conclusion that, despite existing differences, a growing convergence of national models can be observed.

In the following sections, developments are presented which may reinforce the trends towards convergence by policymaking, e.g. through policy learning as described in the fourth section and through implementation of the Lisbon ambition of modernization of the different European social models, as presented in the fifth section. The sixth section deals with the contents and evolution of the European model itself. The chapter leads to the conclusion that, taking into account a gradual Anglo-Saxonization or Americanization of the economy within European countries, the possibility of a future downward convergence cannot be excluded.

DIVERSITY AND DIVERGENCE

Cross-national comparative research usually emphasizes considerable differences between EU Member States in areas like social security, the labour market and labour systems (European Commission 2000; European Foundation for the Improvement of Living and Working Conditions 2000, 2001). As far as industrial relations are concerned, there still exist differences concerning for instance the relationship between collective bargaining and legislation, the levels on which collective bargaining takes place, the membership of unions and employers' organizations, the role of bipartite and tripartite institutions and of social dialogue processes (European Foundation for the Improvement of Living and Working Conditions 2002). Moreover, decentralization of collective bargaining has been considered to be a major trend in industry for some time (Marginson 2004). Together with the recent enlargement this may lead to more diversity between Member States and a greater heterogeneity in Europe than ever before.

In order to facilitate comparative research, the classification in typologies is a frequently used method. Types or models are used as ideal-types in order to highlight characteristic differences in national systems. A well-known distinction is for instance the typology of capitalism by Michel Albert into a neo-American model and the Rhineland model (1992). Similarly Hall and Soskice (2001) make a distinction between liberal market economies and co-ordinated market economies. Coates offers another typology of three ideal-types of capitalist organization: market-led or liberal capitalism, state-led or Asian capitalism and consensual or European welfare capitalism (2000).

Typologies are also used to classify subsystems in societies, for instance industrial relations systems. Peper (1980) for instance makes a distinction between conflict, coalition and harmonious models of industrial relations. Crouch (1994) develops also a threefold model consisting of contestative, pluralist and corporatist systems. Another frequently used typology is the classification by Ebbinghaus and Visser (1997) into Anglo-Saxon pluralism, Nordic coordination, Continental social partnership and Latin polarization.

Other typologies are developed to classify welfare states. Esping-Andersen (1990) draws the distinction between three types of European welfare states: the Scandinavian or social-democrat model, the Continental or corporatist model and the Anglo-Saxon or liberal one. Using the typology of Esping-Andersen, others have added the Southern-European model as a fourth category (Leibfried 1992; Kvist 1993). Essential for the classification by Esping-Andersen is that the different models are characterized by the extent to which they combine essential socio-economic objectives, such as a high labour participation rate, a large degree of social equality and a moderate level of public expenditure. The difference between the types has to do with the degree of joint optimalization of the three objectives. In practice it seems impossible to achieve the objectives of social equality, high labour participation and budget control simultaneously. Generally speaking the liberal states fail to achieve a low poverty rate, the social-democrat welfare states have a considerable taxation and the corporatist ones show rather low employment rates. This kind of 'natural' incompatibility (Iversen and Wren 1998) implies that European welfare states will have to choose between sacrificing social equality or cohesion, high labour participation and/or welfare sustainability, as it turns out in practice: a trade-off between equality and jobs (Esping-Andersen 1996).

The historical diversity of European welfare systems as captured by Esping-Andersen's typology is a good reference point for assessing recent developments. During the 1990s there appeared to be a substantial political resistance against a further strengthening of European co-ordination, especially in the area of social protection systems. This resistance was translated into the political principle of subsidiarity, the notion that a transfer of national authority to the European level can only take place 'if and in so far as the objectives of the proposed action cannot be sufficiently achieved by the Member States' (Article 3b Maastricht Treaty). This can be interpreted as an attempt to ensure that the bargaining power lies more clearly on the side of the Member States (CEPR 1993).

In 1998 the Cardiff process was initiated to ensure structural reform and liberalization of national product and capital markets. As this policy is ideologically based upon neoliberal microeconomic orthodoxy, the intention is to eliminate impediments to freely operating markets through structural reform and deregulation (Green 2002). From this perspective, harmonized social policy systems or common minimum standards in social welfare are considered to be unnecessary or even counterproductive: unnecessary since there are sufficient policy options for the separate Member States to safeguard social cohesion via their own systems (CEPR 1993); counterproductive since it would only stand in the way of adequate reactions to international competition. Diversity in labour conditions and social protection arrangements is called for in order to respond flexibly to the consequences of regional or sectoral economic shocks (Den Butter and Hazeu 2002). European coordination of labour costs and arrangements for income redistribution could only result in less regional/national flexibility (Hartog and Teulings 1999). From this angle it might be illusory to speak of a convergence of national (social) systems. However, this economic integration implies also neoliberalization and a residualization of social models (Hay 2000, p. 529). As Hyman (2001, p. 291) – when quoting Castells (1998, p. 326) – has argued: the process of European unification is often presented as marketization, 'as the necessary adaptation to globalization, with the corollary of economic adjustment, flexibility of labor markets, and shrinkage of the welfare state'. Indeed, such a position might be at the heart of the British-French controversy following the 2005 referenda on the Constitution in France and the Netherlands.

DIVERGENCE OR CONVERGENCE?

The focus on diversity and divergence can be associated with the (neo-) institutionalist approach which stresses the specific national institutional architecture and cultural configurations (Hay 2000, p. 511). Comparative research using structural indicators like union density, often suggests national institutional stability and divergent tendencies between national systems (Cortebeeck, Huys, van Gyes and Vandenbrande 2004). Nevertheless, the possibility of convergence has been debated already for several decades. When analysing possible trends to convergence within Europe it is therefore relevant to further explore the nature of this concept and the evidence that has been found for convergence and divergence between national models.

Almost simultaneously with the start of the European Community, Kerr, Dunlop, Harbison and Myers (1960) had already stated that there is a global tendency for technological and market forces associated with industrialization to push national (IR) systems towards uniformity or convergence. This point of view was largely rejected in later years, but got a renewed impetus in the 1990s, following the political changes in the former communist countries. Reviewing the convergence-divergence debate

Bamber, Lansbury and Wailes (2004) classify various perspectives in the literature into three categories: a simple globalization approach, an institutionalist approach and an integrated approach. They suggest that the simple globalization approach assumes that international pressures associated with globalization are so overwhelming that they leave little scope for national differences. Criticism of this approach shows that there nonetheless still exists considerable diversity in monetary and fiscal settings across countries (Garrett 1997). Other critics contribute to the development of the institutionalist approach suggesting that international trends are mediated by relatively enduring differences in national-level institutions (Bamber et al. 2004, p. 31). The integrated approach stresses the importance of the interaction between interests and institutions in the context of international economic change.

According to Hay (2000) the simple globalization approach can be associated with neoclassicism which is less sensitive to institutional factors channelling common challenges in specific ways and thus more likely to identify convergent tendencies. From his point of view it is useful to differentiate between four senses of convergence: (1) convergence in the pressures and constraints placed upon a particular economy (input convergence); (2) convergence in the politics pursued by particular states (policy convergence); (3) convergence in the consequences, effects and outcomes of particular policies (output convergence); and (4) convergence in the process sustaining the developmental trajectories of particular states (process convergence). His point in this distinction is that policy convergence can bring about divergence in outcomes, while policy divergence may sustain convergent outcomes (Hay 2000, p. 515). This point is made in order to suggest that European convergence is not so much the result of globalization, which might as well heighten competition between states, but of Europeanization, of regional economic integration.

Clearly the process of European integration implies a considerable input into national systems. In the first place it refers to the supranational level with its own body of regulations and standards for harmonization of national laws, especially with respect to the creation of the European common market. The Single Act of 1986 introduced the possibility to remove nontariff barriers for free movement of goods and introduced also the free movement of capital, as well as the free provision of services. Application of European competition law to social security bodies and also the application of the principle of equal treatment of men and women have led to a great number of cases before the European Court of Justice. According to Leibfried and Pierson (2000, p. 267) the dynamics of market integration have created a multi-tiered pattern which is largely law- and court-driven and imposes significant constraints on national social policies. As a consequence they describe the European Court of Justice as 'the key actor of European social policy'.

Secondly, it is important to note the fact that there have been efforts towards greater social policy co-ordination at European level during the 1990s. The changes in the Treaty effectuated in 1991 and in 1997 strengthened the social dialogue at the central European and sectoral levels. They did this even to such a degree that Vandenbroucke (2002) could speak of 'the recognition of the primacy of bargaining levels over legislative channels'. Also, during the 1990s harmonizing directives were adopted in some areas like quality of work, the improvement of equal treatment and workers' participation and consultation, forcing Member States to adapt their own systems, thus stimulating policy convergence.

The process of monetary integration with the Economic and Monetary Union (EMU) also implied that Member States had to consolidate national budgets and to reduce collective expenditure. When looking at output convergence of collective bargaining it can be noted that EMU has stimulated convergence of wage increases: purchasing power increases still varied from 2.5 to 7.1 per cent in the 1960s, but fell between 0.2 and 2.1 per cent a year in the 1990s (EIRO 2000). At the same time economic growth in the 1990s enabled several Member States to raise their social security expenditures, which has led to a reduction in the social expenditure variance (Goudswaard, Kees and van Riel 2004). Also, attempts to reconcile the EMU with a higher profile in social policy resulted in the introduction of the Open Method of Co-ordination (OMC), 'soft' co-ordination of employment, social inclusion and pension policies. This European institutional creation can be considered as an important driver of regional (European) convergence, especially since more recent European initiatives in the area of policy learning intend to create greater policy convergence.

POLICY LEARNING

Despite continuing diversities, all the Member States are facing comparable challenges. This was once again underlined by the Lisbon strategy, which required that all Member States would achieve the same goals. The Member States agreed to proceed by a combination of EU legislation and via the Open Method of Co-ordination (OMC). Under the OMC process Member States cooperate voluntarily in areas of national competence and make use of best practices from other Member States.

The Lisbon strategy was adopted in 2000, at a time that turned out to be a point of return, during the last years of a decade with economic and employment growth. From 1995 to 2000 the EU-15 showed an average economic growth of 2.6 per cent GDP and an unemployment decrease from 11 to 8 per cent. Such a positive trend ended in a period of decline which appears to be difficult to overcome. It implies that the already well-known challenges, like globalization, international competition, the growing use of ICT, ageing and individualization in society, have greater impact and are more difficult to meet. Five years since the start of the Lisbon strategy, Europe has to face budget deficits, an ageing workforce, stagnant economic and employment growth that endangers the realization of the objectives set for 2010 by the Lisbon Strategy. Actual policy questions are: how to support innovation and the transformation into a dynamic knowledge-based economy under the present social and economic conditions? How to create more and better jobs when economic growth is no longer sustainable? How to enhance social cohesion inside a Union with more diversity than ever?

In order to find answers to these questions an Employment Taskforce chaired by Wim Kok was established in March 2003. The main ambition was a relaunch of the Lisbon strategy. The Taskforce presented its report, titled *Jobs, Jobs, Jobs: Creating more employment in Europe,* to the Commission on 26 November 2003. One of the main recommendations of the Taskforce was that to boost employment and productivity, Europe should make better use of the many examples of good practice that exist (European Communities 2003, p. 8).

As a next step a High Level Group, headed – again – by Wim Kok, was established in March 2004 in order to contribute to the mid-term review of the Lisbon process. The report of this group, with the title 'Facing the Challenge: The Lisbon strategy for growth and employment', was submitted to the Commission by 1 November 2004. In this report the process of policy learning is stretched so far that – according to one of the recommendations – the European Commission must be prepared to 'name and shame' those Member States that fail to achieve the Lisbon priorities as well as to 'fame' those that succeed (European Communities 2004, p. 17).

Conventional wisdom suggests that it is impossible to export policy successes from one country to another, because of the fundamental differences in national welfare states. As former Dutch minister Melkert stated in 1997: 'There are no models of eternal bliss to copy' (Visser and Hemerijck 1998). This has not kept delegations all over Europe from visiting neighbouring countries in order to study interesting policy initiatives. Since the 1990s 'modelling' became an accepted practice for policy learning. Well-known European examples in this respect are for instance the 'Celtic Tiger', the Irish model of social partnership, the 'Golden Triangle', the Danish model of activating labour market policy and the 'Polder Model', the accomplishments of the Dutch consensus economy during the last decade. More recently the Scandinavian model draws attention because it succeeds to combine high ranking in global competitiveness and in achievement of the Lisbon objectives with a rather generous welfare state. But, taking into account for instance the Swedish case with two-thirds of the population employed by the state or on state benefits and a tax-take equivalent to 50 per cent of GDP, this model will be hard to copy elsewhere. It confirms the continuity in characteristics of the Scandinavian model: high labour participation, social cohesion and a high level of public expenditure.

Nevertheless, the practice of 'modelling' can also illustrate an evolution in the process of policy learning and the use of best practices. Models may no longer be considered as simplified presentations of reality or instruments for analytic comparison only, but to a certain extent also as examples to be copied. As far as growing consensus on social policy objectives and joint policy learning result in policy convergence and in process convergence, in the sense of the adoption of similar policy instruments, there will be all the more reason to agree on the contents of a European social dimension.

MODERNIZATION OF THE EUROPEAN SOCIAL POLICY

The High Level Group's report just mentioned, underlines the challenges for Europe: besides globalization and intensifying international competition as an external challenge there is (1) the declining economic growth rate, (2) the ageing population as an internal challenge to the sustainability of pensions and healthcare and (3) the enlargement as a challenge to the internal cohesion of Europe.

1. Over the period 1996-2003 Europe's economy is growing less quickly than the US, and the EU-15 productivity growth rate averaged 1.4 per cent, as opposed to 2.2 per cent for the US (European Communities 2004). Such a picture does not offer a strong case for social policy as a productive factor, which might explain why modernization of the social model as an overarching Lisbon objective will essentially imply modernization of the national welfare state arrangements. Meanwhile the ingredients of modernization of the social models are well-known: higher labour participation to be achieved by all Member States simultaneously, also for special categories like women, elderly and vulnerable groups on the labour market, in order to increase competitiveness, but also social inclusion and sustainability of social protection to be supported by flexibilization of the labour markets and more activating social security systems.

2. Under influence of the challenges mentioned before, like ageing and increasing dependency ratios, sustainability of welfare state regimes came

under pressure, not only in the sense of financial sustainability, but also because social security has become more a 'safety trap' then a 'safety net'. Since having a job was considered to be the best way of social inclusion, a redesign of existing arrangements towards activating social security was considered to be necessary. This point of view is also accepted by the European trade union movement. While defending statutory social protection systems, unions' spokesmen are also in favour of adapting social protection systems to new needs and in favour of individualizing social protection rights in order to safeguard the financial viability of social security systems (Hutsebaut 2003). In fact in social security and labour market policies the US originated conception of workfare, stressing individual responsibility and social inclusion through activation, seems to replace the more traditional European human capital approach (Nuys 2004). In this respect the Danish model of flexible and activating labour market policies is considered to offer an outstanding example.

3. As stated above, social cohesion is also one of the objectives of the Lisbon Summit. In fact, fostering social cohesion and solidarity has been a European ambition ever since the Treaty of Rome. The social agenda of Nice has implemented this ambition by underlining the need for reduction of social inequality and poverty. Key objectives here include the integration of people excluded from the labour market and more and better job opportunities for vulnerable groups, for instance via measures to correct regional imbalances in Europe and in the Member States. The recent enlargement however, has enhanced the social diversity in the Union. Despite marked growth rates, the new Member States still show substantial income disparities compared to the EU-15. Moreover it should be noted that especially large regional differences exist inside the central and eastern Member States. In countries like the Czech Republic, Estonia, Latvia and Slovakia the GDP per capita of the population in and around the capitals is about twice the GDP in other regions. Also the level of unemployment in the capitals is about half the level in rural areas. These regional disparities are probably growing instead of declining (Vos 2004). But it is not only a question of catching up by the new Member States. In fact in all Member States social cohesion seems to decline because of growing income inequalities. Thus, former commissioner Romano Prodi (2003) observed that if one looks at figures for the distribution of income within individual countries one has to acknowledge that inequalities, after falling between 1970 and 1980, have widened again, to a point where at the end of the last decade they were back where they had been 30 years before. Recent (2002) OECD figures point into the same direction. This could confirm the statement of Esping-Andersen cited earlier about the trade-off between equality and jobs, or, to put it differently: under the present

conditions, cohesion and sustainability might be or may become incompatible.

Using the Esping-Andersen distinction mentioned earlier, the conclusion can be that all Member States focus their reform policy on the two objectives of budget control and labour participation. With the exception of the Nordic states, this coincides with increasing income inequality and growing poverty rates. In this respect one might speak of a continuing convergence of the social systems, be it that the joint optimalization of the two objectives is hardly compatible with social cohesion. This means that in the end modernization of the national social models will imply American-style redistribution of responsibilities from public to private (Vos, de Beer and de Gier 2004).

THE EU SOCIAL MODEL

The question to be answered now is: can convergent tendencies as described above justify reference to one European social model? To answer the question, five stages in the evolution of the model will be distinguished.

1. The notion of an EU social model was originally developed to mark the difference between European and US social and economic performance. According to Albert (1992) it is the continental or Rhineland model which is more efficient and just, and therefore socially as well as economically superior to the neo-American model. One year later, the publication of Delors' White Paper on growth, competitiveness and employment (European Commission 1993) initiated the European-level political debate on the comparison of EU with US accomplishments. By that time Europe was facing a high level of unemployment, while the US showed strong job growth. At the same time Europe showed a high level of labour productivity, while labour productivity in the US was stagnating. To put it differently: in those years Europe showed a significant but jobless economic growth, while the US showed a moderate economic growth with a high 'employment intensity' (European Commission 1993, p. 50).

2. At a later stage, comparisons between both continents focused on the fundamental differences between social security arrangements. The differing balance between public and private responsibilities was supposed to make the difference. The US economy was considered to be built on the individual pursuit of happiness and the EU economy on

fundamental social rights. In Europe prevention of social risks was considered to be a public or government responsibility, since it is society itself that ultimately demands protection against the dysfunctional effects of social exclusion (Berghman, Douarge and Govaerts 1998). In this perspective the EU model was considered to be a reflection of social values and policies common to most Member States. Larsson (1995) characterizes the model as follows:

> First of all, at the heart of this model, we find a deep sense of solidarity, whose roots are in Christian and trade union traditions, developed by political parties into public policies. Secondly, the model implies a concept of public responsibility for social protection, in the widest sense of the word. The model takes concrete form in fundamental social rights, guaranteed by legislation and at times even in constitutions; rights which have gone on to become part of the European Social Charter (Larsson 1995).

As stated by the Commission, social cohesion, reduction of social inequalities and improvement of social protection were some of the basic values of the social model (European Communities 2001). The European buzz word of 'social policy as a productive factor', meaning that an activating welfare state can enhance economic prosperity (e.g. Larsson 1996), does reflect the principles just mentioned.

3. As a consequence, the Lisbon (2000), Nice (2000) and Barcelona (2002) Summits – as important steps in the development of a European employment strategy – more or less assumed the existence of a European social model. The Lisbon process coupled the economic objective of sustainable growth with progress towards social objectives of more and better employment, greater social cohesion and modernization of the social model, while stressing the significance of social policy as a productive factor. The European Council of Nice referred to the model like it was developed in the past 40 years on the basis of a substantial 'acquis communautair' (European Communities 2001). The Barcelona Summit described the European social model as 'based upon good economic performance, a high level of social protection, education, and social dialogue'. These statements look however, more like political programmes than definitions of reality. Common to all policy statements made at this stage is the assumption of a potential joint optimalization of the three objectives: a balanced budget (economic performance), high labour participation (more employment) and social equality (cohesion).

4. The Social Policy Agenda 2000-2005 added the notion of promotion of quality in all areas of social policy: quality of training, quality in work,

quality of industrial relations and quality of social policy (Diamantopoulou 2001). Since then, quality of industrial relations especially became a topic on the European agenda. In the European Commission's perspective, quality is considered in terms of the contribution of social partnership in implementing the Lisbon strategy (Weiler 2004, p. 6). Social partnership relates to the Commission's objective of capacity building, especially in the new Member States, the promotion of social partners' involvement at all levels: national, sectoral, regional, local and enterprise level (European Communities 2004). By promoting consensus and cooperation oriented industrial relations the Commission in fact supports the introduction of the continental or Rhineland model of industrial relations. The final outcome can be described in terms of a 'multi-level system of regulated autonomy' or a 'multi-tiered EU social and employment community' (Chouraqui and O'Kelly 2001; Esping-Andersen, Gosta, Gallie, Hemerijck and Myles 2001). These descriptions refer to the existence of social policy arrangements at European level in combination and interaction with national level systems.

5.   Since modernization was a key objective of the Lisbon strategy, stagnating economic growth rates may have led to a refocusing of policy goals. Gradually priority was given to the sustainability and the activating effect of social protection systems, and labour market flexibility and social security reform became the key elements in the Lisbon process, suggesting that realization of the Lisbon objectives would be impossible without a fundamental renewal of the EU social model. Right at the start of his EU presidency in 2005, British Prime Minister Blair has echoed such a position by announcing something like a crusade against the EU model. To cite Hay (2000, p. 521): in this respect European integration, initially social and political in nature, tends to mutate into little more than economic liberalization and marketization and 'threatens to become the altar upon which the European social model is ultimately sacrificed'. Because of the fact that labour market policies and social protection mainly are the domain of national policy such a refocusing of values and policy goals does affect national models in the first place, thus promoting (downward) policy convergence.

The different stages as distinguished above characterize the evolution of the European social model. The European employment and industrial relations policy, as part of the European integration, has developed from a rather stylized way of looking at Europe as a region with typical features differing from the US and other regions in the world towards an integrated model of production with participation and training as essential elements.

As it is however, hardly possible to determine whether this model is also the heart of social reality in Europe therefore it is even harder to determine whether this implies a convergence between national models. The picture of a European social model that arises from the gradually developed European social policy is of a distinctive nature when looked at from the national level. When more detail is added to the analysis the picture becomes more blurred.

The European social model, as leading the development of European policies with regard to employment and employee relations was however, never intended to be an ideal-typical, analytical instrument, but was always conceived as a political instrument to present US-EU differences in a stylized way and it always had also the nature of a model that was constructed as an ideological, normative model for the purpose of the European political debate. In the end it was not so much the result of convergence of national systems or models, but primarily an instrument to promote (upward and downward) convergence.

CONCLUDING REMARKS

Following the approach in this chapter it may be concluded that European integration created a substantial input in the different national models. The dynamics of market integration, followed by processes of policy learning, especially stimulated the convergence between policies and their output. The Lisbon strategy, designed to boost economic and employment growth, could even reinforce convergent tendencies if it would lead to the realization of policy objectives as formulated. At the national level, however, many Member States followed neo-liberal economic policy agendas, therewith challenging traditional European values and practices. In many Member States the role of the state as a defender of values of social inclusion and preventing poverty is undermined and financial-monetary objectives have sometimes overruled basic values of social protection. As argued, this redesign of national arrangements does affect the existing balance of public and private responsibilities in many respects and therefore underlines a trend towards increased Americanization of the national social models.

Taking into account the classification of welfare state models we can at least observe an increasing interaction between the two dominant models, e.g. the Anglo-Saxon (or American) and the Rhineland or continental model. Since both models seem to be focusing now on high labour participation and balanced budgets, Europe has become more or less a platform where the different models meet and mix. In this context it can be argued that those who claim that there is little evidence of globalization driving a process of regional convergence (cf. Hay 2000, p. 524) do not take into account sufficiently that the Anglo-Saxon model may serve as the Trojan horse of Americanization. The Scandinavian model seems to be the exception in this trend towards policy convergence, though also there some new, more neo-liberal concepts can be noticed like the adoption of the workfare conception in the Danish labour market model and the Swedish additional private pension system.

The notion of a European social model initially designed as a tool for comparison, evolved from a combination of common values, in the sense of the main characteristics of various national models, to a 'model' (as part of the *acquis social*) to be copied as part of a political programme, eventually with a view on the modernization of social protection arrangements. In this sense it functioned to some extent as an instrument to promote upward convergence, be it that stagnant economic growth and the urgency of more international competitiveness caused a refocusing of the Lisbon ambitions.

In order to relaunch the Lisbon strategy, the 2004 High Level Group report asked for a wide range of reform policies in order to accelerate employment and productivity growth, offering Europe a new frontier for the European economic and social model. This position may suggest that realization of the Lisbon objectives would be impossible without a residualization of the EU social model. Time will tell whether or not the new frontier will imply a European model promoting downward convergence in the future.

REFERENCES

Albert, Michel (1992), *Kapitalismus contra Kapitalismus*, Frankfurt am Main/New York: Campus.
Bamber, Greg J., Russell D. Lansbury and Nick Wailes (eds) (2004), *International and comparative employment relations*, London/New Delhi: Sage Publications, fourth edition.
Berghman, J., D. Douarge and K. Govaerts (1998), 'Social Protection as a Productive Factor', Report on the request of the Commission of the EU – DG V, Leuven: EISS.
Castells, M. (1998), *End of Millennium*, Oxford: Blackwell.
CEPR/Centre for Economic Policy Research (1993), *Making Sense of Subsidiarity: How much Centralization for Europe?*, A CEPR Annual Report.
Chassard, Yves (2002), 'Towards a new architecture for social protection in Europe?', *Belgisch Tijdschrift voor Sociale Zekerheid*, **44** (3), 441-450.
Chouraqui, Alain and Kevin O'Kelly (2001), 'Which European Social Model? A Challenged Balance between Regulation and Deregulation', Paper presented at the Aix-en-Provence Seminar, 11 and 12 September.
Coates, D. (2000), *Models of Capitalism*, Oxford: Polity Press.

Cortebeeck, Veerle, Rik Huys, Guy van Gyes and Tom Vandenbrande (2004), *Quality of industrial relations: Country Profiles*, Katholieke Universiteit Leuven/European Foundation for the Improvement of Living and Working Conditions, second draft.

Crouch, C. (1994), *Industrial Relations and European State Traditions*, Oxford: Oxford University Press.

Den Butter, F.A.G. and C.A. Hazeu (2002), 'Arbeidsmarkt- en sociaal beleid in Europa: Tussen coördinatie en concurrentie', in Cock Hazeu and Gerrit Kronjee (eds), *De vitaliteit van de nationale staat in een veranderende wereld*, The Hague: WRR/Stenfert Kroese, pp. 111-126.

Diamantopoulou, A. (2001), 'Social and labour market policies: Investing in quality', European Conference Brussels, http://europa.eu.int/comm/dgs/employment_social/speeches/010222ad.pdf.

Ebbinghaus, B. and J. Visser (1997), 'Der Wandel der Arbeitsbeziehungen im westeuropäischen Vergleich', in S. Hradil and S. Immerfal (eds), *Die westeuropäischen Gesellschaften im Vergleich*, Opladen: Leske & Budrich.

EIRO (2000), *Wage policy and EMU*, European Foundation for the Improvement of Living and Working Conditions.

Esping-Andersen, G. (1990), *The Three Worlds of Welfare Capitalism*, Cambridge: Polity Press.

Esping-Andersen, G. (1996), 'Equality or employment? The interaction of wages, welfare states and family changes', *Transfer*, **2** (4), 615-634.

Esping-Andersen, Gosta, Duncan Gallie, Anton Hemerijck and John Myles (2001), 'A new welfare architecture for Europe?', Report submitted to the Belgian Presidency of the European Union, final version.

European Commission (1993), *Growth, Competitiveness, Employment: White Paper*, Luxembourg: Office for Official Publications of the European Communities.

European Commission (2000), *Industrial relations in Europe*, Luxembourg: Office for Official Publications of the European Communities.

European Communities (2001), 'European Social Agenda', approved by the European Council of Nice 7, 8 and 9 November 2000, PB C 157, 30 May.

European Communities (2003), 'Jobs, Jobs, Jobs', Report of the Employment Taskforce chaired by Wim Kok, Luxembourg: Office for Official Publications of the European Communities.

European Communities (2004), 'Facing the Challenge', Report from the High Level Group chaired by Wim Kok, Luxembourg: Office for Official Publications of the European Communities.

European Foundation for the Improvement of Living and Working Conditions (2000), *Eiro Annual Review 2000*.

European Foundation for the Improvement of Living and Working Conditions (2001), *Eiro Annual Review 2001*.

European Foundation for the Improvement of Living and Working Conditions (2002), *Towards a qualitative dialogue in industrial relations: Five years of developments in collective bargaining and social dialogue from the European Industrial Relations Observatory,* Luxembourg: Office for Official Publications of the European Communities.

Garrett, Geoffrey (1997), *Partisan Politics in the Global Economy*, Cambridge: Cambridge University Press.

Goudswaard, Kees and Bart van Riel (2004), 'Social Protection in Europe: do we need more co-ordination?', *Dutch Journal of Labour Studies*, **20** (3), 236-248.

Green, Roy (2002), 'Structural reform in Ireland: deregulation and the knowledge-based economy', in David Foden and Lars Magnusson (eds), *Trade unions and the Cardiff process: Economic reform in Europe*, Brussels: European Trade Union Institute, pp. 27-65.

Hall, P. and D. Soskice (eds) (2001), *Varieties of Capitalism: the Institutional Foundations of Comparative Advantage*, Oxford: Oxford University Press.

Hartog, J. and C. Teulings (1999), 'Euro-corporatisme voor de Arbeidsverhoudingen?', *ESB*, **23** (4), 304-307.

Hay, C. (2000), 'Contemporary capitalism, globalization, regionalization and the persistence of national variation', *Review of International Studies*, **26** (4), 509-531.

Hutsebaut, Martin (2003), 'Social protection in Europe: a European trade union perspective', *International Social Security Review*, **56** (1), 53-74.

Hyman, Richard (2001), 'The Europeanisation – or the erosion – of industrial relations?', *IRJ*, **32** (4), 280-294.

Iversen, T. and A. Wren (1998), 'Equality, Employment and Budgetary Restraint, The Trilemma of the Service Economy', *World Politics*, **50**, 507-546.

Kerr, C., J.T. Dunlop, F.H. Harbison and C.A. Myers (1960), *Industrialism and Industrial Man: The Problems of Labor Management in Economic Growth*, Cambridge: Harvard University Press.

Kvist, J. (1993), 'Social Protection for all', Paper presented at the seminar 'Möglichkeiten und Grenzen des Wohlfahrtstaates; Beiträge zu einem Vergleich zwischen USA und Europa', Internationaler Arbeitskreis Sonnenberg.

Larsson, A. (1995), *The European Social Model: Can we afford it?*, Netherlands Institute for International Relations Clingendael.

Larsson, A. (1996), 'Social Policy: Past, Present and Future', *Transfer*, **2** (4), pp. 724-737.

Leibfried, S. (1992), 'Towards a European Welfare State? On integrating Poverty Regimes into the European Community', in Z. Ferge and J. Einvind Kolberg (eds), *Social Policy in a Changing Europe*, Boulder Colorado: Westview Press, pp. 245-279.

Leibfried, S. and P. Pierson (2000), 'Social Policy: Left to Courts and Markets?', in H. Wallace and W. Wallace (eds), *Policy making in the European Union*, Oxford: Oxford University Press, fourth edition, pp. 267-292.

Marginson, Paul (2004), 'The changing relationship between sector- and company-level bargaining', introduction at the EU-presidency conference 'Recent developments in European Industrial Relations', The Hague, 7 and 8 October.

Nuys, Otto (2004), 'Sociaal beleid met twee gezichten: Europa en de Verenigde Staten', *SISWO Cahiers sociale wetenschappen en beleid*, **5**.

OECD (2002), *National Accounts of OECD Countries*, volume 1, Main aggregates 1970-2000 (CD-ROM); Social expenditure database (http://www.oecd.org).

Peper, A. (1980), 'Een nieuwe fase in de studie der Arbeidsverhoudingen?', *Sociaal Maandblad Arbeid*, September, 605-617.

Prodi, Romano (2003), 'Europe: the dream and the choices', *Bulletin Quotidien Europe*, 21 November, No. 2339/2340.

Vandenbroucke, Frank (2002), 'The EU and social protection: what should the European Convention propose?', Paper presented at the Max Planck Institute for the Study of Societies, Köln, 17 June.

Visser, Jelle and Anton Hemerijck (1998), '*Een Nederlands Mirakel*': *Beleidsleren in de verzorgingsstaat*, Amsterdam: University Press.

Vos, K.J. (2004), 'Les relations industrielles en Europe centrale et orientale', *Travail et Emploi*, **99** (Juillet), 55-62.

Vos, Kees, Paul de Beer and Erik de Gier (2004), 'Social Cohesion and the European Social Model', in Kees Vos, Paul de Beer and Erik de Gier (eds), 'Modernising Social Europe, Special issue on the occasion of the Netherlands' presidency of the European Union', *Dutch Journal of Labour Studies*, **20** (3), 336-343.

Weiler, A. (2004), *Quality in industrial relations: Comparative indicators*, European Foundation for the Improvement of Living and Working Conditions/Publications Office.

3. Work and Employment Conditions in New EU Member States: A Different Reality?

Daniel Vaughan-Whitehead [1,2]

INTRODUCTION

No doubt the various EU enlargement processes adopted with Central and Eastern European countries – in May 2004 and again for those joining in 2007 – contribute to explaining why the 'European Social Model' has returned to the heart of the policy debates both at EU and individual EU Member State level. The lower economic and social standards in the new EU Member States in particular have led to fears of social dumping – that is of unfair competition based on local practices in a number of social areas. In the recent national policy debates surrounding the referendum on the European Constitution, the opponents to the Treaty clearly used such uncertainties after EU enlargement to highlight the lack of a social Europe and the lack of harmonized employment and working conditions in an enlarged European Union.

It is thus a pressing need to clearly identify the realities of working and employment practices in the new EU Member States and how much these diverge from those in the older EU Member States, and especially try to distinguish the changes that have taken place since the recent EU enlargement.

A first question is whether working conditions follow similar patterns in all the new EU Member States, and whether they have started to converge significantly towards the standards in the older Members? Alternatively, do we find diverging trends in certain areas? Consequently, we attempt in this chapter to identify any general direction being followed in work and employment conditions in the EU-25 and even the future EU-28. To begin, we scrutinize all the working and employment conditions in the new EU Member States, and how they differ from those in the former EU-15, before trying to establish their temporary or more permanent nature.

ALREADY RALLIED TO THE SIRENS OF EXTREME FLEXIBILITY?

Work under the previous communist regimes tended to be characterized by very low wages but with a guarantee of lifelong employment. The shift to a free market economy has brought radical changes in patterns of employment and working conditions. During the transition years, new enterprises started to leave former corporate models behind and adopt new forms of employment and working conditions; arrangements to better fit with the newly competitive environment. The opening up of trade, required as a condition of EU membership, also led enterprises to accelerate their adaptability processes, while the negotiation process itself influenced all policy areas including the world of work. Can we say that these processes have assisted in moving towards harmonization in this field – as is desired by all those concerned with a Social Europe – or do certain practices in the new EU Member States continue to lag far from EU standards?

Massive Recourse to Atypical Forms of Employment

The first significant change has been a move towards atypical employment forms: fixed-term contracts, self-employment and, more recently, employment through intermediate agencies.

Although these forms of employment were rare in the early years of transition – with most workers benefiting from permanent contracts – fixed-term work has become a major form of employment and is being increasingly used as an important source of flexibility. While the growth in fixed-term contracts occurred in the early 1990s in the EU-15 Member States, they have only started to emerge in most of the ten new Member States and three candidate countries in the last few years. However, their use has increased rapidly, with this type of contract, unheard of in the early 1990s, used with more than 15 per cent of the workforce in the ten new EU Member States in 2005. Figure 3.1 below, covering the period 1998–2005, shows that this process shows no sign of abating. This form of employment is already more widespread in the ten new Member States (15.6 per cent) than in the EU-15 (14.0 per cent). The most noticeable increases have been in Poland (from 11.9 per cent of employees in 1998 to 25.5 per cent in 2005) and Slovenia (from 11.5 per cent to nearly 17 per cent). Polish legislation with regard to this type of contract is particularly permissive, encouraging most employers to switch to such flexible forms of labour contract. However, Spain remains the Member Country with the highest percentage of fixed-term contracts at 33.3 per cent.

For employers, the use of such contracts has the major advantage of reducing costs in the event of employment termination.

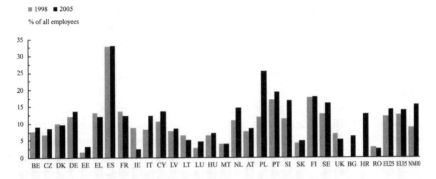

Note: CY, MT, PL: 1998 data are for 2000; LU: 2005 data are for 2004

Source: Eurostat, EU Labour Force Survey

Figure 3.1 Employees on fixed-term contracts in Member States, 1998 and 2005

A new phenomenon is also emerging in the new Member States: the use of intermediate employment agencies to provide employers with a constant supply of employees. Although this type of employment is only in its infancy, in all the new Member States, with usage well below the EU average, a growing proportion of work contracts seems to be concluded through an employment agency. Of the new Member Countries, they are most widespread in Latvia, Slovenia and Malta. Although such contracts remain limited in the other newcomers, this is often attributed to use being made of other forms of irregular contract.

The form of flexibility that seems to have recently grown the most is self-employment, now 'enjoyed' by 13 per cent of workers in the new EU Member States, compared to 10 per cent in the EU-15. Self-employment is particularly common in certain countries, affecting in 2005 more than 20 per cent of workers in Romania, 16 per cent in Poland, 14 per cent in Cyprus and 12-13 per cent in the Czech Republic and Lithuania. It has also recently increased significantly in Slovakia and the Czech Republic. The percentage of self-employed workers is thus already above the EU-15 average in many of the EU new Member States, at levels matched in the EU-15 by only Greece, Italy and Portugal (see Figure 3.2).

However, two aspects should not be overlooked: (i) it is important in analysing the data and developments to consider the significance of agriculture since the proportion of self-employed is generally very high in that sector and agriculture is particularly important in certain countries including Poland; and (ii) it is important to focus on the self-employed 'who do not work for a dependent employer' (as indeed is shown in Figure 3.2), i.e. leaving out those who are self-employed in little more than name.

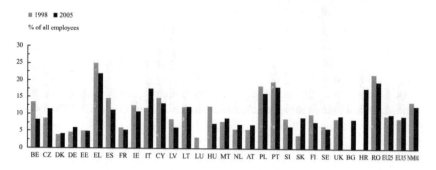

Note: CY, MT, PL: 1998=2000; LU: 2005=2004

Source: Eurostat, EU Labour Force Survey

Figure 3.2 Self-employed in Member States, 1998 and 2005

Self-employment represents, as a form of temporary work contract, a new source of flexibility, often convenient for employers since it allows them to achieve maximum flexibility more easily, and largely avoid social contributions and labour regulations. Use of this approach is significant in Poland, Hungary, Lithuania and Latvia, but also to be seen in Estonia and other new Member States. Compared to the EU-15, recourse to this approach not only seems to be more extensive already, it may capture a different phenomenon – of regular employees shifting from a conventional labour contract to self-employed status, although it must be admitted that the self-employed in the EU-15 also include a significant number of small 'businesses' run by ex-employees continuing to work for their old employer. The concerns of the Commission regarding this problem were expressed in a recent report on free movement of workers across the enlarged EU: 'The problem of persons posing falsely as self-employed workers to circumvent the law should be dealt with by Member States'.[3]

In addition to this form of self-employment, with employees being moved from a regular to a self-employment contract, while continuing to work for the same 'employer', we have also observed a second form of self-employment in which an employer supplements an employee's normal labour contract with an additional self-employment contract (Vaughan-Whitehead 2005). In this situation, the two different employment statuses may reflect distinct forms of activity and the additional activity may be covered by the Civil Code rather than the Labour Code. This approach, that is the use within the same enterprise and with the same employee of 'multiple contracts', seems to be developing rapidly in many of the new Member States with a regular labour contract being supplemented, for extra working time or additional work assignments, by a civil contract or a self-employment contract. This phenomenon seems to be particularly widespread in Poland, Hungary and the three Baltic States, but is also prevalent in all the other new Member States in Central and Eastern Europe.

In Estonia, not only are civil contracts widely used by employers as a major source of flexibility, but also a not insignificant proportion of workers – 5 per cent in 2002 albeit down from 11 per cent in 1998 – continues to work without any written labour contract. Their employment and working conditions are agreed orally with their employer, a practice that circumvents Estonian law and seems to be most common in new enterprises, especially in Tallinn and in rural areas (7 per cent of enterprises in 2002).

Another practice that is used in some of the new EU Member States, especially in Lithuania, Latvia and Estonia, to enable an employer to achieve flexibility without breaking the law, is to make an employee sign, alongside their individual labour contract, a supplementary 'extra agreement' which, in fact, amounts to a resignation letter that can be used at any time the employer so desires. While this practice is decreasing in Estonia (from 10 per cent to 6 per cent between 1999 and 2002) it continues to gain popularity in Latvia and Lithuania, where it affects nearly 10 per cent of the labour force. The employees' 'willingness' to accept such a practice is clearly related to the existing high unemployment and the poor prospects of finding a job.

Part-time work is also an employment area where the mechanisms seem different to those in the former EU-15. It is first of all a form of contract that remains poorly developed, and it often takes on a non-voluntary nature for employees. A recent survey in Hungary found that most people on part-time contracts were unable to find full-time work. Only one-third agreed to such contracts by choice, particularly women.

Part-time work seems to have been developing as a flexible form of employment rather than as a way of reconciling work and family, as it is the case in many of the EU-15 countries, most notably in the Netherlands (see Figure 3.3). Part-time work in most of the new EU Member States is used in employing particular categories of workers, such as retired people, the disabled, young first entrants and the previously unemployed, who generally already receive social allowances but desperately require additional income. In Hungary, nearly one-fifth of the 4.8 per cent of employees who work part-time are disabled. In Poland, 40 per cent of part-time workers are either pensioners or disabled.

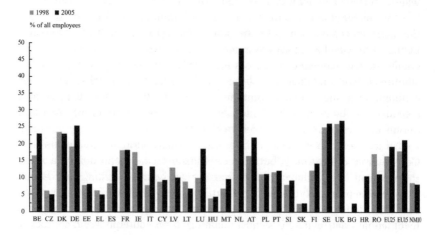

Note: CY, MT, PL 1998=2000; LU 2005=2004

Source: Eurostat, EU Labour Force Survey

Figure 3.3 Part-time employment in EU Member States, 1998 and 2005

Wages Lag Well Behind

Undoubtedly, wages constitute the variable which, in the transition process as well as in the period following EU enlargement, shows the greatest lag; and wages do not seem to be catching up despite the better economic prospects.

The reasons are first to be found in the type of policymaking implemented during the transition years, with a rapid price liberalization process that exerted an immediate downward pressure on real wages despite wages having already been kept at artificially low levels during the previous communist regimes. The downward trend in wages reflected the adjustment variable of choice by governments during the early transition years, with wage earners, along with those dependent on social allowances, bearing the brunt of the burden of transition. It is not by chance that the most conspicuous gap between the new and the older EU Member States today is in terms of wage levels.

As a result, poverty remains a major issue in most of the new EU Member States. A large part of the population continues to find itself below or not far above the subsistence minimum or poverty line. While the unemployed, and especially the long-term unemployed, are first in line, along with pensioners, the disabled and those trying to cope on only social benefits, one can also observe an increasing phenomenon of a working poor, confirming that low wage levels are another major source of poverty.

From Table 3.1 we can see that the minimum wage, one of the most important tools against workers sinking into poverty, and also average wages in the new Member States continue to be well below those in other EU countries. The average wage across the ten new EU Member States was only slightly above one-quarter of the EU-15 average in 2004. The large differentials in the levels of minimum wage make it unrealistic to attempt to establish an EU-25 minimum wage level, as was in fact frequently proposed during the recent debates on the European Constitution, especially in France and in the Netherlands, where a majority of the electorate voted against the Constitution, often it is believed because of a feeling of a lack of a social Europe and the failure to harmonize wages and working conditions. However, a progressive levelling-up of the national minimum wage in the new EU Member States, where it has often remained at a rather symbolic level, could contribute to a steady social catch up and help avoid sources of destructive competition.

Another practice observed at the enterprise level in some of the new Member States is the widespread payment of bonuses in exchange for accepting very poor working conditions, especially in terms of occupational health and safety, a practice which both workers and trade unions seem content to accept, rather than demanding a progressive improvement in health and safety conditions and the removal of such bonuses, a 'choice' very much influenced by workers' needs to increase their incomes. Working long hours has also become a significant way to increase living standards. One interesting development that seems to be taking place is that, over the last few years, there has been a steady decrease in the number of workers with a second or even a third job, the typical way of coping during the early transition years for many workers. In Estonia, for instance, the percentage of people having two jobs decreased from 9 per cent in 1997 to 4.5 per cent in 2002. Instead, workers now seem to concentrate on one activity but work longer hours to increase their wages and increase the likelihood of being retained by their employer.

Wage levels also contribute to the limited interest in working on a part-time basis reported in all new EU Member States; part-time work leads to a decrease in wages and lower living standards. In Estonia, the main reason for working part-time (according to 51 per cent of part-timers) is their failure to find a full-time, and thus higher paid, job. The situation is the same in Poland where 40 per cent of part-timers would like a full-time job and where part-time work is generally associated with social exclusion. This is especially the case given the high cost of urban transport in cities like Warsaw (which can

Table 3.1 Minimum wage and average wage levels, 2003–2004, EU-25

	Monthly minimum wage 2003 (€)	Monthly minimum wage 2003(PPP)	Annual average wage 2003	Annual average wage 2004
Austria	-	-	-	-
Belgium	1 163	1 162	29 880	30 622
Cyprus	-	-	17 667	18 495
Czech Republic	199	389	7 042	7 465
Denmark	-	-	36 785	37 332
Estonia	138	264	5 292	5 874
Finland	-	-	27 126	28 048
France	1 154	1 150	26 517	27 230
Germany	-	-	26 282	26 397
Greece	605	725	17 676	18 721
Hungary	212	384	7 721	8 544
Ireland	1 073	910	33 666	35 539
Italy	-	-	21 572	22 218
Latvia	116	239	3 741	4 148
Lithuania	125	252	4 495	4 803
Luxembourg	1 369	1 338	60 733	64 037
Malta	535	752	13 599	13 801
Netherlands	1 249	1 225	27 218	27 719
Poland	201	351	6 486	6 559
Portugal	416	543	12 259	13 497
Slovakia	118	265	4 519	5 197
Slovenia	451	668	14 903	15 641
Spain	526	617	19 627	20 235
Sweden	-	-	26 984	27 826
United Kingdom	1 105	983	31 133	33 079
EU-15	-	-	25 939	26 678
EU-25	-	-	23 342	24 015

Note: PPP (Purchasing Poverty Power)

Source: Minimum wages: Eurostat, EC Employment in Europe 2003, p. 80; Average wages: Eurostat, National accounts data.

absorb up to 15 per cent of the average part-time wage); moreover, a part-time wage is probably insufficient to cover child-care costs. In addition, where part-time work is a voluntary choice, this is often because it is a second job for those already working full-time (this situation reflects 12 per cent of part-timers in Estonia).

Another way of reducing labour costs in the new Member States seems to consist of employers declaring that a majority of their employees are on the minimum wage, and then making extra 'under the table' payments, i.e. undeclared cash-in-hand. This enables employers to make significant savings in terms of social contributions and other taxes. Nearly half of the Hungarian employers who responded to a recent survey (see Ecostat 2003) reported that this was general practice in Hungary. As such, it represents the most quoted method (by 46 per cent of respondents) of reducing the cost of labour. Other popular methods included employment through a civil contract (mentioned by 27 per cent of employers), making use of trial periods (12 per cent) and part-time employment (15 per cent).

In Estonia, 10 per cent of employees received such 'under the table' payments in 2002 (an improvement on 1999 when this practice was reported by 19 per cent of employees). In Poland, this affected nearly 20 per cent of employees in micro-enterprises (i.e. those with less than five employees) in 2003, between 10 per cent and 15 per cent of those in small and medium-sized enterprises (six to 150 employees) but less than 5 per cent of employees in large companies (over 150 employees).

The general practice of under-declaring wages has implications for many other working conditions: for instance, overtime payments according to national laws are calculated on the basis of the basic wage. Given these under-declared wages, instead of being regulated by law, overtime rates are in practice at the employers' discretion. Further, other sources of income (social benefits) are systematically deflated by such wage under-reporting.

Longer Hours and More Stress at Work?

The length of the working week is undoubtedly an area where significant differences continue to prevail between the EU-15 and the ten new Member States, with employees appearing to work longer on average in the latter (see Figure 3.4). Workers in several of the new EU Member States, such as Poland (43.3), the Czech Republic and Slovenia (42.9), Latvia (42.8) and Cyprus, seem in particular to work more hours. What is also interesting is to try to capture the trends in new EU Member States compared to the older Members. Here, at least, we can undoubtedly talk about convergence since the average working week in the new EU Member States has been approaching the EU-15 average between 1998 and 2005.

To an extent, this is due to a slight increase in working hours in the EU-15 – notably through the greater use of overtime – but primarily it can be attributed to a steady decline in working hours in the new EU Member States. Such a relatively rapid decline in working time has been achieved mainly through changes in national labour laws – for example, a reduction in the maximum weekly working time in Poland from 42 to 40 hours between 2001 and 2003 – mainly implemented to fall into line with the EU working time directive. Average working time decreased significantly in many new Member States between 1998 and 2005, for instance by two hours in the Czech Republic and Slovakia.

In the opposite direction, ten of the EU-15 countries experienced an increase in their weekly working time between 2004 and 2005. In contrast, only two out of the ten new EU Member States, Lithuania and Slovakia, experienced an increase, and then only a very modest one.

However, we would caution that the above assessment on convergence in working time should be balanced by four other important factors.

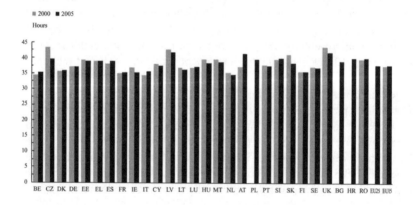

Note: PL: 2000=2001; LU: 2005=2004

Source: Eurostat, EU Labour Force Survey

Figure 3.4 Average usual hours worked by full-time employees, 2000 and 2005

Firstly, the recorded figures also contain information on the percentage of employees working more than 50 hours a week, and these show that this is much more common in the new EU Member States. According to Paoli, Pascal, Parent-Thirion and Persson (2002), in 2001, 79 per cent of workers in the 12 candidate countries (that is, the ten new Member States plus Bulgaria and Romania) – compared to 48 per cent of workers in the EU-15 – worked more than 40 hours a week on average. More recent case study evidence seems to confirm these long working hours in the new EU Member States and this is also observed in the three candidate countries (European Commission 2005). In Croatia, for instance, according to national survey results, the average self-reported working week stands at 45.5 hours, with 75 per cent working in excess of 40 hours, 22 per cent more than 50 hours and 6 per cent more than 60 hours.

Much of this overtime work is not included in official statistics leading to our second remark: that there are good reasons to believe that, in the context of a strong informal economy – where by definition the number of working hours is unregulated and therefore potentially much greater (often above 50 hours a week) – official statistics on working time regularly under-represent the real number of working hours. Employers also have a tendency to under-report the total number of working hours when using civil contracts, for which working time does not seem to be fully counted, and unpaid overtime is also relatively common and certainly does not appear in official statistics. Moreover, there can also be intensive periods with very long working weeks (in excess of 50 hours), while the average working time remains low because the reference period used in calculating the average is often defined by the employer (as a result of very weak social dialogue and works councils).

Overall, it seems that the extension of working hours has become a way of coping for both employers and employees, at least during the transition period. On the employers' side, it is a way of responding to peak periods of activity without needing to increase the number of workers, and in this way they can limit social security contributions and avoid costly hiring and firing procedures. From the employees' side, increasing the number of hours worked has been the main way of topping up the low basic wages and obtaining the means necessary for family survival. It is mainly the low wages that drive workers to longer working hours. However, longer working hours are often imposed to meet the employers' requirements. As an illustration, it is suggested that 30 per cent of overtime is involuntary in Poland and thus does not reflect a free choice by the employees.

Thirdly, weekend or unsocial hour working has also increased rapidly in some of the new EU Member States and, in 2005, was most common in Slovakia, Malta and Estonia (see Figure 3.5). Since 2000, such working has increased the most in Slovakia and the Czech Republic and also markedly in Slovenia and Croatia, where the issue – and in particular Sunday working in the retail sector – has recently been a hot topic of public debate, with not only political but also religious representatives becoming involved.

Finally, our fourth point is that we also observe more arduous working patterns in the new EU Member States (also observed by the Dublin

European Foundation, see Paoli et al. 2002) as well as a systematic introduction of shift work in order to facilitate round-the-clock operations (Vaughan-Whitehead 2005).

The countries with the highest levels of shift work (in both industry and services) are Poland, Croatia, Slovenia, Slovakia and the Czech Republic. In Poland for instance, 40.6 per cent of women and men in industry (compared to 18.7 per cent and 21.5 per cent respectively in the EU-25) and 37 per cent of men and 27 per cent of women in services (18.3 per cent and 15.3 per cent respectively in the EU-25) are affected by shift work.

This phenomenon has other direct implications for employees regarding other working conditions. The increased recourse to shift work has also often led to a parallel development of weekend working. Longer or more stressful working weeks are associated with greater health and safety risks and also with more difficulties in reconciling work and family demands.

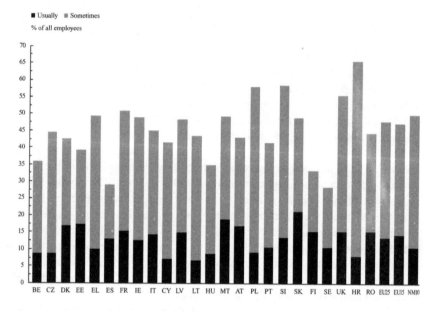

Source: Eurostat, EU Labour Force Survey

Figure 3.5 Proportion of employees working both Saturday and Sunday, 2005

Poor Safety at Work

Enterprises in most new EU Member States have so far not paid much attention to health and safety, particularly because this is an area in which they would have to spend significantly to meet the numerous EC directives without any immediate bottom-line return. A health and safety index which we established using results from the 2001 Dublin Foundation Survey shows that the health and safety risks in most new EU Member States are far higher than in the EU-15 countries.

Even when there is significant legislation in place, it is rarely applied at the enterprise level, especially among the new private small and medium-sized enterprises. In Estonia, for instance, according to the Labour Inspectorate only 15 per cent of enterprises were complying with legal obligations in this area. The main violations included the absence of a contract with an occupational health service specialist (70 per cent were found not to have one), no risk assessment or plan of activities (60 per cent of enterprises are not in compliance), no internal control (absent in 49 per cent of enterprises), no training (not even discussed in 44 per cent) and no elected working environment representatives (in 37 per cent).

Although the general situation seems to be slowly improving according to several recent reports by the European Commission, the picture is still worrying in most new EU Member States. The fact that many enterprises still have problems in this area is reflected in the statistics on occupational accidents and diseases in Estonia: their number increased by almost 50 per cent between 1999 and 2002. In other countries, such as Poland, while the number of accidents at work is decreasing, it remains at a high level. Further, most victims of such accidents are on short-term or temporary contracts indicating that there is a direct correlation between employment security and the risk of accidents. We would caution that the recent increase in accidents in a few new Member States may not be due to a real increase in absolute numbers but due to better reporting since the true figures have frequently and systematically been hidden over the first 15 years of transition and EU accession, by both employers and employees. This is a sign that these countries are moving towards greater transparency and reflecting greater public concern in relation to occupational health and safety issues.

ARE THESE SHORT-TERM OR LONG-TERM TRENDS?

No doubt there are significant differences in the world of work between the new and the older EU Member States. However, these may be largely due to the different levels of economic development, and so one might expect a catching up process to be underway following EU enlargement. Nevertheless, there does seem to be structural differences in the functioning of labour markets and the actors concerned. One may also wonder whether the newcomers have in fact already adopted a much more liberal approach in their policymaking. In this section, we attempt to identify important processes that may help explain the differences observed so far, and enable one to predict the possible long-term outcomes.

The Social Context: Wages and Employment Conditions are Not, so far, Catching Up

The general social context clearly has a direct effect on working conditions. In fact, almost all the working and employment conditions at the enterprise level in the new EU Member States can be traced back to the general social situation, particularly the high unemployment levels and the low wages. Most case studies recently carried out at individual enterprises show that the main reason why employees accept poor working and employment conditions, without complaining or going to court, is fear of losing their job. In particular, the prevalence of long-term unemployment in these countries acts as a strong disincentive for employees to complain about their working conditions or to apply elsewhere for another job with hypothetically better working conditions. This situation demotivates workers and lowers productivity in the enterprises. It also results in a very low worker turnover and little mobility between enterprises. To overcome this problem, more concrete action is needed to fight long-term unemployment in these countries, where efforts to introduce active labour market policies remain rather weak. In fact, it seems that not only do the long-term unemployment rates, especially for young people, remain higher than in other EU Member States but also that the employment situation does not seem to have improved as a result of the higher economic growth recently experienced in these countries.

Another reason why employees generally accept tough working conditions such as long hours – often without extra compensation – and stressful working rhythms is the urgent need to raise their living standards. In this regard, most new EU Member States are lacking a long-term strategy on incomes policy and mechanisms to enable progressive catching up in terms of incomes and real wages. Only when the situation becomes somewhat rosier with regards to wages and employment can any improvement in working conditions, as well as with reconciling work and family, be seriously envisaged.

The Influence of the Large Informal Economy

The presence of a large informal sector is to an extent a result of the unintended processes brought about by the transition. This, together with the serious collapse in production that occurred during the early transition years, was not foreseen by external advisers, including those from international monetary institutions, and has yet to be documented and explained. The emergence of the informal economy was seen at the time as a temporary phenomenon that would fade as the economy grew and employment expanded.

Contrary to such initial predictions, the presence of an informal sector remains a key, and seemingly a permanent, feature of most transition economies. Partly fed by the disengagement in the official sector as part of the restructuring process, long-term unemployment in particular has encouraged informal activities. The informal sector is also rooted in the general economic and social situation of these countries with different motivations on both the supply and the demand sides. For the employers, that is from the demand side, informal activities are a way of avoiding what they consider as the 'over-taxation' of the labour market. These are most commonly found in the small and even micro-enterprises whose life expectancy is very short – less than two years. Although the development of myriad small private businesses has contributed to increasing official employment, it has been paralleled by a similar development of small units in the informal sector. From the supply side, i.e. those providing a service or doing the work, the informal sector represents a way of obtaining additional income and avoiding taxation and social security contributions as well as other constraints that come with an official job such as obligatory working hours (which makes it difficult to hold down two or three jobs). In general, however, most have been forced by circumstances to accept a job in the informal sector where they work under very precarious conditions, and lose the right to unemployment benefits and other social allocations should they lose their job. It is also important to note that there is also a thriving demand from the consumer side, since buying items on the black market is a way to survive for many households.

The informal sector remains enormous throughout the region: in Hungary, for instance, it has been estimated from surveys that it may well generate more than one-third of GDP. Similarly, in Latvia, this sector has more than doubled, reaching more than 35 per cent of GDP, and even this figure is probably an underestimate. In Poland, as well, the black economy has expanded enormously, estimated as being worth more than 27 per cent of GDP by Schneider (2002). There is also a significant informal sector in Slovenia, although reliable data are not available. The use of hidden employment is also well advanced in Estonia (it was estimated the equivalent of 39 per cent of GDP by Schneider (2002)), especially in sectors such as construction, agriculture, trade, hotels and restaurants and other services. It should be emphasized that the size of the informal economy expressed as a percentage of GDP, while serving as an approximate measure of the phenomenon, has limitations since many informal activities do not generate much added output as regards GDP (small jobs exchanged between neighbours, and so on), but rather represent lost opportunities for the formal sector – the time that people dedicate to the informal sector in effect being deducted from the formal economy. Other complementary and generally more appropriate measures should be used, such as the number of people involved in informal activities; the amount of time they dedicate to the informal sector; the proportion of total income earned in the informal sector; or even the share of expenditure in informal markets. Information of this kind can generally be collected through representative household surveys. So far, however, information remains limited. This is partly due to the purposeful neglect of the phenomenon (and even of its promotion as a way of deflecting difficulties during periods of restrictive macroeconomic policy) [4] which has unfortunately contributed to it being tolerated and developed at all levels.

Unquestionably, the presence of a large informal sector heavily influences working and employment conditions in the formal economy. The informal sector effectively represents the most extreme form of 'flexibility' within the labour market. For managements, the informal sector constitutes a permanent reserve of cheap and flexible labour, and this helps them in pressurizing their employees to accept poor employment conditions. The presence of a significant informal sector has also played a role with regard to the prevalence of long working hours, unpaid overtime and the increasing recourse to self-employment. In fact, making use of the self-employment status represents an open door to the informal sector, a path to informalizing a previously formal activity. In such a context, one cannot expect to see improving working and employment conditions, unless timely and adequate action is taken to control the informal economy.

Social Dialogue, the Missing Lever for Improving Work

It is clear that social dialogue, especially in the sense of collective bargaining at the local level, can serve as an important lever for improving conditions at work. Not only can it lead to significant improvements in the individual work issues discussed above, it can also help to address these various areas within a combined and coherent approach. This is especially the case since social dialogue has become a transversal governance tool at the EU level.

Nevertheless, the outcomes in enterprises of the new EU Member States are rather mixed. Case studies at enterprise level (see Vaughan-Whitehead 2005) show that working and employment conditions have definitely improved where there are trade unions or where collective agreements have been signed at enterprise level. However, the general weaknesses of trade unions and of employer organizations have seriously limited the achievements in this field. Employer organizations do not seem to have much influence over the myriad of small business entrepreneurs who have emerged in the new private sector. Trade unions, on their part, have yet to find an effective strategy for achieving representation in small private companies. Moreover, they continue to face a fall in membership and limited mobilization capacity.

Direct forms of workers' participation – such as seats on boards of directors or on works councils, including European works councils – are also little developed as yet. These have been found to have a direct impact on working conditions elsewhere, especially where a clear role is foreseen for workers' representatives, such as in the implementation of EC directives on health and safety which require health and safety committees to be established. Among the new EU Members only Slovenia and Hungary, and more recently Slovakia and the Czech Republic, have implemented a role for some types of works councils. In the other new Member States, worker participation is still surprisingly, given their history, missing. In some countries including Poland and the Baltic States, works councils and other forms of worker involvement in decision making, considered as vestiges of socialism, have been completely dismantled, along with self-management forms, such as cooperatives, and often with the full cooperation of the trade unions. For example, one may recall the fierce opposition during the early years of reform by the Polish trade union Solidarnosc to works councils because they were considered to contradict the effective functioning of a free market economy.

Worker participation and forms of information exchange and consultation are most likely to be found in larger companies, which generally also continue to have trade union representation. Conversely, small private enterprises generally do not have trade unions or works councils, or indeed any other participatory mechanisms that could act as a counterbalance to management.

Moreover, and contrary to the tripartite structures envisaged for social dialogue and bilateral negotiations, independent channels continue to be poorly developed in most new EU Member States. Worrying trends continue to be observed at the enterprise level, which often seems to be beyond the control of social partners. At the same time, in contrast to the wider EU experience, there is a lack of collective agreements at the sectoral and regional levels, indicating a similar lack of intermediate social dialogue. These various features explain the low coverage of collective bargaining currently found in most new EU Member States. The majority of workers – sometimes as many as 80 per cent as for instance in Latvia and Lithuania – is not covered by collective agreements. This contrasts with the general trend in the EU-15 where, in 2000-2002, coverage rates were as high as 100 per cent in Belgium and Austria, above 90 per cent in Sweden, Finland and France, and covered more than two-thirds of employees in Denmark, Spain, the Netherlands and Germany. Only Cyprus, with an estimated coverage rate of 65-70 per cent, was comparable with the above-mentioned EU Member States. Slovenia is a special case since its high coverage rate is due mainly to an obligatory system of collective agreements, signed between relevant sectoral trade unions and relevant sectoral organizations of the Slovenian Chamber of Commerce (rather than with the national employers' association). Thus, a fully voluntary collective bargaining system has yet to emerge.

However, even if the coverage rate is high, enterprise characteristics may limit the effectiveness of collective bargaining. In Hungary, where the coverage rate is relatively high, micro- and small enterprises account for more than 1.5 million jobs, thus absorbing half of the labour force. In such enterprises there is little likelihood of seeing any form of collective industrial relations. Rather, working conditions will continue to be governed by the employers through individual employment relationships with their employees. We would also emphasize that employees who switch to self-employment status fall outside any legal social dialogue.

Not only does the number of collective agreements remain very low in the new EU Member States, their contents are also limited. They generally reproduce the minimum requirements of the applicable legal texts. A recent study of the contents of agreements in Estonia revealed that, in some cases where a collective agreement had been signed, the contents were sometimes even more modest than what was enshrined in the law, reflecting the social partners' lack of knowledge of the existing legislative provisions on working conditions (Eamets, Raul, Raal and Masso 2005).

Collective agreements also cover a very narrow range of issues, generally only wages and bonuses and rarely also working time. All the other key working conditions described in this article such as health and safety, working rhythms, working time flexibility, payment of overtime and employment contracts are not covered by social dialogue, explaining the crisis observed at enterprise level.

This absence of collective bargaining naturally helps to explain the excesses found in employment and working conditions described in the previous sections. Employers seem to have become the dominant decision makers on working and employment conditions, and so any changes that do occur may well continue to depend for some time into the future on employers using their discretionary power.

This leads to a final important realization: as working conditions have been weakened as a result of the lack of social dialogue, they will only be reinforced in the future through a significant strengthening of social dialogue.

CONCLUSIONS

While work under the previous communist regimes was characterized by very low wages but with the compensation of a guarantee of lifelong employment, the shift to a free market economy has brought radical changes in both patterns of employment and working conditions. During the transition years, which brought with them the unprecedented, in these societies, phenomenon of restructuring with associated dismissals and growing unemployment, and the emergence and development of a private sector, new enterprises started to abandon former corporate models and adopt new forms of employment and working time arrangements to better adapt to the newly competitive environment.

This is confirmed from our assessment at the firm-level of working and by the current employment conditions in the new Member States. This leads to an initial major conclusion: not only is the general responsiveness of new Member States to change very strong, but they have also shown an ability to introduce innovative policies and practices in all aspects of working conditions.

At the same time, reality at the enterprise level shows that adapting to new difficult circumstances has clearly led to a number of excesses and has often generated extreme behaviour. This is observable in a number of areas related to working conditions including employment status, working time, payment of overtime and wages and occupational health and safety.

While new Member States are witnessing a growth in atypical forms of contract, such as temporary contracts or engagements through intermediate employment agencies, self-employment is the most commonly used form of flexibility. This type of contract is often the most attractive for employers, since it allows them to achieve maximum flexibility while avoiding and circumventing social contributions and labour regulations.

Since these various forms of flexibility – temporary work, self-employment, agency work – already exist in the EU-15 countries, where they are also increasingly used by employers and are even becoming recognized by the trade unions, it could be argued that the changes in the new Member States reflect convergence towards the practices developed in the original EU free market economies. However, if we compare the two groups of EU Members, the recourse to these atypical contracts seems not only to be already more extensive in the new Member States, but also to sometimes reflect a different phenomenon. This seems to be the case with self-employment which, in the new Member States, is often used as a means of converting regular employees into a more flexible workforce, rather than reflecting a true growth in self-employed entrepreneurs. Part-time work also seems to capture a different phenomenon in the new and future EU Member

States, offering at least some income to the weakest groups in the labour market who cannot get a full-time job.

Working time is another area in which there are some differences between the EU-15 and the ten new Member States: employees seem, on average, to be working more hours in the latter and also varying working hours much more as a form of flexibility tool. However, the fact that the average working week has already decreased in many of the newcomers – for instance by two hours a week in the Czech Republic since 1997 – is an encouraging sign of convergence.

Finally, what is perhaps the largest and most important gap, namely in the levels of wages and incomes, between the older and the new EU Member States seems to be slow to close.

So, overall, there do seem to be positive signs of both convergence and increased diversity. What should not be overlooked, however, is the general context of the new as well as the future EU Member States. The growth of new forms of employment and working conditions in these countries has taken place within a context of total economic restructuring and alongside the emergence of a new type of entrepreneur, especially in SMEs, for whom profits and short-term survival are the priorities. This has often taken place within an environment that lacks a tradition of human resources and industrial relations with the result that the outcomes have often been large imbalances between the employers' desire for flexibility and the workers' aspirations for security in employment terms and working conditions. High unemployment and low wages have pushed workers to accept almost any working conditions to retain their jobs, and so trade unions, if and where they are present, find they can do little more than support the workers' choices. This explains why the few collective agreements that are found, tend to define only employment conditions and wages, and ignore other working conditions. The existing context puts the employer in a dominant bargaining position which only a radical improvement in the economic and social situation is likely to change.

Even then it is not certain that a better balance would be achieved since this really requires an improvement in the labour markets and especially a better matching of labour demand and supply. So far, the persistent long-term unemployment in these countries has shown little sign of falling, even in those countries displaying strong economic growth. This suggests that the working and employment conditions imposed by employers may well prevail for some considerable time into the future. Perhaps the upward trend in 'self-employment arrangements' will continue as a replacement for regular labour contracts at the enterprise level. However, according to Eurostat, the percentage of self-employed workers has been decreasing recently, although it is too early to tell if this is a permanent trend.

Nevertheless, the fact that the world of work at the enterprise level seems to be over-influenced by the fear of falling by the wayside into deprivation and social exclusion, highlights the importance of developing appropriate social protection policies. The fight against social exclusion, especially with notably high long-term unemployment rates, requires a comprehensive policy especially since the macroeconomic context also plays a role. The obligations for new EU Member States to adopt the EMU criteria, which are very demanding given the current state of their economies, will not leave them with much flexibility, something that may well comfort the neo-liberal options and ideologies of many of the policymakers in these countries.

At the same time a greater sense of solidarity is clearly needed from the European Union, so that its redistributional tools, such as the structural funds, can contribute, especially at regional level, to these countries' economic catching up processes. This would allow these countries to meet the competition while retaining their basic elements of social protection and solidarity.

NOTES

1. Many of the observations in this article are based on a recent research study carried out at enterprise level in the new EU Member States. For more detailed information and case studies, please refer to the following report edited by the author of this chapter: *Working and Employment Conditions in new EU Member States: Convergence or Diversity?*, Geneva: ILO, 2005.
2. This paper remains under the responsibility of the author and does not necessarily reflect the position of the International Labour Office.
3. Report on the Functioning of the Transitional Arrangements set out in the 2003 Accession Treaty, Commission of the European Communities, 2006, p.15.
4. The World Bank for instance has taken little account of the informal sector, with only very rare mentions of the phenomenon in all its reports on the transition period (see Vaughan-Whitehead 2003, pp. 177-183).

REFERENCES

Eamets, Raul, Rail Raal and Jaan Masso (2005), 'Estonia: Towards a Rather Mixed World of Work', in D. Vaughan-Whitehead (ed.), *Working and Employment Conditions in New EU Member States: Convergence of Diversity?*, Geneva: ILO, pp. 99-159.

Ecostat, Institute for Economic Analysis and Informatics, Budapest (2003), 'Economic Trends in Hungary 2003', *Economic Trends in Hungary*, 1.

European Commission (2005), *Industrial Relations Report 2004*, Brussels.

Paoli, Pascal, Agnès Parent-Thirion and Ola Persson (2002), *Working Conditions in Candidate Countries and the European Union*, Dublin: European Foundation for the Improvement of Working and Living Conditions.

Schneider, Friedrich (2002), 'The size and development of the shadow economies of 22 transition and 21 OECD countries', IZA Discussion Paper No. 514 (June), Bonn.

Vaughan-Whitehead, Daniel (2003), *EU Enlargement versus Social Europe – The Uncertain Future of the European Social Model*, Cheltenham, UK and Northampton, MA, USA: Edward Elgar.

Vaughan-Whitehead, Daniel (ed.) (2005), *Working and Employment Conditions in New EU Member States: Convergence or Diversity?*, Geneva: ILO.

4. European Labour Standards' Impacts on Accession Countries: The Hungarian Case

László Neumann

INTRODUCTION

Immediately after the accession of the Central Eastern European Countries (CEECs) to the European Union, at a conference held in Prague on the impact of German-owned subsidiaries on CEECs, a German colleague asked the Czech deputy Minister of Labour what his understanding of the 'European Social Model' was. The unequivocal answer was that the Czech Republic had adapted the whole *acquis communautaire* including the directives on employment and social policy issues and consequently it had already met all of the European requirements. Certainly some sort of formal 'Europeanization' of labour laws and institutions had taken place in the course of preparing for accession and the above view also prevails among many politicians of other new Member States.

In contrast with this rosy evaluation, a growing bulk of western literature reflects a deep concern about labour relations in the CEECs. Western 'stakeholders' in the enlargement have been fearing a 'Trojan horse' of deregulation and 'Americanization' coming from the East for a long time (Meardi 2002). Others argue that the enlargement of the EU puts the European Social Model in serious jeopardy (Vaughan-Whitehead 2003). The views of experts on the impact of the formal transposition of the *acquis communautaire* on the reality in the CEECs are fairly sceptical and they consider the gap between the law in the statutes and the law in action to be worrisome. For instance, according to Mária Ladó and Daniel Vaughan-Whitehead: 'The low coverage of collective bargaining, combined with the insufficient development of forms of workers' participation at enterprise level, represents serious obstacles to the introduction of the Community regulations into the everyday life of enterprises in the candidate countries' (Ladó and Vaughan-Whitehead 2003, p. 80).

Arguably, if lower wage costs, as the major competitive advantage of the new Member States, cannot be eliminated in the short-term, at least the labour standards laid down in Community legislation should be enforced effectively in order to prevent 'social dumping'. The search for common labour standards seems to be a shared objective of all regional treaties on free trade zones. As Gitterman puts it:

> The political conflict between nations at different stages of economic development, and the regional responses in the EU, NAFTA, MERCOSUR, and ASEAN all follow a similar pattern, with the more advanced economies pressing for some harmonization that would moderate the competitive advantages of developing countries. Given this cleavage, various compromises have been struck, which confirmed national policy control but also amounted to an incremental convergence toward common minimum standards (Gitterman 2003, p. 99).

This sums up the focus of this paper: whether the Hungarian application of EU law amounts to such an incremental convergence.

The specific solution chosen by the EU for regional integration relies on the principle of subsidiarity, and consequently Member States, to a certain extent, retain control over the implementation of minimum and enforceable rules through legislation, administrative regulation and collective bargaining. 'Thus, in reality, a significant gap continues to exist between regional standards and their actual implementation in domestic law' (Gitterman 2003, p. 110). However, in the fields of employment and social regulation, where the Member States are not willing to give up their national decision making competence, the EU increasingly relies on 'soft law' methods (such as the Open Method of Co-ordination (OMC) in pursuing the European Employment Strategy) to achieve its common policy objectives through voluntary co-ordination of national policies. Any study of the effectiveness of European regulation obviously needs to take into account both the impacts of EU law and those of the OMC, especially if both of them, through their intertwined regulations, affect the behaviour of certain actors in the workplace reality.

It needs genuine research to determine the extent to which the transposed laws affect workplace reality. There is not only insufficient knowledge of the depths of this process, it is also not clear which elements function properly, what sorts of dysfunctions emerge and, in the worst case, which components of the EU instruments are completely inadequate for transplantation, given the lack of western-style industrial relations institutions. This paper examines the transplantation and enforcement of two directives from this perspective: firstly, the so-called 'acquired rights' directive of 1977 (Council Directive 77/187/EEC on 'safeguarding of employees' rights in the event of transfers of undertakings, businesses or parts of businesses'), which was seen as of paramount importance in restructuring post-communist industries, when thousands of former state-owned or cooperative businesses were reorganized and then privatized; secondly, the so-called 'working time' directive of 1993 (Council Directive 93/104/EC 'concerning certain aspects of the organisation of working time') which is of interest due to more recent concerns. Working time flexibility is not only a legal policy of the European Commission, it is also one of the key elements of the European Employment Strategy.

The methodology used in the research included interviews with trade unions and with associations for the self-employed, as well as detailed case studies at different types of employers where businesses were actually transferred in 2000-2002. For the research into the working time directive, the research methodology combined statistical analysis with the analyses of the legal language used in collective agreements, as well as case studies in enterprises on the practices of employers and the bargaining position of local trade unions. Other sources used in the research were the rulings of the labour courts and the database of the collective agreement registry run by the Hungarian Ministry of Employment and Labour.

TRANSFER OF UNDERTAKINGS DIRECTIVE

Transposition

The Labour Code, which came into effect in July 1992, apparently 'forgot' to regulate business transfers in the spirit of Council Directive 77/187/EEC, which was designed to smooth the coming restructuring and privatization of state enterprises. It definitively ruled out acknowledging years of service with former employers counting towards severance pay. However, the decentralization of former large enterprises was moving so fast and so many workers were losing their 'acquired rights' in the course of setting up legally independent companies based on former internal company units, that, as early as in November 1992, a Hungarian Supreme Court decision provided a juridical guideline for lower level courts. According to the Supreme Court's position, the employment relationship established with the transferor must be maintained by the transferee: with unchanged conditions, especially those concerning the notice period and severance pay; and further, periods of service at different employers should be added up. This ruling has been highly debated ever since from the legal theory point of view but, in practice, it replaced earlier inadequate legislation in the heydays of privatization.

As privatization speeded up in the early 1990s, a series of laws regulated such ownership changes.[1] Among economic reformers and politicians there was, however, a general conviction that heavily unionized manufacturing would delay ownership change and deter direct foreign investment, the only realistic hope of financial underpinning for restructuring the economy. This was why employee representatives had never had the power to veto a privatization process initiated by the State. In terms of employee representation rights, Hungarian law required only access to information and consultations about privatization at the company level. The 1992 law on privatization inserted more stringent stipulations when considering the buyer's required 'Employment Plan'. Later, investors' promises to maintain employment became one of the criteria for evaluating tenders and employment clauses were built into privatization contracts.

Employee representatives also gained co-determination rights over the sale of those parts of the company's assets that were used as a company welfare facility (for instance kindergartens and resort houses). Certainly, such regulations on privatization went further than the 'transfer of undertaking' directive. However, these exceptional stipulations were always based on the special position of the seller, and the State, as the owner of the public property, was forced to waive some of its rights (Neumann 2000).

In 1997, the Parliament passed an amendment to the Labour Code that was designed to transpose Council Directive 77/187/EEC. However, when it comes to upholding the employment relationship, the Hungarian Labour Code fails to adopt the full text of the Directive. It fails to explicitly enumerate the possible reasons for lawful dismissal and neglects the guarantees in the Directive that preclude substantial changes in working conditions to the detriment of the employee. As a new feature, the 1997 amendment requires the transferor and the transferee to inform trade unions and consult with them, in due time concerning any proposed measures that affect employees. Interestingly, this amendment 'forgot' to regulate for the succession of works councils. Since 1997, the Labour Code requires any work conditions stipulated by a collective agreement with the transferor to be respected by the transferee, with the exception of any stipulations on the system of work schedules and forbade any unilateral termination of the agreement for one year following a transfer.

The Hungarian transposition of the Directive on Transfers of Undertakings was completed by Act XX of 2003. Since the EU itself had amended the Directive in the meantime, the transposition of the new 2001/23 EC Directive was an excellent opportunity to remove the shortcomings in the previous legislation at the same time.

Juridical Enforcement of Laws Upholding Employment Relationships

Maintaining the individual employment relationship, with its rights and obligations, is the most sensitive issue for both employers and employees.

Court cases have almost exclusively dealt with the rightfulness of claims for severance and other payments; that is, the courts had to clarify whether the given, sometimes rather complicated, series of changes in the organizational setting and/or of ownership qualified as a 'transfer of undertaking' or not. There were many cases in which employees signed a new employment contract with the transferee, while the earlier contract with the transferor was terminated. In other cases, employees claimed severance pay, but their employment continued with unchanged conditions at the transferee. Case studies suggest that the most characteristic abuse of the law by employers is in evading obligations created by the transfer. In the most frequent cases, the employers (the transferor and/or the transferee) do not acknowledge the legal situation of a transfer and therefore initiate the termination of the employment contract with the transferor 'with the mutual consent of both parties' and employees sign a new contract with the transferee. Understandably, the transferee seeks to minimize risks resulting from the lack of information as well as the likelihood of unforeseen obligations.

In the majority of cases, such 'mutual consent' was initiated by the employers and the 'consent' of employees was motivated by fear of losing their jobs. Frequently, the employers could rely on the employees' naïvety and ignorance. Most would trust documents prepared by the firm's lawyers and would not be aware that solutions presented by the employer might be unlawful. Even if suspicious, they did not dare to voice their objection because they considered worsened working conditions to be more tolerable than job-seeking with the label of being laid off. Sometimes, employers would deliberately use the tool of fear; for example, the privatization of one small rural pharmacy started with the would-be owners exclaiming: 'We are privatizing, everyone will be kicked out!'

Poor Information and Consultation Practices, Transfer of Collective Agreements

Essentially, the information and consultation rights of employee representatives are observed at the large former state-owned companies. In these large companies, sound industrial relations have developed and trade unions and works councils with their experts carefully oversee any organizational changes. Also, in such companies, the Human Resource Management department is prepared for giving out information and pursuing consultations and the employing company meets its administrative duties. In best practice cases, trade unions have managed to play a meaningful consultative role in negotiations and, following a series of intense discussions, to sign written agreements.

Some of the transfers have coincided with reductions in the workforce, as in some mergers and bankruptcy cases where the transferor dismissed employees whom the transferee did not want to employ further. In such cases, it is difficult to separate consultations on transfer procedures from those on collective redundancies. In a merger of two large commercial banks, the management and the various employee representatives (negotiators from the unions and work councils) agreed upon the conditions of the transfer through formally negotiating the collective redundancies and an amendment to the collective agreement. The management and the unions had daily contacts and a series of difficult negotiations led to a compromise.

One of the shortcomings of the transposition in Hungary was the lack of clear responsibility for the information to be given to the unions. Therefore, for example, the State Privatization Holding might refuse requests for information and consultation concerning any of the numerous transfers that occurred in the course of privatization, saying that this was the responsibility of the company management. Similar problems tended to occur repeatedly. The fundamental decisions on organizational changes are made in the public administration units responsible for the given service (for instance, in ministries and local governments), whereas the Labour Code defines the employer (namely, the heads of the public service units, such as a school principal) as the one obliged to share information and consult. Hence, the employer becomes responsible for a decision made by a public administration unit and the latter is not obliged to provide information or engage in consultation.

Overall, the current Hungarian understanding of the consultation procedure is not that different from the similar procedures of the State-socialist period. Even the text of the current Labour Code sometimes uses the old wording: 'presenting the opinion' ('*véleményezés*' in Hungarian) of representatives of employees. This term does not include the meaning that the management has to take the arguments of the unions seriously and present counter arguments before refusal. Management that keeps to deadlines, listens to opinions and than imposes measures contrary to the presented opinion satisfies this legal criterion.

Maintaining a role for collective agreements in the course of transfers seems to somehow be more problematic in Hungary than in the majority of the EU Member States, where bargaining tends to operate at the sectoral level and it is very likely that the transferor and the transferee are covered by the same sectoral agreement. In the Hungarian collective bargaining structure, company-level agreements are the most important and almost all ownership transfers in unionized settings need to harmonize the contents of the various agreements. Possible scenarios for employers' measures as they affect the validity of earlier collective agreements signed at the transferor are summarized in Figure 4.1.

The first type of lawful solution is where the transferee accepts the collective agreements of the transferor. This is the most frequent scenario, although they may modify the contents of the agreement at a later date by observing the normal rules for introducing amendments. At the end of the extended validity period (the expiry date of the original agreement or at least one year), the transferee may lawfully terminate the agreement. There is another lawful solution (second type) which – in our opinion – is contrary to the spirit of the Directive. Here, the transferor may terminate the agreement prior to the transfer. In this way the new employer tries to avoid any problems coming from the transfer of the agreement. This latter way of terminating an agreement is not common, but did occur in one of the public-sector case studies.

There are two ways of unlawful termination. Firstly, when the transferor terminates all individual employment contracts 'by mutual consent' and new contracts are signed with the transferee (third type), the collective agreement 'automatically' ceases to exist since there are no employees for it to cover. Then agreements of the first type may be terminated within the extended validity period (fourth type), which amounts to an unlawful act by the transferee. In Figure 4.1 this is labelled as a 'mixed case' since it starts out as a legal action (and the transferor has acted legally throughout). This type of action typically occurs in the course of decentralizing large companies: while the large heir companies maintain the agreement lawfully (first type), the newly-born small companies tend to neglect the transfer agreement (and so convert it to the fourth type).

WORKING TIME DIRECTIVE

Transposition

The main reason for the 2001 amendment (Act XVI of 2001) was to adopt nine directives of the European Union: one of the preconditions for Hungary's membership of the Union. Within the centre-right government coalition led by the Alliance of Young Democrats – Hungarian Civic Party (FIDESZ-MPP), the proposed modifications to the Labour Code were a highly controversial political issue and led to heated disputes. It took a very long time before all the expert debates, consulting and bargaining with the social partners were complete and the necessary amendments to the bill could

Date of transfer → End of validity period extended by the law →

	Action prior to Transfer	Action during Validity Period	Action after end of Validity Period
1. Lawful way of entry	Amendment of the transferor's collective agreement	Amendment of the collective agreement by the transferee	Possible amendment of the collective agreement by the transferee
2. Lawful termination of the collective agreement	Termination of the collective agreement prior to transfer		Possible termination of the collective agreement by the transferee
3. Unlawful termination through new individual contracts	Termination of the employment relationship, the collective agreement then ceases to exist by default		
4. Mixed way (lawful and unlawful actions)		Small transferees 'ignore' the collective agreement	Possible amendment of the collective agreement at large transferees

Time →

Source: WERS Survey 1998.

Figure 4.1 Possible scenarios concerning transfer of company collective agreements

be drafted. Trade unions tried to emphasize their demands through mass demonstrations and the largest opposition party proposed a referendum motion to prohibit Sunday working. Even the Catholic Church became involved and issued a statement which declared Sundays and holidays as non-working days. Despite all the efforts, no agreement was reached with the social partners on an amendment to the Labour Code.

The rather complicated language of the law remained largely incomprehensible for the public, and the public discussions were dominated by political arguments. According to the trade unions, by changing the working time regulations, the government was unilaterally meeting the demands of employers, primarily of multinational companies, and of shopping malls in particular.

Another line of debate concerned the perspectives held on trade unions and collective agreements. The government claimed that since the law permitted collective agreements to depart from several of its provisions to the disadvantage of employees, which had in some way been a feature of the Labour Code since 1995, it provided an incentive for employers to engage in collective bargaining, especially at the multi-employer level. Thus, ran the government's argument, the modifications to the legislation specifically served to strengthen the role of workplace and sectoral trade unions. The opposition retorted that, in such situations, the law also permitted individual agreements and, in the absence of a collective agreement, enabled employers to take unilateral decisions on a number of issues (such as determining work schedules) and therefore employers did not really need collective agreements. Another major issue in the discussions was the compensation for more flexible working time regulations. In the government's argument this should be shaped by local collective or individual agreements as the law could not specify what wage premiums or additional rewards employees should be given in exchange for the burdens imposed by greater flexibility. Opponents, however, saw the whole modification of working time regulations not only as an attempt to create more flexible working, but also as a benefit granted to employers to reduce their labour costs. It was especially through the use of a reference period (working time account) that it was easy for employers to avoid extra payments for overtime work and having to pay people for idle hours.

Implementation through Collective and Individual Bargaining[2]

According to a report by the Ministry of Employment and Labour (FMM) – which maintains the statistical database on collective agreements – about one million people, that is 39.6 per cent of employees at companies and public institutions employing more than four people, were covered by collective agreements in 2002. Private-sector collective agreements are usually found at large enterprises, while the small and medium-sized enterprise (SME) sector is largely unregulated by collective agreements.

The Ministry's collective agreement database also keeps a record of the contents of agreements. Following the 2001 amendment to the Labour Code's provisions on the organization of working hours, 2002 was the first year in which bargaining parties could contractually regulate working time flexibility by adopting various flexibility schemes. Statistics suggest that the social partners did exercise this option and that working time accounting systems have been widely applied with a wide range of reference periods.

Of the relevant company agreements concluded and/or amended in 2002, 32 per cent adopted a reference period of between two and four months and 5 per cent had longer four to six month periods. This reflects a sharp increase in the use of reference periods, as prior to the 2001 amendment only 18 per cent of collective agreements included such regulations. Moreover, 32 per cent of the agreements introduced annualized hours (effectively a reference period of 12 months), an option created by the 2001 legislation. Employers also used a wide range of other means to introduce working time flexibility. For example, two-thirds of firms with collective agreements adopted 'accumulated rest days'. This means that employees cannot take all their rest days off as in the traditional working schedule, but that the employer can now stipulate they be taken during an idle period in the production cycle.

Both the analysis of collective agreements and also the case studies suggest that overtime and extra shifts in the weekend remain important tools for enterprises to adapt to demand, as well as an important source of income for employees through overtime pay. At one extreme, some multinational companies use overtime work excessively – 'it is not necessary to order overtime work, it is enough to announce it and workers sign up voluntarily'. From the analysis of the content of collective agreements, it was quickly established that they vary greatly in terms of the sophistication of the regulations and in the balance between the gains to employers and to employees.

In this diversity, the two extremes are quite clear-cut: at one extreme, there are collective agreements including a wide range of rules which permits one to draw the conclusion that they provide a harmonic balance of rights and obligations and thereby equally serve the interests of labour and capital. At the other extreme, there are collective agreements with very poor content; in many respects they include only explanatory regulations as demanded by the management.

Table 4.1 Frequency of working time issues in individual employer collective agreements

Issue	Percentage of collective agreements	Percentage of employees covered
Use of reference period [a]		
– Less or equal to 2 months	34.6	41.9
– 2–4 months	32.1	45.0
– 4–6 months	5.0	3.7
– Annualized work hours	31.6	42.6
Stipulations on the system of work schedules		
– Shift-work	68.8	79.8
– Split working hours	24.5	41.3
Stipulations on accumulative rest days		
– Up to 1 months	43.4	69.6
– Up to 6 months	21.9	20.8
Maximum days that can be reallocated annually		
– Less than 44	16.6	14.6
– More than 44	21.2	34.0
Maximum days for reallocation, posting and transfer together annually		
– Less than 110	21.5	17.8
– More than 110	11.7	27.3
Way of instruction for overtime [b]	78.9	77.7
Annual hours of compulsory overtime		
– Less than 200 hours	30.3	22.8
– 201-300 hours	57.7	55.1
Annual hours of compulsory standby service		
– 201–300 hours	21.2	32.1

Source: Database of the Ministry of Employment and Labour. The analysis includes collective agreements reported to the Ministry between January 2002 and June 2003, and was limited to single-employer agreements in the so-called competitive sector. In total, 598 firms with 365 127 employees were covered.

[a]   The data on the use of reference periods should not be added up. A collective agreement may include arrangements both for a reference period and for annualized work hours, to be applied in different units for different categories of workers.

[b]   Collective agreements may require another way of instruction for overtime than the default arrangement of the boss' oral instruction, such as a written form or an advance announcement of actual overtime work.

Inappropriate applications of legal regulations are also apparent and there are collective agreements and workplace practices that show a complete misunderstanding of the concept of a reference period. Some of these agreements re-interpret the legal definition of a reference period and its restrictions to the detriment of employees. In one extreme interpretation of the reference period, the employer fails to define when the working day ends; stating it lasts until 'the daily workload is finished'. The most severe violation of the regulations, however, is when, by using a reference period, employees are denied the day off that they are entitled to for working on a Sunday, when Sunday is not a regular workday.

The focus of our research was on what employees get in exchange for the flexibility enjoyed by the employer, i.e. what 'price' they can successfully ask for being flexible. On the whole, in a decentralized collective bargaining system, the organizational strengths and abilities of the leaders of local unions play a direct role, so it is no wonder that results vary just as much as the wage levels in the various companies. Unions can consider themselves successful if they have managed to achieve higher supplements than the minimum required by the law or have retained supplements that the 2001 legislation wanted to cancel (for instance wage premiums for additional assignments). However, such company collective agreements where employers pay some form of extra 'flexibility supplement' to replace lost overtime pay to employees for working flexibly (typically through the use of a reference period) are rare.

In introducing a reference period, an employer is fundamentally driven by the goal of saving money as, provided the work schedule is announced in advance, this is a legal way of reducing labour costs, specifically overtime and weekend supplements as well as wages for idle time. Here, what is advantageous for the employer is clearly a disadvantage for the employees, who want to maximize their earnings. If the trade union was too weak to have forced some form of compensation for introducing a reference period, employees tend to understand the new work schedule and working time accounting system as 'the new law deprives employees of the overtime supplement'.

The overwhelming majority of employees and trade unions believe that employees should receive financial compensation for such flexibility. In only one of the case studies, as described below, did we find a collective agreement in which it was stated that this flexibility would strengthen employment security.

CASE STUDY

One of the largest road construction enterprises lays off 80 per cent of its 2 500 strong manual workforce in the winter. Traditionally, the company used fixed term employment contracts that expire in December and then in March of the following year the company rehires these workers. Now, the company is to create continuous employment for some employees by using the newly introduced annualized working time budget opportunity ('working time saving system' – as it is euphemistically called in company documents). According to the latest modification of the collective agreement, overtime on longer workdays in the summer can be accumulated and workers can make use of these 'saved' hours, with a 25 per cent bonus, in wintertime. In practice, 250 hours of such overtime plus the annual paid holiday may be enough to span the idle winter months. This development also means a further segmentation of the internal labour market at the company with two additional categories on top of workers with permanent contracts: traditional seasonal workers laid off in the wintertime and the new-type of seasonal worker with continuous employment through an annualized time budget.

Not only collective agreements but also 'the agreements between the parties' deviate from the requirements of the Labour Code. The 'agreement between the parties' in practice is mostly concluded on an occasional basis. Most of them only exist verbally and therefore it is very hard to decide whether they constitute a genuine agreement duly negotiated between the parties or a demand/instruction from the boss which is obeyed by employees. Both in small businesses and at the shop-floor level of large companies, the organization of work heavily relies on such 'agreements between the parties'.

Problems of Enforcement

The informal aspects of using a reference period is highlighted by another issue. Many employees reported that before the introduction of the reference period and depending on their relationship with their boss, they would occasionally ask the boss to let them leave earlier because of family duties. And this was not registered. Nowadays, however, it has become possible to officially account for such extra leave, but there is no rule.

With this somewhat informal allocation of working hours it is often unclear whether employees are given the correct amount of time off to compensate for working extra hours. Unpaid overtime can also result from employers – unlawfully – not recognizing the phases of preparation and finishing work as part of working hours. This not only extends the working time: the employer is also avoiding the overtime supplement as required by law or the collective agreement.

It is our general experience that, in the retail sector, such irregularities – even if uncovered by the labour inspectorate and the employer fined – are easily covered up by the computerized working time recording programs:

either false data are entered or the program itself refuses to accept a working day longer than 12 hours. In this way, one of the minimal standards in the EU directives to protect employees is easily circumvented.

Evidence from the case studies shows that shop-floor practices often breach the law and are even ignored in the written rules and contracts. It is well known that the legal or contractual overtime limitations can be easily evaded by falsifying written reports. In a work situation where the activity is accounted for and paid for based on actual results, it is very easy not to report a period of overtime and account for this as an 'over-fulfilment of the work norm'. Based on the empirical research findings, one can conclude that legal regulations and collective agreements play a relatively limited role in shaping actual working hours, especially in small and medium-sized businesses as well as in larger non-unionized establishments. We have to conclude that informal agreements between workers and shop-floor supervisors, one-sided managerial decisions and even breaches of the law and of contracts remain important factors in shaping working hour patterns in Hungary.

What about 'Flexicurity' as a Policy Objective?

By and large, flexibility was introduced primarily to meet employers' fluctuating need for labour and agreements left little opportunity to provide employees with some sort of security or to facilitate a balance between work and family life. While this is largely attributable to the weakness of unions, such endeavours also lacked any political encouragement from the national and sectoral levels. The 2001 amendment to the Labour Code seems to be a rather unilateral governmental approach to the 'flexibility and security nexus'. The government basically adopted the relevant EU directives and then added a component favouring employers by expanding and making more economically attractive, the use of internal flexibility. It is worth noting that workers' security outside of workplaces also deteriorated under the right-wing government as it tightened the eligibility criteria for unemployment benefit and shortened the period for which it would be paid out using the fashionable rhetoric of 'making work pay' (Nagy 2002). Therefore, the increased flexibility within companies was not counterbalanced by any strengthening of social security outside the firm. This compares unfavourably with many West-European countries where a 'flexicurity' approach, including both a strengthened labour market and social policies, was implemented to safeguard disadvantaged workers in the labour market (Wilthagen and Tros 2004).

CONCLUSIONS

In Hungary, the prospect of EU accession led to enormous harmonization efforts in relation to the institutions and practices of the 'old' Member States. While harmonization of legal systems with the *acquis communautaire* was a prerequisite of accession, there was also some harmonization in terms of building deliberative institutions that come with a 'European-style' social market economy. This was the case, for instance, in the creation of work councils in 1992, well before Hungary submitted its formal EU candidacy (Tóth, Neumann and Ghellab 2004). The process of adoption of the 'transfer of undertaking' directive commenced as early as 1992 when, in the heydays of privatization, the Hungarian Supreme Court practically overruled the then valid Labour Code and established the upholding of employment relationships in the spirit of the EU regulation in the event of business transfers, which can be seen as the backbone of the directive. The story of the transposition of these two directives indicates that, besides the significant role of the EU law, it is largely the influential role of the legal profession in the country (be they judges of the Supreme Court or advisors to the government and its social partners) that matters in the development of national legislation, as well as in the ever changing power balance between various political parties and social partners. With the accession period over, internal forces (political parties, governments, social partners and the legal profession) will presumably have greater autonomy to shape labour regulations in the country. As Hungarian politicians increasingly consider labour relations to be a competitiveness issue,[3] it is very likely that the trend towards 'deregulation' will be maintained or even enhanced, as far as this is possible in the context of EU membership.

Finally, it is difficult to fully grasp to what extent the already achieved degree of 'Europeanization' of labour relations in the 'new' Member State differs from the workplace labour relations in the 'old' Member States. Although a growing bulk of research has recently addressed the issues of transposition, non-compliance and the application of EU law in the 'old' and 'new' Member States (Falkner, Treib, Hartlapp and Leiber 2005; Leiber 2005), it is much more problematical to compare real company practices and the functioning of shop-floor institutions. In terms of the transfer of undertakings, industrial relations research in Western Europe has mainly been focused on merger and takeover cases (Armour and Deakin 2003; Macaire and Rehfeldt 2001). With the 'working time' directive there has been more field research; largely due to the recent hype on flexibility and the envisaged revision of the directive. Overall, comparable research findings from the older Member States on shop-floor practices do show a certain degree of similarity with our findings. For instance, informality is a phenomenon of growing importance, especially in the SMEs and the high-tech sectors (Dupré and Lallement 2003) and the flexibility gained by adopting reference periods does seem to serve the needs of employers rather than those of employees, who tend to come under increasing stress in trying to harmonize their work and family obligations (Eberling, Hielscher, Hildebrandt and Jürgens 2004). Similarly, it is not only in the low-wage new Member States that employees voluntarily take on large amounts of overtime or work longer hours in order to increase income. Trade unions and employee representative bodies, although they are in place, often encounter resistance from their own members if they try to reduce the volume of overtime (Freyssinet and Michon 2003).

Research findings by and large verify the convergence hypothesis that compromises have been struck between the European Union and the new Member States resulting in an incremental convergence towards common minimum standards, that is in terms of adhering to the codified law. However, the adaptation of 'soft law' policy objectives, for instance those formulated in the European Employment Strategy, has been less successful. This failure is all the more worrying in the light of expected future developments at the EU level, particularly because the proposed Constitution envisages relying more heavily on 'soft law' methods, rather than directives with a clear juridical enforcement mechanism. Fully fledged implementation, to the extent it is required not only by the formal directives but also by EU 'soft law' instruments, will certainly take a lot of time due to the cumbersome social learning processes involving the state, the social partners as well as civil actors.

As the implementation of (European) regulatory initiatives depends so much on institutions for social dialogue, it seems obvious to observe that strengthening employee representation at the workplace, in particular to assure they have some representation at non-union workplaces, is crucial. Unfortunately, knowing the controversial history of works councils in Hungary, one cannot with confidence predict a swift solution to this problem (Tóth et al. 2004). The failure to implement European policy objectives through collective bargaining allows one to draw another lesson for policymaking: governments in 'new' Member States should not delegate such responsibilities to sectoral- and company-level negotiators without developing national strategies, building supporting institutions and enhancing the economic actors' attitudes and capabilities to conduct meaningful negotiations in line with the desired policy objectives.

NOTES

1. It is important to distinguish between privatization and a business transfer. The 'transfers of undertaking' directive does not apply where there is a share transfer only or where there is only a sale of assets without 'maintaining a going concern'.
2. The analysis of the wording of agreements was made by Beáta Nacsa.
3. The first instance when Hungary transposed an EU regulation at the same time as other (older) Member States was the recent adoption of the European Company (SE) Statute (2157/2001 EC regulation) and the 2001/86 EC Directive concerning worker involvement within the SE. In his parliamentary speech, the State Secretary of Justice stressed that 'in this case the national rules constitute an issue of competitiveness' as, in his understanding, the effective and flexible rules may have a favourable impact on the incoming foreign investment and thus on job creation in the context of the single European market (Neumann 2004).

REFERENCES

Armour, J. and S. Deakin (2003), 'Insolvency and employment protection: the mixed effects of the Acquired Rights Directive', *International Review of Law and Economics*, **23**, 1-23.

Dupré, M. and M. Lallement (2003), 'The regulation of working time in the SMEs of the information and communications technology sector in France', Paper presented to IIRA World Congress, Berlin.

Eberling, M., V. Hielscher, E. Hildebrandt and K. Jürgens (2004), *Prekären Balancen, Flexible Arbeitszeiten zwischen betrieblicher Regierung und individuellen Ansprüchen*, Berlin: Sigma.

Falkner, G., O. Treib, M. Hartlapp and S. Leiber (2005), *Complying with Europe: EU Harmonisation and Soft Law in the Member States*, Cambridge: University Press.

Freyssinet, J. and F. Michon (2003), *Overtime in Europe*, EIRO, http://www.eiro.eurofound.eu.int/2003/02/study/tn0302101s.html.

Gitterman, D.P. (2003), 'European integration and labour market cooperation a comparative regional perspective', *Journal of European Social Policy*, **13** (2), 99-120.

Ladó, M. and D. Vaughan-Whitehead (2003), 'Social dialogue in candidate countries what for?', *Transfer*, **1**, 64-87.

Leiber, S. (2005), *Implementation of EU Social Policy in Poland: Is there a Different 'Eastern World of Compliance'?*, Düsseldorf: Institute of Economic and Social Research, http://www.mpi-fg-koeln.mpg.de/socialeurope.

Macaire, S. and U. Rehfeldt (2001), 'Industrial relations aspects of mergers and takeovers', *European Industrial Relations Observatory*, **1** (Supplement), http://www.eiro.eurofound.eu.int/2001/02/study/TN0102401S.html.

Meardi, G. (2002), 'The Trojan Horse for the Americanization of Europe? Polish Industrial Relations towards the EU', *European Journal of Industrial Relations*, **8** (1), 77-99.

Nagy, Gy. (2002), 'Unemployment benefits forms, entitlement criteria and amounts', in K. Fazekas and J. Koltay (eds), *The Hungarian Labour Market*, Budapest: Budapest Institute of Economics, HAS, pp. 158-162.

Neumann, L. (2000), 'Privatisation as a challenge for Hungarian trade unions', *Gewerkschaften und Industrielle Beziehungen in Mittel- und Osteuropa*, Berlin: Otto Brenner Stiftung, **13**, 21-38.

Neumann, L. (2004), 'The Hungarian transposition of the European company (SE) Statute and the Directive concerning worker involvement within the SE', http://www.seeurope-network.org.

Tóth, A., L. Neumann and Y. Ghellab (2004), 'Works councils examined', *EIRO*, http://www.eiro.eurofound.eu.int/2004/01/feature/hu0401106f.html.

Vaughan-Whitehead, D.C. (2003), *EU Enlargement versus Social Europe? The Uncertain Future of the European Social Model*, Cheltenham, UK and Northampton, MA, USA: Edward Elgar.

Wilthagen, T. and F. Tros (2004), 'The concept of "flexicurity" a new approach to regulating employment and labour markets', *Transfer*, **2**, 166-186.

5. Slovenia's Integration into the European Market Economy: Gradualism and its 'Rigidities'

Miroslav Stanojevic and Urban Vehovar

INTRODUCTION

Slovenia has endured many transitions since gaining its independence in 1991. Offe, for instance, sees the 'triple transition' of post-socialist regimes: the transition to statehood, the transition to a capitalist economy and the transition to a democratic political regime (Offe 1991). Similarly, Mrak, Rojec and Silva-Jauregui define Slovenia's triple transition as the transition from the socialist to a market economy, plus the 'parallel transitions from a regional to the national economy, and from being a part of SFR Yugoslavia to becoming an independent state and an aspiring member of the enlarged European Union' (Mrak, Rojec and Silva-Jauregui 2004, p. xx). The latter, the transition to EU membership, can be viewed as crucial.

From the very beginning, the process of Europeanization, perceived as the development of a social market economy, has strongly determined the Slovenian transition. This was consensually accepted among all the social actors and political parties who tacitly agreed that a 'big bang', i.e. a 'shock therapy' approach, was inappropriate for Slovenia's inclusion in the European market economy. Constitutionally defined as a social market economy, Slovenia proceeded with a practice of historically-conditioned institutional isomorphism that strongly resembled the German model. At the same time, it was exposed to the constraints common to other European countries – the process of European monetary unification, unfavourable demographic trends, and also to the wider and well-known general escalation of international competition within a global market.

Compared to other 'post-communist' societies, the transition in Slovenia was atypical. Here the transition was gradual: slow and very cautious reforms have been a distinctive feature of the Slovenian transition towards the European market economy. This chapter aims to present evidence and develop arguments supporting the thesis that the gradual integration of Slovenia into the European market economy implied the gradual formation of an inclusive industrial relations system and, in accordance with that, a corresponding version of a co-ordinated market economy – a distinctly different result to that in other 'post-communist' societies, where systems approximating to liberal market economies came into being (see Hall and Soskice 2001).

Within the recent critical and increasingly influential approach adopted towards the Slovenian transition, the Slovenian industrial relations system is perceived as highly rigid and identified as an important cause of the presumed sub-optimal performance of the Slovenian economy. Here we attempt to evaluate this diagnosis and conclude that some of the system's defining features, i.e. the presumed labour market rigidities, are far more complicated than they first appear. We will also relate the situation, albeit briefly and tentatively, to the further development of industrial relations in Slovenia.

Even though the adoption of gradual and cautious market reforms, i.e. 'gradualism', amounts to an extremely complex process that is influenced by a range of factors, we assume for simplicity that the reforms have been largely influenced by two factors: labour and the political elites, and further we will primarily focus on the role of organized labour in the transition process. In line with this simplification, we use the terms 'gradualism' and 'labour-influenced transition' interchangeably.

In this chapter, we will first summarize the main features in the development of the Slovenian industrial relations system in order to show its labour-inclusive nature. We then move on to focus on the most important aspects of the labour market and the employment relations system. According to the aforementioned, and increasingly influential, critique of recent Slovenian developments, the rigidity within Slovenian employment relations is a natural and self-evident contribution to, and result of, the (labour-influenced) gradual transition. We will show that this linkage is not at all self-evident. It is true that some signs of 'rigidity' are apparent (e.g. high salaries and relatively good job security for a significant part of the labour force) but, at the same time, there is a striking flexibility within parts of the labour force. We then proceed to describe various aspects of this gradualism, i.e. the 'labour-influenced transition', arguing that it has been an important and positive factor in Slovenia's integration in the European market economy. The question remains, however, as to whether it continues to be a viable option, capable of supporting sustainable development in Slovenia in the future, or whether it has exhausted its potential. There are indications that gradualism – cautious, consensual moderate reforms – has exhausted its positive potential, and is becoming an obstacle to the future development of the Slovenian economy following accession to the EU. We conclude by offering what we see as a more balanced view of gradualism, arguing that its pre-accession nature should adapt to the post-accession realities.

DEVELOPMENT OF THE SLOVENIAN INDUSTRIAL RELATIONS SYSTEM

In the late 1980s, when a range of political groups started to compete on the Slovenian political scene, a reform-oriented, 'social democratic' faction established and consolidated a leading role within the Slovenian communist party. Nevertheless, in the first parliamentary elections in 1990, the winner was the Demos coalition, consisting of new anti-communist right-wing and centre-right parties. Almost simultaneously, the same electoral body elected the leader of the reformed communists, a person symbolizing the above-mentioned 'social-democratic' faction within the former elite, as President of the Republic of Slovenia.

As the national independence manifesto was realized during 1990-1992, the constellation of political forces began to change rapidly. The Liberal Democrats, a political party leaning slightly to the left on the political spectrum, won the largest vote, and held on to its leading position throughout the entire decade. This party formed coalition governments and co-ordinated the Slovenian transition into a market economy over a period of 12 years. The continuity of the coalitions led by the major centre-left party was the most important political factor in the Slovenian transition up to the end of 2004.

In 2004, only a few months after Slovenia's formal acceptance as a full EU Member, the relatively long domination of the broad liberal-democratic (LDS) coalition ended. In the autumn of that year, a right-wing coalition, the inheritors of the Demos legacy, won the parliamentary elections. During the centre-left's period in power, the Slovenian economy had relatively high growth rates, achieving '. . . one of the highest average economic growth rates among the transition economies . . . and having had by far the least volatile growth during the transition process. Moreover, this stable and reasonably high growth rate was achieved without any major macroeconomic imbalances over the 1990s' (Šušteršič 2004, p. 400). Further, the unemployment rate was moderate, having stabilized below the EU average in the second half of the 1990s.

These successes were achieved through gradual and cautious market reforms that were systematically applied in Slovenia during the 1990s, and, parallel to these processes, theoretically resumed under the notion of 'the

Slovenian model' ('the gradualist approach' to market reform). For Slovenia, which 'was not only the most developed part of the former SFR Yugoslavia and indeed of the whole socialist block, but also the one where economic reform in the pre-transition period had gone the furthest', the gradual approach was a natural choice (Šušteršič 2004, p. 402).[1]

The development of the Slovenian industrial relations system clearly overlaps with this cautious transformation. It was an organic part of this transformation and as such strongly influenced Slovenian gradualism.

The Labour Influence on Development

In the second half of the 1980s, when Yugoslavia entered an exceptionally serious period of political and economic crisis, strikes and related activities started to increase sharply. This reached its peak in 1987 when, according to somewhat incomplete evidence, approximately 1 700 strikes occurred across Yugoslavia (including 300 in Slovenia) (see Jovanov 1989; Lukan 1992). In Slovenia, the workers continued to apply heavy pressure through industrial action into the next decade and were especially powerful in the early 1990s.

In addition to this spontaneous workers' pressure, in the late 1980s and early 1990s Slovenian trade unions were also exposed to strong pressures from the two antagonistic political camps (the 'old' and 'new' political elites) which induced sharp ideological and political tensions amongst them. However, they were able to successfully reorganize themselves during that period. Despite the politicization and mutual competition, they all managed to focus on defending workers' everyday interests. As the social dissatisfaction amongst the workers – who were the most vulnerable to and most threatened by the transitional processes – became manifest, the unions, which were relatively successful in articulating this dissatisfaction, began to gain power rapidly.

Over the past ten to 15 years, the Slovenian unions have been faced, as have the unions in other 'post-communist' societies, with declining membership. However, this has been relatively gradual in Slovenia, sliding from a 70 per cent union density rate in 1989 to slightly above 40 per cent in 1998. According to public opinion surveys, the rate remains at approximately the same level today (PORC 1989-2003)[2], being amongst the highest within the new EU Member States and also higher than in many of the old Member States. Over this period, the Slovenian unions have, despite the decline in membership, stabilized into relatively strong special-interest organizations. They are usually strong at the company level, covering more than half of all employees at the majority of medium and large organizations.

There are numerous indications that the Slovenian trade unions significantly influenced the development of the industrial relations system, and the major features of the Slovenian transitional trajectory in general. We will now attempt to briefly systematize these.

At the start of the transition, the first significant crossroads in Slovenia's 'post-communist' development occurred in 1992, when the transformational depression reached its lowest point[3] and a powerful strike wave emerged (Stanojevic and Vrhovec 2001). It has already been noted that this was the year when the centre-left started to dominate national politics with the Liberal Democrats taking a leading role.

From that point on, political exchanges between the centre-left governments and organized economic interests became a permanent feature of the Slovenian transition during the 1990s. Exchanges became the key mode in reconciling different interests, enabling adjustments to market reforms that made them socially acceptable while simultaneously restoring some features of the previous coalition between employees and the political-business elite, in particular avoiding a clear differentiation between its political and business wings.

During the early period (up to 1994), the political exchanges were highly pragmatic and weakly institutionalized. In that period the elite was involved in intense, both explicit as well as implicit, dialogues, in other words in political exchanges with the social discontent clearly expressed by the core of the working population.

The exchanges started with massive social transfers, mostly in the form of mass early retirement, this later being combined with and substituted by a somewhat loosely defined unemployment status. Exceptional increases in gross payments in 1993, following large falls in wages in the previous years, could also be classified as falling within these pragmatic exchanges. All these exchanges were primarily focused on preventing and lowering social tensions, while simultaneously securing political support for the government.

The first strategic, and symbolically the most important, political exchange between the workers and the political elite was the Law on Privatization adopted in the 'critical' year of 1992. Strongly emphasizing internal buy-outs in labour-intensive sectors of the economy, the law literally turned striking workers into co-owners of their companies.

The immediate 'anti-strike' effect of the law, combined with the wage increases in 1993 mentioned above, was significant. Although less obvious, an indirect result of this first strategic exchange was even more important: combined with other pragmatic political exchanges, the Law on Privatization laid the foundations for the Slovenian transitional pattern that was to follow. It triggered the institutionalization of the industrial relations system which, unlike in other transitional societies, was tailored to the interests of the employees. The result of these early, largely pragmatic, dialogues between the political elite and the dissatisfied workers was of a strategic nature.

In practice, a specific and labour-friendly balance between social equity and economic efficiency had been established by 1994, when a second period of political exchanges began. The beginning of this new period was marked by the establishment of the Economic and Social Council (ESC). Following this, the political exchanges took the form of an institutionally-regulated tripartite dialogue, materializing in a series of agreements primarily concerning income policies, but also covering other social and economic areas (including social policy, employment and unemployment) within broader social agreements (social pacts). Between 1994 and April 2003, three broad social tripartite agreements (pacts) and five tripartite agreements on income policies were adopted, the last of these broader social agreements covering the period 2002-2005.

Within the ESC, all the proposals for new labour laws and other legislation concerning the interests of social partners have been regularly discussed. The new Labour Code, which has been in force since January 2003, was a compromise which is slightly more restrictive in terms of the workers than earlier legislation, but which still strongly respects the interests of workers. The discussions concerning a new pension system have been especially tense. The topic has been on the Council's agenda as a result of the deep pension fund crisis caused by the mass early retirements at the beginning of the 1990s. Due to the unions' strong opposition to certain aspects of the proposed pension reforms, clearly expressed in the form of mass protests as well as through the ESC, a radical privatization of the pension funds has not taken place in Slovenia (Stanovnik 2002). The ESC also revised the 1998 Act on unemployment insurance. This introduced some new, restrictive approaches towards the unemployed, but would have been significantly more restrictive without the compromises reached within the ESC. In addition to this, the ESC has been influential in establishing a minimum wage in Slovenia.

Complementing the ESC's growing co-ordination role, there has been a stabilization of the highly centralized collective bargaining system. The system was – an inheritance from the former 'communist' regime – highly inclusive. It 'covered' virtually all the labour force through the provisions of collective agreements, with at least minimum standards defined in general agreements.

RIGIDITY IN THE LABOUR MARKET?

This all-inclusive industrial relations system implied a need for labour market regulations that were quite similar to the regulations found within developed co-ordinated market economies. In terms of the increasingly influential neo-liberal critique of Slovenian gradualism noted in the introduction, the

Slovenian labour market is clearly a case of a highly regulated, rigid system. However, there are some features of the Slovenian labour market that do not fit with this supposed 'rigidity'. Certain features, even within the most intolerant streams of the aforementioned discourse, have to be recognized as quite flexible.

There are two features which can be labelled as 'rigid'. The first concerns payments. Slovenian wages, when compared to wages in other 'transitional' societies, have been relatively high in the past decade. The second 'rigid' feature concerns job security: this has also been rather high over the past decade for most of the Slovenian employed workforce. Labour surveys from the end of the 1990s show that approximately 70 per cent of Slovenian employees are in permanent contracts, the most secure form of employment (Ignjatović and Kramberger 2000, p. 454). Other data, collected as part of the annual Cranet surveys and consistent with these findings, reveal comparatively weak labour force fluctuations and internal rather than external labour market mobility. Job security has been combined with markedly soft policies for dealing with redundant workers. These policies reflect the accentuated social nature of the Slovenian 'post-communist' system. In spite of the depression and the other problems that followed the transformation, the reconstruction of companies has essentially retained softer policies than those found in other countries.

Along with the above-identified 'rigidities', there are other features of the Slovenian labour market and employment relations that can hardly be labelled as 'rigid'. Firstly, the 'rigidity discourse' presupposes that the restructuring of the economy was too slow, partial and nowhere near completed (or at best, only halfway there). Data concerning the changes in the labour force structure, however, reveal a different picture. The structure of the Slovenian labour force changed significantly in the 1990s. The labour force was sharply reduced during the transformational depression of 1990-1994: according to contemporary research findings (for 1991-1993), the labour force fell by 12 per cent. In the ten-year period from 1988 to 1998, the number employed in Slovenia fell by more than 200 000 – from 831 000 in 1988 to 592 000 in 1998 (Ignjatović 2002, p. 179). The reduction, which implies a corresponding increase in the number of early-retired and unemployed people, mostly affected employees in large industrial plants (Ignjatović and Kramberger 2000, p. 450). Within the occupational structure, the number of those employed in typical workers' occupational categories had been reduced significantly and more rapidly than those in certain other categories. In terms of percentages, these changes meant a reduction in the typical worker share of the working population from 28.7 per cent in 1993 (230 000 out of a total of approximately 800 000 employed people) to approximately 23.7 per cent in 2001 (140 000 out of the 600 000 employed).

During the ten years from 1988 to 1998, the size of this group was reduced by almost 40 per cent. Roughly one in every four employed people in Slovenia in the 1990s belonged to the 'workers' occupation category, but one in two of those who lost their jobs or were moved to the non-active population (approximately 200 000 in total) were from one of the 'workers' occupational categories (plant and machine operators, assemblers and elementary occupations, etc.). These massive changes clearly indicate that the restructuring of the Slovenian economy, and especially of its manufacturing industry, was, despite the somewhat protracted character, fairly radical.

Secondly, the Slovenian labour force is highly flexible. Recent Cranet research clearly suggests that the work input of the full-time employed has increased (mostly in the form of shift work, overtime and weekend work) and that there is a ubiquitous presence of temporary employment (also in comparative terms) and that these are both widely used to create flexibility in Slovenian organizations. The key finding of the analysis conducted by the Institute of Social Sciences (Svetlik and Ilic 2004) is that the success of the Slovenian transition pattern in the 1990s was strongly 'supported' by the significant increase in work input within Slovenian companies.

All these changes occurred within highly unionized organizations. Given this, it is reasonable to conclude that the various forms of working time flexibility and the significant use of temporary employment mechanisms were the result of (implicit and explicit) bargains between managers and unions within the companies. The extensive use made of flexible working conditions, indicates that these micropolitical exchanges (i.e. the bargaining between social partners) did not in any way limit an organization's internal flexibility. While it is true that in strongly unionized companies all uses of work and employment flexibility are negotiated, selected and adjusted to meet the interests of the full-time workforce, the results of these negotiations are not rigidity. On the contrary, it has resulted in a special, highly advanced form of workforce flexibility. The fully employed Slovenian workers are not rigid – they are selectively flexible.

The selective flexibility of the permanent, full-time employed workforce in the strongly unionized Slovenian organizations is the result of the workers' desire for additional work. The desire is to increase the low wages received for working a standard forty-hour week which are seen as insufficient to meet the 'normal', socially and culturally created, expectations of the employees and their families. For this reason, the average employee in a Slovenian organization is strongly prone to accept some form of additional work that can help to boost income and enable the worker to fulfil their perceived needs. In the majority of Slovenian organizations, the employees' interest in additional work is collectivized, i.e. articulated through the unions' collective demands. Under this pressure, managers usually allow employees to work more than the standard eight hours per day (classified as overtime, weekend work, etc.) and/or allow them to work on better-paying shifts.

The selective flexibility of the permanent, full-time employed workforce, in the strongly unionized Slovenian organizations, represents one aspect of workforce flexibility in Slovenia. The other aspect, which is complementary to selective flexibility, is temporary employment. In the strongly unionized Slovenian organizations, the differentiation and redistribution of the above-mentioned flexibilities among different categories of employees is a common occurrence. The increased job security and the selective flexibility of the long-term employees are complemented by the greater uncertainty attached to workers employed on temporary contracts. In the event of an increase in demand, companies increase the number of hours for the permanent employees and, if needed, also take on more temporary employees. In the event of a fall in demand, the number of temporary employees is immediately reduced, leaving the permanently employed able to continue with their agreed extended working hours. Only with a huge drop in demand do the additional hours worked by the permanently employed workers become open to question. In this sense, the permanent workers are highly protected and only exposed to real risks in extreme circumstances; and, as a consequence, they are fully committed to their companies.

This dual form of flexibility within the highly regulated (i.e. 'rigid') labour market has numerous clearly contradictory effects. Firstly, on the positive side, there is the valuable social capital: the commitment of the established workforce to their companies. As we have seen, this results from the two 'rigidities' (payment and job security) as well as from the flexibilities (additional work and income through selective flexibility). This commitment decisively contributes to workforce timekeeping and the high quality of the products delivered. For Slovenian organizations, strongly integrated into international markets and often part of 'just-in-time' production chains, these workforce characteristics are of crucial importance. Without workforce commitment, the key Slovenian exporters (the most vital part of the Slovenian economy) would simply not be able to survive. Secondly, there are some serious problems with mixing flexibility and 'rigidity' since it also generates some less favourable indirect effects in the social environment. Divisions within a social structure that contains unusually large generation gaps and problems linked to the natural reproduction rate of the population (a low birth rate and low natural growth rate) are to some extent managed by the divided flexibility, with the younger population facing a prolonged period of temporary employment. Further, some researchers (see Malnar 2002) suggest that 'symptoms' of the imbalances between work and family life are clearly evident in Slovenian society, especially among those at the lower end of the social scale, and that these have detrimental effects (accumulation of 'bad habits', high death rates from external causes and a high frequency of specific diseases). These findings reflect how the groups lowest on the social scale are being exposed to extreme pressures and that the living conditions for this part of the Slovenian population are, despite the social transfers, exceptionally difficult.

Market regulations imply two 'rigidities': relatively high payments and relatively high job and social security for most of the Slovenian workforce. These two 'rigidities' (amounting to high labour market standards), however, have been mediated by the strong competitive pressures from abroad. As a result, Slovenian exporters, many of whom naturally gravitated towards competing on price (cheap, labour-intensive production) although a significant group have taken a more knowledge-based and quality-oriented approach, have had to invent a flexibility that would secure their survival within this wider environment. Trapped by the 'rigidity' that led to severe competitive pressures, these organizations have had to develop dual flexibility: a combination of high, but selective, flexibility by established full-time workers on the one hand, and the massive temporary employment of the young workforce on the other.

The two 'rigidities' protected the majority of the workforce and, simultaneously, prevented organizations from slipping into the pure price competition. And because they prevented this slip, the organizations, which inclined towards the pure price competition, were especially forced to invent dual flexibility – a functional substitute for the prevented type of competition.

Does this game make any sense? Yes, in the sense that it shows that the more advanced organizations within the Slovenian economy are able to survive in the international market despite the two 'rigidities' and, further, without needing to make massive use of temporary employment. We believe that these advanced organizations demonstrate a 'high developmental road' that others could follow to position Slovenia as a relatively independent economy in the international market.

This complex 'flexible rigidity' knot lies at the heart of the gradualist transition story. The approach is essential if organizations in markets related to knowledge-oriented production and development are to survive. However, at the same time, it creates system imbalances with signs of socially unsustainable development. Conversely, if the two 'rigidities' were to be removed from the knot, knowledge-oriented development would suffer and the economy would move towards competing purely on price. This would result in an unsustainable type of development – especially in the case of Slovenia which is on the threshold of the third developmental phase, *i.e.* on the threshold of an innovation and knowledge-based economy.

THE CONTRADICTIONS IN GRADUALIST TRANSITION: LATEST DEVELOPMENTS

Of the two approaches to a transition strategy, the orthodox 'big bang approach' and the gradualist approach, Slovenia chose the latter; although there are many arguments in favour of both approaches, as outlined by Rojec, Šušteršič, Vasle, Bednaš and Jurančič (2004). One of the arguments in favour of gradualism stresses that it spreads the costs of transition (i.e. the increasing unemployment and social risks) over a longer period. Further, since the processes of institutional change are necessarily path-dependent, gradualism allows economic actors to gradually adapt to the new, market, economy (Rojec et al. 2004). It should be noted that in Slovenia (and also in Hungary during the initial phase of transition) a gradualist approach was already the traditional way. The socialist regime that ruled Slovenia had, from an early date, adopted a specific form of market economy. The third claimed beneficial effect of gradualism is that it enables economic policy to make 'relevant decisions without risking political instability or social unrest' (Rojec et al. 2004, p. 460). Policies can consistently focus on macroeconomic stability, which can efficiently shelter a national economy. The monetary policy pursued in Slovenia, with the help of managed exchange rates, limited capital inflow and successfully secured macroeconomic stability. Together with the complementary industrial policy, this helped the most vulnerable parts of the Slovenian economy to survive. The evidence from the economic results supports the logic of gradualist transition: over the last decade, Slovenia has enjoyed high and stable levels of growth and this growth has been achieved without any macroeconomic imbalances (Mrak et al. 2004; Šušteršič 2004).

Virtually from the beginning, the gradualist approach has been exposed to a continuous, although muted, critique by neo-liberal economists. Even Jože Mencinger, one of the most influential 'gradualist' economists, has recently stated the Slovenian gradualism has been more gradualist than initially planned (Mencinger 2004). The context leading to this admission was the critique that exploded in the second half of 2004, immediately following Slovenia's formal accession to the EU and overlapping with the recent political changes including the right-wing coalition victory in late 2004. The younger generation of Slovenian economists, the so-called liberals, added an especially sharp edge to the criticism, claiming that gradualism, at best, diminished Slovenia's developmental chances, seeing it as the worst-case scenario and altogether the wrong approach from the very beginning.

It is not easy to distinguish political and ideological overtones from any rational critique of gradualism. There is a lot of suggestions that the interests of powerful (both old and new) players are at stake, and the critique is perceived as preparation for the power and wealth redistribution which is getting underway. In addition, the main paradigm of the critique fits quite well with the latest EU and global deregulatory trends. Despite these doubts concerning the background to the critique, it does seem to reveal some contradictions within the gradualist transformation that could be seen as an obstacle to further development.

The main assertion is that the economic stability achieved in the 1990s, marked by the slow privatization and restructuring of the business sector and only partial privatization of the financial sector, is not sustainable and as such poses a serious obstacle to further economic development in Slovenia (Šušteršič 2004). Rojec et al. emphasize the impact of the gradual transformation on the export sector, arguing that 'too slow a pace of restructuring of the Slovenian economy is weakening its export competitiveness and its ability to achieve the above average long-term economic growth' (2004, p. 477). The key features of the gradualist approach, which led to Slovenia's economic, social and political stability, are now seen to lie at the heart of the dangerously slow structural reforms. Šušteršič summarizes the main point of the critique by saying that every element of the gradual approach has its downside: the monetary policy that efficiently prevented macroeconomic instability 'also effectively prevented some foreign direct investments and created an exchange rate buffer for marginal exporters that would otherwise have been forced into more comprehensive restructuring' (2004, p. 405). The industrial policy has had similar, complementary effects by neglecting the needs of the most innovative companies.

To summarize the prevailing view according to these critiques, 'further application of the gradualist approach might seriously hamper Slovenian economic competitiveness and even backfire on the macroeconomic performance that has so far been remarkably stable' (Mrak et al. 2004, p. xxiii). Within this discourse three major points have become crystallized.

Firstly, corporate governance is a critically weak link in the Slovenian economic system. Rojec et al. (2004) clearly connect this, together with the prolonged restructuring of the economy, to the Slovenian privatization pattern. According to Mrak et al. (2004, p. xxiii), the traditions of the former-Yugoslav self-management system negatively influenced privatization in Slovenia. These resulted in the workers playing an important part in the process, leading to a dispersed ownership structure with the workers, managers and pensioners all preserving their crucial role through internal ownership and, to make matters worse, this has frequently been combined with the state retaining a large share ownership. Such a form of ownership presents an obstacle to efficient corporate governance and to the process of restructuring (Mrak et al. 2004). Within this pattern of mixed ownership, managers as owners are unable to reverse the decreasing levels of economic efficiency found in Slovenian companies.[4] The claim made by all these authors is that – at least in the business sector – a consolidation of ownership is needed, together with the establishment of a form of corporate governance that would lead to long-term strategic ownership and enterprise restructuring. Mrak and his co-authors (2004) emphasized that this would become of crucial importance immediately after Slovenia's accession to the EU. To sum up the argument: the privatization process produced an inefficient ownership structure resulting in inefficient corporate governance (Rojec et al. 2004, p. 477) that seriously obstructs economic efficiency in Slovenian companies.

Secondly, the gradualism was 'privatized', that is it gradually became monopolized and functionalized by relatively narrow interests. Some of the critics claim that one of the drawbacks of the decision to opt for a gradualist approach was 'a stalemate among interest groups, leading to postponed decisions and less-than-optimal compromises, which delayed some crucial structural reforms' (Mrak et al. 2004, p. xxiii). Other critics suggest that gradualism suited the prevailing business and political elites, since it reinforced their position in the process of privatization or provided them with access to positions that enabled political control over capital and companies. Further, they argue that the government systematically postponed necessary reforms, since reforms could have brought about the withdrawal of public support. Since the key macroeconomic indicators have never been problematic, medium- or long-term reforms have never been something of a pressing concern. Further, reforms would have endangered the client networks that formed during the long period in power of the Slovenian grand centre-left coalition which included former members of the old elites, who built special relationships with the trade unions and the *nouveau riche*.

Thirdly, extensive state interventions in the economy, they argue, inevitably reproduce the unsustainable trade-offs between social equity and economic efficiency. Rojec et al. (2004) write that the Slovenian form of a 'soft', gradualist transition merges economic and political aspects. This has meant that redistribution has become 'at least as decisive an element in economic policy decisions as their efficiency aspect' (Rojec et al. 2004). The problem of imbalance, and the need to change the balance between equity and efficiency, can be considered as one of the key factors in lowering the competitiveness of the Slovenian economy.[5]

Therefore, it is hardly surprising that the critics of gradualism propose the introduction of further reforms. According to Šušteršič, Slovenia needs in addition to a reformed private sector: infrastructural and public-sector reforms, a reform of public administration (to reduce the over-regulation of private economic activity), improvements to the legal system (to reduce the impressive backlog of cases), a reform of the healthcare system and pension reform (Šušteršič 2004). Further, Šušteršič criticizes the current pension reforms and claims that 'the difficulty in reaching a consensus has hampered the introduction of a comprehensive labour market reform, and it remains to be seen whether the enacted legislative changes were sufficiently extensive to create a significantly more flexible labour market' (Šušteršič 2004, p. 407).

We have already discussed the contradictory character of the Slovenian labour market and shown that the thesis of rigidity simply does not hold true. However, we are not claiming that reforms in Slovenia are not needed at all. Currently, Slovenia's GDP per capita is far too high to allow it to compete on price alone while, simultaneously, its technological lag is too great to enable a skills-based equilibrium to be maintained. In 2003, Slovenian GDP per capita, in terms of purchasing-power parity, amounted to US \$19 300 (Sala-I-Martin and Artadi 2004; Porter 2004). In general, the threshold for the third developmental phase, in which innovative and knowledge-based societies are to be found, is put at US \$17 000. For this reason, Porter characterizes Slovenia as an 'overachiever', having a level of GDP not justified by its uncompetitive economic system, and argues that therefore the Slovenian GDP is unsustainable in the medium-term (Porter 2004). Moreover, recent comparisons reveal some quite alarming trends; according to the Institute for Management Development's (IMD) World Competitiveness Yearbook (WCY), Slovenia ranked 35th in 2002 and only 52nd in 2005 (of 60 economies analysed). This means that, in only four years, Slovenia was overtaken by 17 economies (WCY 2005).

CONCLUSION: EVALUATING GRADUALISM AND ITS RESULTS

In the early 1990s, Slovenian industrial relations developed a structure which secured and confirmed labour's powerful position within the Slovenian 'post-communism' system. A clearly visible manifestation of this power was the construction of a centralized collective bargaining system with an impressive capacity to regulate the labour market, along with some other 'rigidities' that are typical of co-ordinated market economies (i.e. relatively high job security and a well-paid workforce).

The strength of labour within the system undoubtedly influenced the dynamics as well as the results of the Slovenian transition. Labour significantly contributed to gradualism being even more gradual than its creators had envisaged (see Mencinger 2004). The Slovenian labour market provides a valuable illustration of Slovenian gradualism. Here we have argued, contrary to the aforementioned critique of gradualism and its 'rigidities', that, while the market was undoubtedly highly regulated, the regulations and the rigidities were not as one-sided as the critics would have us believe. We did identify two key regulations (or 'rigidities'), namely high wages and good job security, but found that these are closely related to the high functional flexibility shown by those enjoying these 'rigidities'. We argue that these 'rigidities' are key factors in enabling the Slovenian workforce to display functional flexibility and high commitment, especially in export-oriented and technologically-developed organizations. Moreover, it is precisely these organizations that have the ability to push high-skill equilibrium creation (Finegold and Soskice 1988) and the corresponding developmental acceleration in Slovenia. Deregulation of these labour market 'rigidities' would destroy the commitment shown in these key organizations and their capacity to produce high-quality competitive goods. A deregulatory institutional change would harm the companies by pushing the Slovenian economy towards a low-skill equilibrium (price-based competition) – and towards a form of 'development' that is anything but sustainable.

The analysts of recent developments, even among the critics of the gradualist approach in Slovenia, are forced to accept that, generally speaking, the transition has not been unsuccessful. All the authors cited acknowledge that Slovenia's economic results in the 1990s were fascinating; but all of them claim that significant problems have been building up in parallel. The most critical features highlighted are the inefficient corporate governance structure, the occasional stalemates among key players (social partners) and the unsustainable trade-offs between social equity and economic efficiency. Having been exposed to competitive pressures, and ones that escalated significantly during and especially after EU accession, Slovenia, it is argued, now has to tip the gradualist balance between social equity and efficiency in favour of greater efficiency in order to survive in the current competition.

The present analysis of the labour market, when coupled with the critique of the gradualist transition, suggests that the key question lies not with the gradual nature of the transformation itself, but rather with the main outcome of this transformation – with the co-ordinated market economy. Is it a privileged resource or an obstacle to future development in Slovenia? Based on our labour market analysis, it is not possible to provide a simple 'yes' or 'no' answer to this question. We found that the gradual labour market transformation had produced mixed results. Paradoxically, these results could be evaluated as a privileged resource on the one hand and as obstacles to future development on the other. The problem is that the results are mutually interconnected; 'rigidities' are interlocked with flexibilities, leading to both positive and unfavourable conclusions.

Corporate governance has clearly manifested certain weaknesses, especially in the later stages of the transition when external pressures significantly intensified. However, the roots of corporate governance instability and inefficiency may lie within political formations since the state remains an important co-owner of numerous Slovenian companies. Within the context of the recent, and quite radical, political change, the instability appears as a logical consequence of the state's significant ownership share of many organizations.

From the industrial relations analysis perspective, some other implications of privatization are also important. It has been argued that it was precisely the internal buy-outs that triggered the institutionalization which secured a voice for labour during the transition period. The outcomes include the so-called 'rigidities' that are decisively connected to the development of a knowledge-based economy. Further, irrespective of the identified corporate governance weaknesses, the majority of the technologically most advanced Slovenian exporters has been quite successful – the corporate governance system has seemingly not hindered them at all. How is that to be explained?

We agree that the balance between social equity and efficiency established during the 1990s is no longer sustainable. Change is unavoidable – but what changes should be proposed? What should be the contents of the proposed new balances? What will be the developmental consequences of these new equilibriums?

It appears that the transition period in Slovenia can be split into two main stages. The first period, dating from 1994 to 2004, saw the trade unions co-shaping the Slovenia-specific form of transition (i.e. gradualism) and significantly influencing its integration into the European market economy. This period came to an end in 2004 as Slovenia entered the EU and subsequently elected a centre-right government in the autumn of that year.

The second period is unfolding as we write, and is strongly influenced by globalization processes. The impacts of these processes on industrial relations in Slovenia, and the strategies that trade unions, employers and the government will adopt to handle them, remain to be seen. We believe that the unions will be able to accommodate and survive the external as well as the internal pressures, and retain their power into the future. Given such a situation, they will be able to facilitate a change in the balance between social equity and economic efficiency that will favour future development. Defending workers' job security and fair wages, they will support the creation of a high-skill equilibrium, the only productive and, as we see it in the case of Slovenia, the only feasible developmental solution. In other words, we believe that a significant decrease in the power of trade unions would result in economic efficiency based on growing job insecurity and cheap labour. In that scenario, Slovenia would unavoidably get trapped into competing solely on price and sink to a low-skill equilibrium.

NOTES

1. The Cranfield Network for the Study of Human Resource Management in Europe, Centre for European Human Resource Management, Cranfield University and HRM – Slovenian Surveys 2001 and 2004, Organizations and Human Resources Research Centre, Faculty of Social Sciences, University of Ljubljana.
2. According to the latest survey conducted in spring 2005 by PORC (N = 1002) the overall density rate is 37.1 per cent. PORC is the Public Opinion Research Centre of the University of Ljubljana (Faculty of Social Sciences).
3. Despite comparisons that show that the Slovenian transitional recession was among the less intense ones of that time, the intensity of the crisis and its economic, social and political implications were quite dramatic. In 1992, the GDP 'growth' rate was -11.3 per cent, the worst in the history of the Slovenian transition. The following year, when the first signs of recovery appeared, the negative growth rate had improved to -8.8 per cent.
4. From analysing the performance of Slovenian companies in relation to managerial ownership, Simoneti and Gregorič conclude that empirical analyses 'do not show managerial ownership to have a positive influence on the long-term economic efficiency of Slovenian companies' (Simoneti and Gregorič 2004, pp. 237-8).
5. Pischke claims that one of the main problems facing Europe is the equity-efficiency trade-off, in which the former is favoured. This situation is underpinned by institutions such as 'minimum wages and unions, which redistribute incomes from firms to workers' (Pischke 2004, p. 17). Pischke claims that the difficult question is 'which institutions and how much labour market regulation should European countries retain?' (2004, p. 18).

REFERENCES

Finegold, D. and D. Soskice (1988), 'The Failure of Training in Britain: Analysis and Prescription', *Oxford Review of Economic Policy*, **4** (3), 21-53.

Hall, P. and D. Soskice (2001), *Varieties of Capitalism, The Institutional Foundations of Comparative Advantage*, Oxford: Oxford University Press.

Ignjatović, M. (2002), *Družbene posledice povečanja prožnosti trga delovne sile* (Social implications of increasing labour market flexibility), Ljubljana: FDV.

Ignjatović, M. and A. Kramberger (2000), 'Fleksibilizacija slovenskega trga dela; Statistična omrežna sodelovanja za večjo evropsko usklajenost in kakovostno sodelovanje' (Slovenian labour market flexibilization), in B. Takačik (ed.), *Network of Statitics for better European compliance and quality of operation*, Ljubljana: SORS, pp. 446-460.

Jovanov, N. (1989), *Sukobi; Protagonisti latentnih i otvorenih društvenih konflikata* (Confrontations, Actors of the latent and manifest social conflicts), Nikšić: Univerzitetska riječ.

Lukan, A. (1992), *Problemi institucionalizacije in regulacije stavk* (Problems of strikes' institutionalization and regulation), Ljubljana: Univerza v Ljubljani, Fakulteta za družbene vede.

Malnar, B. (2002), 'Sociološki vidiki zdravja; Družbeni vidiki zdravja' (Sociological aspects of health), in N. Toš and B. Malnar (eds), *Social aspects of health*, Ljubljana: FDV-IDV, pp. 3-32.

Mencinger, J. (2004), 'Transition to a National and a Market Economy: A Gradualist Approach', in M. Mrak, M. Rojec and C. Silva-Jauregui (eds), *Slovenia From Yugoslavia to the European Union*, Washington DC: The World Bank, pp. 67-82.

Mrak, M., M. Rojec and C. Silva-Jauregui (2004), 'Overview: Slovenia's Threefold Transition', in M. Mrak, M. Rojec and C. Silva-Jauregui (eds), *Slovenia From Yugoslavia to the European Union*, Washington DC: The World Bank, pp. xix-lvi.

Offe, C. (1991), 'Capitalism by Democratic Design? Democratic Theory Facing the Triple Transition in East Central Europe', *Social Research*, **58** (4), 865-892.

Pischke, J. (2004), 'Labor Market Institutions, Wages and Investment', NBER Working Paper No. 10735, August, pp. 1-32.

Porter, M.E. (2004), 'Building the Microeconomic Foundations of Prosperity: Findings from the Business Competitiveness Index', in *Global Competitiveness Report 2004-2005*, Geneve: World Economic Forum, pp. 19-50.

Rojec, M., J. Šušteršič, B. Vasle, M. Bednaš and S. Jurančič (2004), 'The Rise and Decline of Gradualism in Slovenia', *Post-Communist Economies*, **16** (4), 459-482.

Sala-I-Martin, X. and E.V. Artadi (2004), 'The Global Competitiveness Index', in *Global Competitiveness Report 2004-2005*, Geneve: World Economic Forum, pp. 51-80.

Simoneti, M. and A. Gregorič (2004), 'Managerial ownership and corporate performance in Slovenian post-privatization period', *The European Journal of Comparative Economics*, **1** (2), 217-241.

Stanojevic, M. and P. Vrhovec (2001), 'Industrial conflict in Slovenia', SEER, **4** (1), 29-37.

Stanovnik, T. (2002), 'The Political Economy of Pension Reform in Slovenia', in *Pension Reform in Central and Eastern Europe*, **2**, Budapest: ILO, pp. 19-73.

Šušteršič, J. (2004), 'Political Economy of Slovenia's Transition, in M. Mrak, M. Rojec and C. Silva-Jauregui (eds), *Slovenia From Yugoslavia to the European Union*, Washington DC: The World Bank, pp. 399-411.

Svetlik, L. and B. Ilic (eds) (2004), *Razpoke v zgodbi o uspehu* (Cleavages in the success story), Ljubljana: Sophia.

World Competitiveness Yearbook 2005 (2005), Lausanne: Institute for Management Development.

6. Consequences of Enlargement for the Old Periphery of Europe: Observations from the Spanish Experience with European Works Councils

Holm-Detlev Köhler and Sergio Gonzalez Begega

INTRODUCTION

The accession of eight, former communist, states to the European Union (EU) on 1 May 2004, raised new challenges and opportunities affecting the institutions and governance mechanisms of this supranational structure. From the perspective of the European Commission, it has been argued that this enlargement implies the culmination of a successful political and economic project initiated after the fall of the Iron Curtain in 1989. However, as a consequence of the special characteristics of the new Members, this enlargement poses some new and complex questions for the social construction of Europe and, as one of its most prominent elements, for the Europeanization of industrial relations.

Experts have offered advice on the difficulties that the political institutions of the EU-25 will surely face. Governance in the enlarged EU will become more complicated as a result of the incorporation of new interests and actors. It is apparent that these difficulties will also spill over into other supranational bodies, in which the political balance between actors coming from different national backgrounds remains a fundamental issue. The role of the European Works Councils (EWCs) has been the most advanced, stable and consolidated attempt in the Europeanization of industrial relations (IR) over the last ten years. However, following enlargement, it is arguable that the incorporation of actors from these eight post-communist economies will mean a fresh start in the life of these bodies.

The aim of this contribution is to put forward the Spanish experience with EWCs, believing that this can be a useful reference in the discussion on the challenges that the social actors from the new Members will have to face. We, however, do not deny that the mid-1980s enlargement towards the Mediterranean (Greece, Portugal and Spain) and the recent Eastern enlargement differ considerably. The European Union has moved rapidly forward during the last two decades and some important economic and social projects, such as Economic and Monetary Union and the Social Dialogue were set in motion in the 1990s. We also know that the political and economic backgrounds of the Mediterranean and Eastern Members on joining the EU were not the same. However, there is some resemblance between these two groups of countries, especially with regard to their national IR systems and in terms of their participation in EWCs. Firstly, none of these two groups of countries had a developed IR institutional framework with mature actors when they joined the European Union. Secondly, there were very few home-based multinational firms (MNCs), although all of these countries were (and still are) perceived by foreign MNCs as competitive locations for their operations. Therefore, experience with EWCs in both Mediterranean and Eastern European countries tends to be through subsidiary firms.

Given these similarities, we consider it reasonable to make some comparisons between the old new Members and the current group of new Members of the EU with regard to EWCs. It is our idea that the opinions, expectations and experiences of actors coming from the former group of countries represent a worthwhile example for actors coming from the latter. Firstly, to contextualize this argument, we will summarize and introduce certain nuances to the debate on the consequences of enlargement for the Europeanization of industrial relations in general, and for EWCs in particular. We consider that this debate has, so far, not given due recognition to the complexity of the EU and its national diversities in terms of institutions and actors, instead presenting two homogeneous groups of countries whereas, in fact, both the old Western Members and the new Eastern European ones show important internal differences. Secondly, we will explain the main features of the Spanish IR system, and we will advance how the Spanish actors are changing their views about EWCs as a result of the negative consequences of the latest enlargement. Finally, we will evaluate if it is possible for actors from the new Member States to draw some positive conclusions from the Spanish experience (as an old new Member State) with EWCs.

QUALIFYING THE DEBATE ON EWCS IN VIEW OF THE 2004 ENLARGEMENT

In 2004, the EWCs were confronted by the challenge of enlargement. Both the European political institutions and the social partners at the European and national levels are being forced to reconsider their views about EWCs and to redefine a debate which has been setting practitioners and scholars at odds for ten years. The traditional stances in this debate reflect two well-known positions. On the one hand, national and European trade union organizations, along with some scholars, consider that with more than 700 MNCs already being covered by an EWC, that this is justification enough to state that EWCs are quite mature bodies (see, for example, Lecher, Platzer, Rüb and Weiner 2002). In contrast, national and European employers' associations headed by UNICE as well as some researchers argue that EWC development is still immature or unsatisfactory (see, for example, Streeck 1997 and 2001).

As Gold and Hall (1994) have argued, the objectives pursued by the European Commission in monitoring the establishment of EWCs in those MNCs with operations in the EU were to move towards a European IR system and to create a firm-level complement to the mid-1990s' European Social Dialogue. From the perspective of the European Commission, EWCs were to become mechanisms to provide firm-level transnational social dialogue between employers and employees. However, as is usually the case with discussions on the topic of EU integration, both the euro-optimists and the euro-pessimists can find justification for their adopted positions in assessing the failure or success of these bodies in promoting European IR (Waddington 2003, p. 322).

For the optimists, the mere existence of these bodies for transnational information exchange and consultation with workers is a sufficient reason to state that EWCs constitute the foundations of the future European industrial relations system: 'EWCs are institutions in development . . . [that are undergoing] learning processes in the revision and negotiation of agreements' (Waddington 2003, p. 322). Lecher, Platzer, Rüb and Weiner (2001, p. 120) argue that EWCs represent 'the most dynamic pole in the process of transnationalisation of industrial relations . . . and they will constitute a central element of any future IR system [at the European level]'. Platzer (1998) underlines the significance of EWCs in the setting up of a European proto-corporatism between social partners and European institutions: EWCs become the firm-level foundations of a framework for the regulation of industrial relations at the European level, grounded in the dialogue between the social partners and the political authorities.

On the other hand, for the pessimists, EWCs are a complete failure and nothing short of a negative evaluation of these bodies and their practical operation is possible, as workers' representatives and trade unions express a high degree of dissatisfaction in reference to the current information and consultation proceedings. 'They are neither councils, nor European', as Streeck (1997) has argued. For these scholars and practitioners, the Europeanization of industrial relations is more a declaration of goodwill than a real process, and the same applies to the creation of the EWCs (Fitzgerald and Stirling 2004). In fact, for the pessimists, the vagueness of the 94/45/EC Directive has allowed companies to avoid obligations and has hindered the fulfilment of the information and consultation rights of workers. Furthermore, EWCs have not become the anticipated locus for workers' representation and trade union cooperation at the European level, but bodies for the hidden competition among national interests which breaks out when it comes to any potential conflict. Quoting Streeck (2001, p. 7), EWCs only constitute 'the establishment of a poor linking mechanism between the different national systems of representation within multinational companies', and probably the only ones to benefit (Streeck 1997, p. 333) 'are the multinational companies themselves . . . [because EWCs] will help them to build new internal management-oriented human resources and labour relations regimes'. Streeck argues that EWCs have turned into another managerial tool to legitimize and to facilitate rationalization and restructuring strategies, and to redesign the corporative culture of the firms.

Whichever view is closer to the truth, the recent enlargement of the EU is going to have a significant impact on European industrial relations, both on Europeanization dynamics and on national systems, institutions and actors (Kohl and Platzer 2003). In particular, the response of EWCs to the enlargement will probably condition their future effectiveness and usefulness. Therefore, any consideration of the future of these bodies should take into account the consequences of incorporating actors coming from the new EU Member States.

ASSESSING THE IMPLICATIONS OF ENLARGEMENT FOR EUROPEAN INDUSTRIAL RELATIONS

One of the first consequences of the 2004 enlargement was the emergence of new problems with governance inside 'the EU polity's multilevel governance system and the EU multilevel industrial relations framework' (Marginson and Sisson 2004, p. 26). As these authors argue 'their [future] trajectory is uncertain . . . and among the more imponderable ingredients is the impact of EU enlargement' (2004, p. 26).

Scholars, social partners and political actors are generally agreed that the enlargement that took place on 1 May 2004 was different to those that had gone before. Although in some specific aspects, the political and social situation of the current new Member States could be considered comparable to those of the early- and mid-1980s new Members, there is a fundamental difference between the latest group of candidates and the existing Members of the EU. The new Members are former communist regimes that have had to face a complicated economic, social and political transition. This has led to new configurations of the IR model appearing within the EU. As Kohl and Platzer (2003) have argued, the IR systems of the new Central and Eastern European (CEE) Member States do not conform to the four traditional Western European IR models: Nordic corporatism, Continental social partnership, Anglo-Saxon pluralism and Latin polarization (see also Ebbinghaus and Visser 2000). Furthermore, they do not even form a homogeneous fifth model to join the existing Western European diversity, but represent a highly heterogeneous reality although sharing some basic characteristics.

Therefore, enlargement has implied an increase in EU heterogeneity, reinforcing the trend towards voluntary and open proceedings in the mechanisms of governance of the EU, and moving the horizon of a convergence of national IR systems further away (Marginson and Sisson 2004). While the enlargement has obscured the old north-south divide of the EU-15, this shallow line has been replaced by a new deeper east-west border in the EU-25. Following enlargement, the European Union has to deal with the problems of having high and low waged areas. Meardi (2002) argues that these social and economic disparities are likely to become the hardest test in the history of the EU.

To date, the debate on the consequences of enlargement has been polarized around two positions: a maximalist stance, reflecting the fears of some Western Europe workers' organizations, which supports a negative assessment of the process; and a minimalist opinion, much less alarmist and founded on reports from the European Commission (ESC 1999; European Commission 2002). Below, we will present the fundamental arguments advanced by these opposing positions and then we will add some riders to this debate by taking into account the foreseeable consequences of enlargement for Spain.

The Maximalist Stance . . .

With regard to firm-level industrial relations, the maximalist stance states that east-west differentials will strengthen some of the practices of transnational capital inside the EU: social dumping threats, coercive comparison strategies, transfer of production or delocation (Kittel 2002, see Table 6.1). All these 'exit option' practices (Hirschman 1970) are essentially linked to benchmarking labour costs. MNCs use them to erode Western Europe's tightly regulated IR systems and, in parallel, introduce new, innovative Human Resources Management policies in the less-developed IR systems of the new Members. Once these policies have been appropriately tested, the corporative management of the MNC is in a position to force these innovations on other locations including Western Europe through competitive benchmarking. In this view, the practices of the MNCs in an enlarged Europe will lead to an inevitable convergence at what the maximalists see as the low end of European industrial relations.

With regard to European IR at the sectoral or inter-professional level (European Social Dialogue), the maximalist position argues that the integration of the Central and Eastern Members' social partners in the European Union 'will go hand in hand with a foreseeable increase in the tensions in the work of the social dialogue structures' (Ladó 2002, p. 116). From this standpoint, the enlargement will hinder further progress in the Europeanization of IR as it has been so far understood in the EU-15, because the model of regulation that is taking shape in CEE Member States clearly diverges from Western European patterns.

After the fall of the communist regimes in Central and Eastern Europe, the new political leaders were confronted with the immediate challenge of creating new institutions for the regulation of IR. In practice, there were two linked objectives motivating the development of new IR systems in these countries: the first to provide a stable social support for the political and economic transition, and the second to introduce democratic practices to industrial relations. However, this process has been assessed as little more than a very shallow effort because, in Central and Eastern Europe, the social actors have not been able to overcome their political backgrounds to effectively represent the interests of employers or workers. Neither the trade unions, anchored in their communist (or anti-communist) heritage, nor employer associations have been successful in creating a new identity and becoming truly representative: the former because they could not release themselves from the tutelage of the political parties; and the latter because of their internal diversity, including as they do public or recently privatized companies and subsidiaries of foreign MNCs among their affiliates (Meardi 2002). The social partners of the new Member States share identity and legitimacy problems with their Western counterparts, but these are aggravated by the particular local circumstances.

A number of factors have hampered the maturing of institutions for dialogue and representation at the national, industry and firm levels. These include the more general democratic shortcomings, the lack of identity and

Table 6.1 Basic convergence indicators (EU average, Spain and eight CEE new Member States)

INDEX/VALUE	EU15	SP	SLV	CZE	HUN	SVK	EST	POL	LTU	LVA
GDP per capita (2003)*	100	87.3	70.8	63.4	55.0	48.3	47.0	42.5	43.8	41.4
Unemployment rate (2003)	8.1	11.3	6,5	7.8	5.8	17.1	10.1	19.2	12,7	10.5
Total employment growth (2003)	0.2	1.9	-0.2	-0.6	3.0	2.3	1.5	-1.2	2.3	1.7
Real growth in GDP (2003)	0.8	2.4	2.3	2.9	2.9	4.2	5.1	3.8	9.0	7.5
Inflation rate (2003) (in HICPs)	2.0	3.1	5.7	-0.1	4.7	8.5	1.4	0.7	-1.1	2.9
Labour Productivity per person employed (2003)*	100	95.6	71.6	61.1	62.7	56.3	48.1	50.3	46.9	38.7
FDI Intensity (inward and outward FDI flows/ GDP x100) (2002)	1.2	3.0	2.4	6.5	0.9	8.1	3.2	1.1	2.6	2.4
Social Protection expenditure (2001)*	100	73.0	93.0	91,2	72,3	69.4	55.6	97.8	50.9	73.4
IT expenditure (2001)*	100	46.3	43.9	73.1	60.1	58.5	73.1	39.0	34.1	48.7

* in % convergence rate; EU15 value = 100%

Source: Eurostat

representativeness of the actors, extreme fragmentation of bargaining structures, material and human resources scarcity and weaknesses in employees' participation rights.

At the national and industry levels, the governments adopted a corporatist orientation from the start and monitored changes by setting up national tripartite and sectoral bipartite institutions. The intention was to provide appropriate institutions to develop social dialogue between the government and social partners, and between the social partners themselves at intermediate levels. However, neither the industry committees, created to strengthen autonomous social dialogue in Poland and Hungary, nor the tripartite bodies established in other countries have been successful in meeting their objectives. According to Cox and Mason (2000), it was the inherent weakness in the social partners that led to the failure of these institutions and to an even greater disorientation in the strategies of these actors.[1]

At the firm level, there has been a defensive preservation of the old structures, causing problems in workers' participation and representation. The majority of these countries have developed a single tier mechanism of representation (the exceptions being Slovenia and Hungary) and difficulties in co-ordinating trade unions and works councils remain.

Essentially, the maximalists promote the negative consequences of enlargement. The increase in diversity in the EU will raise serious governance problems at the supranational level. The heterogeneity itself will hinder social co-ordination at the EU level. It will also reduce the internal coherence of the European social partners and hinder their participation in any decision making concerning the EU social policy as codified in Maastricht and Amsterdam. In the maximalist approach, the 2004 enlargement validates the hypothesis on the Americanization of IR in Europe: the introduction of highly individualized and decentralized national IR systems to the EU will reinforce the hands of MNCs when it comes to benchmarking, social dumping and exit option strategies. The enlargement will put pressure on the governments of the Western Members to deregulate their tight IR systems, and this will lead to a national competition regime in Europe.

The maximalist analysis also points out that the enlargement will cause difficulties in the operation of EWCs. Firstly, the weakness of the social actors in the new Member Countries will not contribute to the consolidation of EWC practice in these countries. Secondly, the under-development of firm-level IR will cause problems in understanding the nature, rights and limitations of the relevant bodies. Thirdly, in the future, differentials in wages and working conditions, and competition for a share of the necessary production will turn EWCs into highly unstable bodies. The distrust and delays already observed in some of the enlarged EWCs suggest that some of these maximalist fears could, to some extent, be well founded.

... and the Minimalist Opinion

The European Commission has always played down the impact of the recent enlargement, grounding its arguments on a positive assessment of the process and restricting its consequences to some soft and indirect effects on European IR (Boeri and Brückner 2000; European Commission 2002).

As Boeri and Brückner (2000) have pointed out, a general delocation dynamic from Western to Eastern Europe is unlikely to occur. While it is undeniable that CEE Countries have become attractive targets for foreign direct investment (FDI), and it is also true that the removal of physical and psychological barriers in Europe has increased the ability of MNCs to put pressure on Western national governments, this does not necessarily imply a scenario of national competition and labour conditions deteriorating in Western Europe. Some authors have even claimed that foreign direct investment in Eastern and Central Europe results in economic incentives for the old Member States. Further, Meardi (2002) has argued that workers representatives are well aware of the negative effects of a competitive strategy founded on labour costs, in fact ' . . . unionists from the two sides of the former Iron Curtain may be more similar than some commentators expect them to be . . . since they are facing similar problems' (Meardi 2002, p. 17). Therefore, enlargement will not necessarily lead to the Americanization of European industrial relations, or to the worsening of wage and labour conditions in Europe, or to a block on the Europeanization of IR. On the contrary, IR practices, labour conditions and wages in the new Member States can improve without harming Western Members' standards.

RECOGNIZING BOTH SCENARIOS IN AN OLD NEW MEMBER PERSPECTIVE

In our opinion, after the enlargement and its immediate consequences have settled down, the resulting European IR arena will reflect both maximalist and minimalist arguments.

Firstly, the enlargement will result in different consequences for each level of dialogue and representation in European IR. At the firm level, the enlargement of EWCs is starting to cause some problems for workers representatives. Naturally, the incorporation of new representatives on these bodies means a redistribution of seats inside an EWC, and this redistribution implies a complex set of negotiations among national delegations to decide the new composition of the EWC. At sectoral and inter-professional levels (European Social Dialogue) the appearance of new actors and interests can increase strain, and problems are also likely to occur.

Secondly, each national IR system in Western Europe will see consequences of the enlargement in a particular way, depending on specific factors such as its size, geographical position, economic situation, labour-related costs and the degree of internationalization of its domestic firms. We cannot compare the impact of enlargement in Poland and in the Czech Republic with that in Germany and in Spain, because neither the new nor the old Members form perfectly homogeneous groups. The economies whose MNCs are leading foreign direct investment to the new Member States will probably take advantage and profit from the full opening up of the new markets (Gradev 2001). As argued in the minimalist approach, high productivity and technology levels in the core Western European countries ensures the new Members' industrial dependency, although it is also true that small and medium-sized German firms are starting to relocate eastwards as a result of pressures from their domestic contractors (MNCs). However, the less advanced and peripheral old EU Members will probably experience the consequences of the enlargement in a very different way. We will use Spain as an example to explain this (see Table 6.2). Firstly, cutbacks in EU cohesion funding would jeopardize the recovery of depressed and de-industrialized regions in such countries. Secondly, as the Spanish (and also the Portuguese) foreign direct investment has traditionally been oriented towards Latin America, MNCs based in Spain will find it more difficult to reorient their strategy and benefit from the opening up of Eastern European markets.

In the opinion of the Spanish social partners, the maximalist arguments reflect the challenges these economies will face in the near future. The medium-level technological and productive capacity of their industries, and their dependency on investments by foreign MNCs, will lead to them suffering the consequences of competitive benchmarking, delocations and sourcing strategies. Eastern European operations will compete with advantages in terms of labour costs over Southern European plants. The geographical proximity of the new Members to the core markets of Europe, and the limited sunk costs by MNCs into their Southern European facilities,[2] are additional arguments that should not be underestimated. Therefore if social dumping in the enlarged EU market does take place as a result of the activities of the MNCs, it will probably bring the old Mediterranean Members and the new Eastern Members face-to-face.

Table 6.2 Characteristics of the Spanish IR system

Contextual factors

Despite its radical modernization over the last 25 years, the Spanish IR system is still immature, although it can be placed within Ebbinghaus and Visser's (2000) *Latin Polarization* IR model.

Its evolution is characterized by the development of a detailed legal framework, a progressive stabilization programme and the adaptation of actors to democratic practices.

After an initial phase of *trilateralism* resulting in the Moncloa Pacts in 1977 and the Workers' Statute in 1980, and which was promoted by the State during the political transition (1975-1982), IR in Spain are defined by the government's interest in promoting autonomous *bipartite* social dialogues between employers and employee representatives at national and sectoral levels.

Despite the efforts to promote consensus, democratic IR in Spain have been conditioned by high unemployment and frequent industrial disputes.

Characteristics

Intensive and detailed regulations, but with a limited coverage in real terms.

Low union membership, between 15% and 20% of the workforce.

Dual system for employee representation at the firm level: through works councils and trade unions.

Fragmented and complex structure for collective bargaining at different levels.

Recent and pronounced trend towards the decentralization of collective bargaining. However, labour reforms from 1997 onwards have attempted to limit this trend, reserving certain topics for national and sectoral level collective bargaining.

High coverage rate for collective bargaining (70% to 80% of the workforce are covered) due to the automatic extension of agreements (*erga omnes* clause).

As a result of the pessimistic expectations of the consequences of enlargement on Spanish industry, there has been a recent and interesting shift in the attitudes of trade union officials and workers representatives towards EWCs. We have detected that enlargement is contributing to a change in the image of EWCs; from pointless bodies to platforms for transnational cooperation among workers.

CONSEQUENCES OF THE RECENT ENLARGEMENT FOR SPANISH PARTICIPATION IN EWCS

Until the recent enlargement, labour costs in Spain represented a competitive advantage that attracted a steady inward international investment. Therefore, as they were not being directly threatened by delocation or transfer of production, workers in Spain were not that concerned about European or transnational issues, and EWCs became, in a way, an alien process. Essentially, trade union organizations and workers representatives in Spain have shown very little interest in EWCs until very recent times. In general, they joined and participated in EWCs with a considerable lack of enthusiasm.

Aragón (2001) identified two reasons that could explain why EWCs have had such a limited impact on Spanish IR practices and actors. Firstly, Spanish MNCs directed their foreign investments towards Latin America rather than within Europe. Before the recent enlargement, there were only 36 Spanish-owned MNCs affected by Directive 94/45/EC, and only five had actually established an EWC (CES 2004). Secondly, workers in Spain have generally experienced EWCs from a subordinate position, working for subsidiaries of MNCs based elsewhere. This has distinctly coloured their views, expectations and attitudes towards such bodies.

We (Köhler and González Begega 2004) found evidence for some additional structural causes to explain this disinterest in EWCs (see Table 6.3).

Table 6.3 Further hindrances to EWC development in Spain

The Spanish IR tradition, which sees employers and employees as *adversaries*, leads to very different practices than in the Continental and Nordic *consensual* IR systems which inspired the EWCs.

The lack of national firm-level structures for workers' representation (national or group works councils) leads to a disconnection between an EWC and the immediate representatives of workers at plant level.

Low trade union density rates in Spanish MNCs, in both domestic and in overseas operations, cause problems in terms of representation and participatory shortcomings.

The lack of a 'multinational culture' amongst Spanish managers and social partners, resulting from the late internationalization of Spanish MNCs, has perpetuated the maintenance and export of *adversarial* IR policies. In general, Spanish managers distrust information and consultation rights and thus consider EWCs as nuisances.

As we have already pointed out, many Spanish workers representatives have joined these pan-European bodies without having taken part in the setting up of the EWCs and without appreciating their exact meaning and the specific extent of their rights. This confusion is a consequence of the disinterest shown by Spanish workers and their representatives towards the dynamics of Europeanization. Further, the novelty of the consensual practices of EWCs, the difficulty in gaining access to information and consultation rights from a minority position, and with associated language and cultural barriers, have led to general discontent among Spanish representatives. In many cases, they developed passive attitudes towards these bodies after comparing local, national and European structures for representation and participation. They concluded that EWCs would not be useful until they developed bargaining rights. However, the prevailing view has suddenly changed as a result of some brutal delocations from Spain to Central Europe (Samsung, Lear, Panasonic, Valeo). Trade unions officials and workers representatives have developed a renewed interest in EWCs, considering these transnational bodies to have the potential to counteract such processes.

Also, EU enlargement has seen a significant increase, from 36 to 58, in the number of Spanish-owned firms affected by the Directive. In 2004, two noteworthy EWC agreements were signed in Spanish MNCs. Both took into account the new conditions of the enlarged EU. However, most of the newly-covered Spanish MNCs are quite small in terms of workforce and resources and, as a consequence, will probably find it hard to establish and support an EWC.

Nevertheless, the increase in the number of Spanish firms, affected as a result of enlargement and the new view of EWCs, could encourage a cultural change in national IR practices. If actors do have to participate more directly and actively in EWCs following enlargement, they will have no choice but to take a more participatory and proactive attitude towards these bodies. A greater involvement in EWCs could also lead to a better understanding of the rights that ensue and also of the consensual IR practices they entail.

DISCUSSION

The EU's enlargement to include CEE countries seems to have improved Spanish participation in EWCs. Firstly, the Spanish trade unions are now attempting to co-ordinate the activities of their members in EWCs. Although serious difficulties in terms of resources and discipline have arisen, the first steps are being taken in Spain to tackle the question of EWCs in a more appropriate manner. As a result of the greater concern over transnational processes, the Spanish trade unions are becoming increasingly engaged in

European IR. For example, they are supporting the demands of the European Trade Union Confederation (ETUC) to enhance the competency of the EWCs in issues such as health and safety, flexibility and productivity, working time and environmental policies; and they are also stepping up their participation in the European Industry Federations to help in the co-ordination and monitoring of EWCs at the European level.

However, the expectations on the consequences of EU enlargement on those EWCs with Spanish participation are fairly pessimistic. Trade union officials and workers representatives believe that the enlargement of EWCs will have negative effects on minority delegations. The incorporation of representatives from the new Member States will lead to changes in the balance of EWCs and might lead to confrontations over the distribution of seats among national delegations. From their perspective, the enlargement will cause further fragmentation within EWCs. This leads to two possible and equally negative scenarios: (1) if the EWC was already controlled by a single national delegation, the enlargement will reinforce its dominant position and hinder alliances between minority representations; and (2) if the EWC composition was balanced, enlargement will introduce further fragmentation and heterogeneity, and so it will become increasingly difficult for workers representatives to reach common standpoints.

Nevertheless, as a result of the perceived negative consequences of the enlargement for some EU economies (including their own), the commitment of the Spanish actors towards EWCs has been strengthened. It seems that, after ten years of somewhat casual participation, the enlargement offers a good reason to set aside past attitudes and to start considering EWCs as relevant bodies with the potential to boost transnational cooperation among workers.

Given the similarities between the process initiated after the recent enlargement and the situation when the Mediterranean countries were incorporated into EU industrial relations in the 1990s, actors from the new Member States can probably learn valuable lessons from the Spanish experience with EWCs. It is possible to join these bodies, it is possible to make good use of information and consultation rights, even from a minority position, and it is also possible to learn from them. However, it would probably be beneficial if the new representatives developed a sense of compromise towards these bodies before they start to suffer from competitive pressures from other countries. Cooperation among workers at the transnational level can be a win-win solution even for those countries that are now favoured in international competition because of their low labour costs.

NOTES

1. Tripartite experiences have been relatively successful only in the Czech Republic, where it seems that a consensus-oriented industrial relations system is being developed, and Slovenia, where a stable collective bargaining system has been established at the industry level.
2. In many cases, the initial move of foreign MNCs into Southern Europe during the 1980s was state co-funded. As a result, amortization costs were low. Furthermore, many of the subsidiaries are not deeply embedded in domestic chains of suppliers or subcontractors, and so MNCs can easily leave if a better opportunity comes along.

REFERENCES

Aragón Medina, J. (2001), 'Los Comités de Empresa Europeos en España', *Cuadernos de Información Sindical*, **14**, CSCCOO.

Boeri, T. and H. Brückner (2000), *The Impact of Eastern Enlargement on Employment and Wages in the EU Member States*, Brussels: Report for the European Commission.

CES (2004), 'Diez años de la Directiva de Comités de Empresa Europeos: Avances y nuevos retos en 2004', *Boletín del Observatorio de Relaciones Industriales del CES*, 67.

Cox, T. and B. Mason (2000), 'Interest Groups and the Development of Tripartism in East Central Europe', *European Journal of Industrial Relations*, **6** (3), 325-47.

Ebbinghaus, B. and J. Visser (2000), *Trade Unions in Western Europe since 1945*, Basingstoke: Macmillan.

ESC (1999), 'Opinion of the Economic and Social Committee on the impact of the enlargement of the Union on the single market', INT/002, 22 September, CES 852/99, Brussels.

European Commission (2002) 'Towards the enlarged Union: Report on the progress towards accession by each of the candidate countries', http://europe.eu.int/comm/enlargement/report2002.

Fitzgerald, I. and J. Stirling (2004), 'Employee participation in Europe', in I. Fitzgerald and J. Stirling (eds), *European Works Councils: Pessimism of the intellect, optimism of the will?*, London: Routledge, pp. 1-13.

Gold, M. and M. Hall (1994), 'Statutory European Works Councils: The Final Countdown', *Industrial Relations Journal*, **25** (3), 177-86.

Gradev, G. (2001), *CEE countries in EU companies strategies of industrial restructuring and relocation*, Brussels: ETUI.

Hirschman, A. (1970), *Exit, Voice and Loyalty*, Cambridge, Mass.: Harvard University Press.

Kittel, B. (2002), 'EMU, EU Enlargement and the European Social Model: Trends, Challenges and Questions', MPIfG Working Paper 02/1.

Kohl, H. and H.W. Platzer (2003), 'Labour relations in central and eastern Europe and the European Social Model', *TRANSFER* **1**, (3), 11-30.

Köhler, H.D. and S. Gonzalez Begega (2004), '¿Hacia un sistema de relaciones industriales europeo? La experiencia de los Comités de Empresa Europeos (CEUs)', *Cuadernos de Relaciones Laborales*, **22** (1), 7-34.

Lado, M. (2002), 'EU Enlargement: Reshaping European and National Industrial Relations?', *International Journal of Comparative Labour Law and Industrial Relations*, **18** (1), 101-124.

Lecher, W., H.W. Platzer, S. Rüb and P. Weiner (2001), *European Works Councils: developments, types and networking*, London: Gower.

Lecher, W., H.W. Platzer, S. Rüb and K.P. Weiner (2002), *European Works Councils: Negotiated Europeanisation: Between Statutory Framework and Social Dynamic*, Aldershot: Ashgate.

Marginson, P. and K. Sisson (2004), *European integration and industrial relations*, Houndsmills: Palgrave MacMillan.

Meardi, G. (2002), 'The Trojan Horse for the Americanization of Europe? Polish Industrial Relations Towards the EU', *European Journal of Industrial Relations*, **8** (1), 77-99.

Platzer, H.W. (1998), 'Industrial Relations and European Integration: Patterns, Dynamics and Limits of Transnationalization', in W. Lecher and H.W. Platzer (eds), *European Union: European Union Relations?*, London: Routledge, pp. 81-117.

Streeck, W. (1997), 'Neither European Nor Works Councils: A Reply to Paul Knutsen', *Industrial Economic Democracy*, **18** (2), 325-37.

Streeck, W. (2001), 'La transformation de l'organisation de l'entreprise en Europe: Une vue d'ensemble', in R.M. Solow (ed.), *Institutions et croissance: Les chances d'un modèle économique européen*, Paris: Bibliothèque Albin Michel Économie, pp. 175-230.

Waddington, J. (2003), 'What do representatives think of the practices of EWCs? Views from six countries', *European Journal of Industrial Relations*, **9** (3), 303-325.

7. Testing Times: Remaking Employment Relations through 'New' Partnership in the UK[1]

Mark Stuart and Miguel Martínez Lucio

INTRODUCTION

Whether UK employment relations have been 'remade' in recent years through new forms of labour-management cooperation or partnership-based approaches to employment relations, has been the subject of significant academic debate (Stuart and Martinez Lucio 2005a). The partnership approach has occupied a central place in the UK Labour government's approach to employment policy and the modernization of employment relations (Martinez Lucio and Stuart 2002a), and, until relatively recently, has been widely endorsed by the UK labour movement. In simple terms, it has a twofold appeal. First, that adversarial, zero-sum approaches to labour-employer relations are considered not to be conducive to either business performance or high trust employment relations, whilst cooperative labour-employer relations, in contrast, organized around more integrative rather distributive concerns, are more likely to generate high trust relations and 'mutual gains' (Kochan and Osterman 1994). Second, that against a backdrop of declining membership and influence, 'partnership' offers the only route for trade unions to increase their 'institutional centrality' in the workplace, and policymaking process more generally (Ackers and Payne 1998). Thus, partnership-based approaches to employment relations have been widely debated in the context of trade union renewal and revitalization, both in the UK and more broadly (Huzzard, Gregory and Scott 2004; Terry 2003).

Against this backdrop, this chapter assesses the development and nature of new forms of partnership in the UK and the extent to which it represents a remodelling of its system of employment relations. The extent to which this is influenced by 'Europeanization' is also considered. The chapter is split into four sections. We begin by considering the 'making' of partnership, both in definitional and conceptual terms and the broader terrain supporting the development of partnership in the UK. Next, we consider the potential 'breaking' of partnership, with reference to recent debates between leading advocates and critics of partnership. We then consider the implications of the UK environment for partnership and outline three key imperatives by which to understand recent developments: first, the economic and organizational imperative to increase efficiency through management's involvement of trade unions and workers; second, the social imperative for partnership that emerges from trade unions in their attempt to enhance the voice of workers within the firm; and third, the political interest in designing new forms of economic governance that are cooperative and based on reciprocal interests and behaviour from management and unions. In conclusion, we consider the extent to which there has been a recent turn away from partnership, or whether partnership should be seen in terms of the ongoing modernization of UK employment relations around labour-management cooperation. The implications of such an Anglo-Saxon model for the Europeanization of industrial relations, and in particular the social dialogue pillar of the European social model (see Introductory Chapter), are that there are competing models of trade union involvement and participation in terms of the firm and the state. The question of partnership is therefore becoming increasingly contested, both in the UK and across the EU, and the object of a broader set of interventions and political projects.

MAKING PARTNERSHIP

Whilst the definitional status of partnership is a matter of some debate, with most commentators arguing that it is a vague, ambiguous concept, formally there has been an astonishing amount of interest in the concept (Ackers and Payne 1998; Guest and Peccei 2001; Haynes and Allen 2001; Huzzard et al. 2004; Martinez Lucio and Stuart 2004). Whatever the point of view, it is generally accepted that in rhetorical terms, partnership is related to an approach to employment relations based on a belief – whether well founded or not – that there are employers that find it both ethically responsible and economically effective to cooperate with trade unions (and workers) on strategic matters of organizational change, and, that there are also strategic opportunities for trade unions in engaging with such matters of organizational change.

Key Interventions in the Partnership Debate

Kochan and Osterman's (1994) work in the USA on the 'mutual gains' enterprise has been particularly influential in the development of the partnership debate. Drawing from a more long-standing engagement on the potentially positive contribution of trade unions to economic competitiveness, Kochan and Osterman's (1994, p. 46) intervention stressed a series of guiding principles of mutual gains enterprises, based on the extension of worker voice at three levels of organizational decision making: the strategic, the functional level of human resource policy and the workplace. By respecting and guaranteeing the rights and roles of organized labour – sustainable through supportive public policy – it was argued that employers and managers have much to gain in negotiating and involving for change. It is important to recognize that the role of organized labour within such partnerships is seen as distinct from more macro-level and politically-driven understandings of labour involvement. Some would prefer to use micro-level corporatism as a term to describe such developments, especially as the state plays a uniquely different, supportive role when compared to the direct economic role it played in the past (Martinez Lucio and Stuart 2002a).

In the UK context, the emergence of interest in partnership was summarized in the wake of the Labour Party's electoral victory in 1997 by Ackers and Payne (1998). Given the ongoing difficulties management faced in responding to the imperatives of change, the pressures for more ethical business practice and the likely impact of a potentially more labour friendly political environment (in the UK, but also increasingly from the EU), Ackers and Payne argued that management could not proceed to progress change without bringing unions on board in terms of decision making. Partnership was thus seen to afford the union movement a clear opportunity for increased social and economic influence after almost two decades in the political wilderness. This echoes Regini's (1995) point, that the new politics of partnership between capital and labour within Europe is less ideological and more pragmatic an approach that will find trade unions favour in the longer term, as they become involved in strategic issues such as training and quality management (Huzzard et al. 2004).

Regulating and Securing Partnership: the National and the European Context

This academic endorsement of partnership coincided with a certain amount of practitioner support for the concept. This needs to be set within the historical context of partnership, the contemporary and distinctive role of the British state and the input of key peak organizations and national bodies and the principles and benchmarks that they have advanced. Sensitivity to these contextual factors is a vital prerequisite to any dynamic evaluation of partnership.

The origins and motives of partnership approaches are long-standing. Historical attempts at labour-management cooperation can be seen, for example, in the concerns with the poor state of industrial relations and the prospect of international shifts in labour politics during the First World War that led to the Whitley Commission, and its industrial relations frameworks subsequently enacted in the UK public sector. Similarly, the deterioration of industrial relations in terms of unofficial industrial action, the lack of management co-ordination within industrial relations and the impact of tight labour markets brought the Royal Donovan Commission's recommendation for a greater 'formalization' of industrial relations in terms of management-union bargaining relations in the late 1960s.

It can be argued that, just as with worker involvement and participation more generally, there are a series of cycles where interest in partnership of one form or another of labour-management cooperation is followed by periods of disinterest (see Ramsay 1977). Varying levels of industrial conflict, labour market shortages and the political context of organized labour, along with other factors, may drive these cycles. For Ramsay (1977), employer interest, and that of the state, in cooperating with labour coincided historically with periods of labour strength. Yet, as Ackers, Marchington, Wilkinson and Dundon (2005) note, the contemporary engagement with partnership is dependent on a broader range of factors, although it would be fair to say that the involvement of labour (although not necessarily via organized labour) for business and efficiency purposes is a paramount determinant. In addition, the current role of the state and regulation is of an indirect and supportive nature (perhaps even 'hands off' at times), which makes for a highly variable experience of worker involvement, in what is a highly decentralized context of industrial relations (Kersley, Alpin, Forth, Bryson, Bewley, Dix and Oxenbridge 2005).

Paralleling these domestic factors has been the emergence of the European social dimension within the space of British industrial relations. The impact of the European Works Council Directive and the re-inclusion of the United Kingdom in the social dimension of the European Union in 1997 (one of the first acts of the Blair Labour Government) contributed to an anticipation amongst industrial relations actors that a new post-Thatcherite modus operandi would be needed based on 'working together' (Martinez Lucio and Stuart 2004). Further directives on consultation and involvement have reinforced this. However, it could also be argued that the advocation of micro-level/firm-based partnership was in part a response to the prospect of such further regulation of the employment relationship and enhancing of trade union rights and a way of ensuring that it did not provide too many institutional rigidities to capital (Martinez Lucio and Stuart 2004). Hence, the process of Europeanization was mediated if anything by such new approaches to partnership. This does not mean that Europeanization has been negative, but that it has been contextualized by the national political and strategic context and therefore modified in terms of its impact.

Thus, Tony Blair's Labour Governments since 1997 have sought to advance an agenda of employment relations' modernization through micro-level exhortation and via the wider role of the state as employer, but without a strong commitment to collective rights and systems of regulation. At the micro-level, its partnership agenda has been supported by the (now defunct) Department of Trade and Industry's (DTI) Partnership Fund, which invited project proposals from employers and unions aimed at modernizing and improving employment practices and joint working (see Terry and Smith 2003). In terms of the state as an employer, various partnership initiatives and models have been advanced in relation to the conduct of employment relations in the public sector. The objective has not just been the restatement of the philosophy of the state as a 'good employer' after almost two decades (1979-1997) of conservative governments and their anti-union rhetoric. Many of these policies are concerned with new forms of individually oriented Human Resource Management practices and workplace strategies, and not simply union-oriented ones (Stuart and Martinez Lucio 2000). The partnership discourse attempts, therefore, to locate and mediate new management-union relations within the context of a broader set of interests, such as those of the individual and, in particular, those of the employer and the customer. In this discourse the state acts not as a third party and major guarantor of partnership, but as a facilitator of network and learning processes relevant to it (Rainbird 2005). Partnership represents an attempt to coax social actors into new forms of behaviour without directly intervening into the substance of employment relations. In this respect, it does not represent the simple extension of the European social model; the European social dimension has indeed had a positive impact in alerting actors to the need for a new modus vivendi, but does not dictate what this will be.

This state policy of partnership depends on key institutions within civil society overseeing and providing rules and knowledge resources for the development of partnership. Hence, government policy has been supported by parallel behaviour amongst certain non-state institutions. The Involvement and Participation Association (IPA) has played a particularly important role in this regard. As an independent body, the IPA has sought to disseminate partnership best practice, provide guidance and advice and has established an underpinning set of partnership principles and practices. As Stuart and Martinez Lucio (2005b) explain, these principles allow us to delineate not just the meaning of partnership, but the subtle supports required for its development. The principles distinguish between the expected commitments to and building blocks of partnership (IPA 1997, p. 2). 'They are in effect "rules from below" in anticipation that the government is unlikely to extol "rules from above"'.

The Trade Union Congress (TUC) has also developed its own interest in partnership, as a way of renewing and extending the role of organized labour within the workplace and moving beyond the traditions and legacies of adversarial industrial relations. The TUC has developed six partnership principles (TUC 2001, p. 2): shared commitment to the success of the enterprise; recognition of legitimate interests; commitment to employment security; focus on the quality of working life; openness; and adding value.

These are presented as the vital preconditions required for the establishment of a new accord between unions and employers. Once again, there is an emphasis on recognizing the need for a common understanding of market imperatives, but the principles also identify the centrality of voice mechanisms, job security and investments in the quality of workers' working conditions to sustainable and effective partnerships. The principles represent in other words an attempt to marry efficiency issues with social ones – a leitmotif of current partnership practices and interests (Martinez Lucio and Stuart 2002b). The TUC has utilized these principles to gain a legitimate stake in the 'market' for partnership.

We have seen, then, the emergence of a broad constituency of interest groups and propagators of partnership that are driven by establishing voluntary guidelines and institutional supports. The modernization of employment relations is thus underpinned by a new language and network of actors (which also includes the Advisory Conciliation and Arbitration Service: ACAS) that facilitate the government's indirect approach. However, the presence of key employer and management groups such as the Confederation of British Industry (which represents most employers) and the Chartered Institute of Personnel and Development (which in the main represents management and professionals involved in personnel issues), is not so common. This absence of a transparent direction and active political support from such employer bodies raises concerns as to the ambivalence of organized employer interest.

BREAKING PARTNERSHIP?

Much of the debate on partnership has been located in terms of an evaluation of the specific manifestations of partnership and, specifically, assessments of the merits of putative partnership-committed organizations. The central point of debate has tended to focus on whether partnership 'diminishes trade union representative capacity (critics) or enhances it (advocates)' (Terry and Smith 2003, p. 2), although a more recent body of evidence has also started to examine the experiences of workers in partnership companies and the broader extent to which genuine mutual gains for all stakeholders are being delivered. Advocates can point to a number of high profile organizational examples of partnership agreements and initiatives, such as those at the retailer Tesco, the financial services firm Legal and General, the utilities company Transco and the widely cited Welsh Water, to name just a few. These agreements, it is argued, have allowed trade unions to extend their remit of influence and to participate, to varying degrees, within management's decision making processes (see Haynes and Allen 2001; Samuel 2005). In contrast, others have questioned the coherence of the 'partnership model' and its ability to reshape the terrain of management-union relations, noting that trade unions face significant difficulties and political risks in adopting the partnership approach (Danford, Richardson and Upchurch 2002; Kelly 1996; Marks, Findlay, Hine and Thompson 1998; Taylor and Ramsay 1998).

Kelly (2005), for example, has argued that when comparing and contrasting partnership and non-partnership firms (something that assumes we can identify partnership) the former do not appear to exhibit significant differences in terms of employment (job security) and profitability. Taylor and Ramsey (1998) have further argued that partnership-based arrangements may draw trade unions into a management strategy of enhancing surveillance and work intensification. For example, in the process of engaging with partnership trade unions may end up legitimating workplace change programmes that trade-off employment security with greater work intensification, with a concomitant impact on membership commitment. Danford et al. (2002) and Richardson, Stewart, Danford, Tailby and Upchurch (2005) develop a series of arguments that point to some of the broader effects of this. Firstly, the emphasis on partnership as a strategy may lead unions to downgrade their development of membership-led and resistance strategies. Partnership may also lead to an undermining of workplace activism, which can in turn lead to a long-term weakening of union structures. Secondly, as Richardson et al. (2005) show, levels of work intensification, work-related stress and job insecurity may actually increase even in supposed partnership-based workplaces.

We would argue, however, that there is a need to supplement such lines of enquiry with an understanding of why partnership can be unstable in weak regulatory contexts, such as the UK's, regardless of the perceived positive or negative outcomes in social and political terms. Partnership is not just about outcomes; it is a development that represents the emergence of a new approach to employment relations that attempts to reconfigure the form and content of management-union relations, as well as the role of the individual within the workplace – in other words: it raises broader questions about the regulation of employment relations.

THE DIMENSIONS OF PARTNERSHIP

Having discussed the broad conceptual, historical and regulatory dimensions and briefly considered the concerns of critics, we now turn our attention to the forces shaping the nature of partnership and its specific characteristics and tensions. Critics of partnership, whilst prevalent, have not always underpinned their discussion of partnership with sensitivity to the distinct, and at times contradictory, dynamics that have driven its development. In what follows, we aim to build on this by evaluating the distinct, and at times divergent, imperatives and forces that have underpinned the partnership agenda, in terms of: economic/organizational factors; trade union engagement factors; and the regulatory and governance dimension.

Economic and Organizational Motives

In organizational terms, the broad economic drive around stakeholding is imprinted within a micro-level imperative for partnership (Deakin, Hobbs, Konzelmann and Wilkinson 2005). At this level, partnership with trade unions and/or workers coalesces around three key concerns: the importance of involvement and what Leadbetter (2003) calls somewhat loosely 'authorship', whereby workers are viewed as virtual owners of their effort and creativity; the need to seek legitimacy for management change; and the need to constantly renew strategies for people management. Firstly, Ackers et al. (2005) have systematically examined the centrality of worker involvement to continuous corporate and product improvement. Their longitudinal analysis documents a shift away from the more individualist experiments in involvement during the 1980s towards a greater concern with representative and integrated structures of involvement by the mid to late 1990s. These forms are not to be conflated with traditional forms of collective representation, based solely on trade unionism. Inscribing workers within the workplace as authors is also seen as imperative to their motivation, commitment and performance (Leadbetter 2003).

Secondly, trade unions can involve themselves in the internal marketing of change to their members, the process of selection and retraining that may come with restructuring and the overall monitoring of fairness and consistency that is vital in broad projects of change. As Oxenbridge and Brown (2002) explain, this is often utilized by management to help legitimate the process of organizational change. There is therefore an economic and organizational utility in involving trade unions within the decision making remits of the firm. However, thirdly, such involvement may not only be about legitimating processes of change, but contributing to and ensuring their ongoing renewal. As a large body of research has shown, the systematic implementation of high performance Human Resource Management practices has proved problematic (Richardson et al. 2005). Yet, it could be argued that there is now a desire to renew and legitimate this 'tired' project of HRM and organizational change using the format of representative dialogue and negotiation instead (Ackers et al. 2005; Martinez Lucio and Stuart 2004).

These economic and organizational imperatives place involvement strategies centre stage on the partnership agenda, to the extent that this will contribute to the economic benefit of the firm and mutual gains more broadly. The question of mutual gains is at the very heart of the partnership debate and is something that has come under increased empirical scrutiny (see, for example, Guest and Peccei 2001; Kelly 2005; Richardson et al. 2005). However, as we have already noted, the evidence suggests that the potential gains from partnership, for both trade unions and workers are often far from obvious. Kelly (2005), for example, interrogates the performance of partnership and non-partnership firms and finds little on offer for trade unions (or firms in terms of higher levels of profit). Wages and conditions were no better in partnership firms and labour shedding appeared to have been more pronounced. Worker gains may also be lacking; with Richardson et al.'s case studies (2005) revealing increased levels of work intensification, stress and job insecurity in so-called partnership environments. Other studies, such as those by Suff and Williams (2004) and Roche and Geary (2005), suggest that the gains from partnership may be more complex and contingent, but again question the appropriateness of (and evidence to support) 'mutuality as a device for conceptualizing the employment relationship under partnership regimes' (Suff and Williams 2004, p. 30).

These findings are informative, yet, at the same time, raise deep challenges for trade unions because they may, according to Ackers et al. (2005), have no option but to engage with partnership. Furthermore, even where there has been the potential for 'alternative' union strategies based around highly politicized struggles against labour-management cooperation, this has not deterred the drive by employers to pursue involvement-based routes to advance organizational change (or resulted in clear alternative wins for trade unions) (see Beale 2005; Gall 2005).

Trade Unionism and Partnership

Trade union interest in partnership is not solely driven by an assessment of economic gains and losses. In this context, partnership is perceived to represent an opportunity for trade unions to advance their historic concern to ensure that the rights of workers in terms of the working environment, such as issues of health and safety, and the extension of learning and training in work and non-work related matters, are enacted and enhanced by employers.

Trade unions do not, therefore, see the adoption of the economic and organizational logics discussed above as being engaged with in isolation. They are part of a new operationalizing of historic trade union concerns. However, this operationalization is premised on the social obligations of the firm and the fundamental shift in the view of labour from being 'economic resource', 'external political mediator', and 'mode of regulation' to 'partner' capable of acting as a voice for both worker and corporate issues. Hence the extension of voice mechanisms at the strategic, functional, and workplace level is a vital prerequisite for the success of partnership as far as trade unions are concerned; something that is largely absent in the UK.

The processes by which worker voice can be enhanced and enacted at the workplace-level and the implications of this for trade union position, strategy and identity have been widely considered (Beale 2005; Gall 2005; Oxenbridge and Brown 2005). Typically, the centrality of voice tends to vary within different forms of partnership arrangements and agreements, which suggests that partnership offers in itself no simple route or strategy for union renewal. In this context, Oxenbridge and Brown (2005) argue that it useful to explore the specific internal and external organizational conditions that foster either 'robust' or 'shallow' partnerships. They assert that 'robust' and effective labour-management cooperation is far more likely in 'nurturing' organizations, where traditional bargaining relations are well established and recognized by management and trade union membership. In contrast, labour-management cooperation is far more likely to be 'shallow' where trade union organization is weak and specific partnership agreements more likely to be constraining of union influence. This supports the position that effective partnership working requires the involvement of strong and independent trade unions (Terry 2003). It also suggests, at a broader level, that engagement between managers and unions is contingent on the character of employment relations processes and the manner by which joint regulation is developed.

Regulation, Governance and Partnership

Finally, there are political imperatives for partnership that go beyond the enhancing of the voice and roles of social actors within employment relations. The main political driver has been the resurrection of Dharendorf's (1959) desire to wither the cold front of class conflict. Whilst corporatist ventures in many European countries attempted this historically at the national political level, via macroeconomic tripartite structures (Berger and Compston 2002; Lehmbruch 1984), current forms of partnership tend to establish the firm as the arena around which class differences should mutate into common economic and social concerns. At the political level, then, there is a strong 'ideological' dimension to partnership, both in the UK and across Europe (see Huzzard et al. 2004).

The need to find broader bargaining agendas, a greater recognition of the centrality of productivity, efficiency and competitiveness and the location of union-management collaboration at the strategic, functional and workplace levels is, as noted above, nothing new. Politically, it links social-democratic concerns from the British Labour governments of the 1960s and 1970s with the post-1997 Blair government (Martinez Lucio and Stuart 2002b). The difference in contemporary terms is the way such developments are understood and shaped by a greater reference to business process and entrepreneurial cultures.

In terms of its promotion of partnership, the role played by the state in the UK is more that of a supportive mechanism and less as a direct actor. The consequences of this facilitative approach and the broader UK regulatory context for partnership have been considered in terms of public policy developments and the British system of corporate governance. For example, the issue of lifelong learning is often considered to be an area ripe for union-management partnership for mutual gains (Rainbird 2005). Yet despite strong rhetoric support from the UK government for partnerships related to learning, little formal regulatory support has been forthcoming. Operating within a voluntary context, with limited obligations on employers, trade union-led partnerships for lifelong learning are typically far from widespread and generally piecemeal in nature. In terms of broader corporate governance, Deakin et al. (2005) argue that an emphasis on shareholder value and corresponding gaps in representative and democratic corporate governance threaten the sustainability of mature forms of labour-management cooperation and partnership in the UK and the development of the long-term investment strategies considered so essential for the maintenance of trust-based partnership approaches.

It may well be, however, that it is in the sphere of regulation that some potential seeds of (and for) change are starting to emerge. Thus, for Rainbird (2005) the increasing influence of European Union regulation, through legal rights for individuals and regulation on information and consultation, may facilitate the remaking (via partnership) of UK employment relations. It is to the European dimension that many British commentators look for alternatives and change, and strong conceptual similarities are often identified between the partnership concept and the 'new' European social model, as we have explained (Ackers and Payne 1998; Sisson 1999). Sisson (1999, p. 460), for example, whilst identifying the potential limits of advancing an approach based on partnership in the UK (due to the paucity of forms of worker representation compared with the rest of Europe), nonetheless asserts that, 'the "new" European social or "partnership" model has a great deal in its favour', since 'it combines the best of the "HRM" and the pluralist collective bargaining models . . . while at the same time minimising many of their weaknesses'. However, Hyman (2005) notes that the obsessive labelling of a continental model of partnership (counterposed to the British experience) is often far from straightforward and that many of the concerns of British critics of partnership run parallel with similar debates in other European countries. Most significantly, the emphasis on strengthening the voice of workers may often isolate this feature of regulation from other more socially and economically oriented ones. This raises the key issue related to this text. Debates on partnership must be conducted in terms of the way national models actually develop in terms of the following factors. Firstly, at what level is worker voice institutionalized within any one system? Secondly, over what issues is the voice of workers and trade unions constructed and how is this supported within the broader system of regulation? Thirdly, how does micro-level partnership correspond to macro- and meso-level involvement for social actors and partners? Kochan and Osterman (1994) were very clear in their critique of mutual gains-based partnership as a long-term prospect and model if it was not underpinned by very clear policies and state supports on questions of union involvement and broader training and quality of working life issues. Fourthly, what traditions of social and economic policy involvement exist within any one industrial relations system and how are these articulated in the employer-union relation and roles? These are the basic factors that configure the manner and level of bipartite and tripartite relations within industrial relations. In the UK, levels of worker voice are weakly institutionalized, tied formally to a lower level of employment related issues, weakly or in some instances not articulated with macro or meso forms of involvement and disconnected from the state in a strong formal sense.

Hence, whilst the EU's EMU criteria may have impacted in terms of the development of various national social pacts (Fajertag and Pochet 1997), in the case of the UK such considerations are not central to the partnership model. Firstly, the pattern of national social pacts is sparse and traditions are weak. Secondly, the impact of the EMU convergence criteria has influenced British policy only in an indirect manner given the monetary policy of the country. And, thirdly, the ongoing decentralization of the system of industrial relations (Kersley et al. 2005) means that macro or meso forms of joint regulation are limited and provide scant space to trade unions for influencing core economic criteria and wages. In effect, there appears to be a disconnection between the industrial relations system, in terms of its governance, and the broader macro economic policy system.

CONCLUSION

This chapter has briefly considered the development of partnership-based approaches to employment relations in the UK. Whilst partnership has been high on the policy agenda in recent years, we argue that it is important not to overstate the underlying aims of partnership-based approaches to employment relations, and instead recognize purpose in relation to the broader socioeconomic context, organizational environment and organizational strategies. This helps to explain competing takes on the issue and different concerns with partnership. That said it is fair to say that there is an Anglo-Saxon and managerialist model emerging that is capturing the imagination of key policymakers within and beyond the United Kingdom. This language of partnership contrasts in some aspects with the traditional regulatory and legislative approach to industrial relations present in many continental European countries (see Huzzard et al. 2004). It provides a counterpoint which does not involve extensive state regulation; instead it points to cooperation being based on the axis of business interests and questions of efficiency within the firm which then mediate the social aspects of work and tie them to the firm's prospects. Partnership redraws the role of trade unions as business and competitive partners, hence its appeal to the more neo-liberal and less socially-committed constituencies of the European project which lurk in more locations than the UK.

In the UK context, concerns have been raised with regards to the challenge of building more cooperative partnership-based relations between management and trade unions and establishing high-trust relations at work. There is also concern at the very different meanings and approaches to partnership that are emerging in economic, organizational, social and political terms. This raises deep questions around motive, the absence of effective preconditions such as the regulatory support for worker voice mechanisms in the Anglo-Saxon context and the costs and distributions of risks related to establishing joint working relations (Martinez Lucio and Stuart 2005).

Given the above, it is hardly surprising that the employment relations climate in the UK has started to move 'against partnership', albeit while interest in the EU for such an Anglo-Saxon model appears to be increasing. Certainly, set against a body of empirical evidence that is largely dismissive of the rhetoric of partnership, the concept may be going through something of a reappraisal. The number of high-profile partnership agreements has always been limited and those that deliver 'genuine' mutual gains appear to be even more illusive. More significantly, a number of 'new' trade union leaders (often referred to as the 'awkward squad') have openly distanced their unions from the partnership approach and levels of formal industrial conflict were up significantly during 2004 as a result of a number of large public-sector disputes (although remaining very low in historical terms). There is also some evidence that the network of agencies active in the 'market' for partnership may be withering. Yet it is likely that the partnership 'model' will find new uses at a policy level and re-emerge through hybrids of European models that are themselves becoming more decentralized – fitting the UK's recent legacy of exporting ideology and less practice.

NOTE

1. This chapter is a unified and revised version of our introduction and conclusion of our edited book *Partnership and Modernisation in Employment Relations* (London: Routledge, 2005).

REFERENCES

Ackers, P. and J. Payne (1998), 'British trade unions and social partnership: rhetoric, reality and strategy', *International Journal of Human Resource Management*, **9** (3), 529-549.

Ackers, P., M. Marchington, A. Wilkinson and T. Dundon (2005), 'Partnership and Voice, With or Without Trade Unions: Changing UK Management Approaches to Organisational Participation', in M. Stuart and M. Martinez Lucio (eds), *Partnership and Modernisation in Employment Relations*, London: Routledge, pp. 23-45.

Beale, D. (2005), 'The promotion and prospects of partnership at Inland Revenue: employer and union hand in hand?', in M. Stuart and M. Martinez Lucio (eds), *Partnership and Modernisation in Employment Relations*, London: Routledge, pp. 137-153.

Berger, S. and H. Compston (eds) (2002), *Policy Concertation and Social Partnership in Western Europe: Lessons for the 21ˢᵗ Century*, New York and Oxford: Berghahn Books.

Danford, A., M. Richardson and M. Upchurch (2002), '"New unionism", organising and partnership: a comparative analysis of union renewal strategies in the public sector', *Capital and Class*, **76**, 1-27.

Deakin, S., R. Hobbs, S.J. Konzelmann and F. Wilkinson (2005), 'Working Corporations: Corporate Governance and Innovation in Labour-Management Partnerships in Britain', in M. Stuart and M. Martinez Lucio (eds), *Partnership and Modernisation in Employment Relations*, London: Routledge, pp. 63-82.

Dharendorf, R. (1959), *Class and Conflict in Industrial Society*, Stanford, CA: Stanford University Press.

Fajertag, G. and P. Pochet (eds) (1997), *Social Pacts in Europe*, Brussels: ETUI/OSE.

Gall, G. (2005), 'Breaking with, and breaking, "partnership": The case of the postal workers and royal mail in Britain', in M. Stuart and M. Martinez Lucio (eds), *Partnership and Modernisation in Employment Relations*, London: Routledge, pp. 154-170.

Guest, D. and R. Peccei (2001), 'Partnership at work: mutuality and the balance of advantage', *British Journal of Industrial Relations*, **39** (2), 207-236.

Haynes, P. and M. Allen (2001), 'Partnership as union strategy: a preliminary evaluation', *Employee Relations*, **23** (2), 164-187.

Huzzard, T., D. Gregory and R. Scott (2004), *Strategic Unionism and Partnership: Boxing or Dancing?*, Basingstoke: Palgrave MacMillan.

Hyman, R. (2005), 'Whose (Social) Partnership', in M. Stuart and M. Martinez Lucio (eds), *Partnership and Modernisation in Employment Relations*, London: Routledge, pp. 251-265.

IPA (Involvement and Participation Association) (1997), *Towards Industrial Partnership: New Ways of Working in British Companies*, London: IPA.

IPA (Involvement and Participation Association) (2001), 'Definitions of Partnership', http://www.Partnership-at-work.com/pardefs.html, accessed on 17 October 2001.

Kelly, J. (1996), 'Union militancy and social partnership', in P. Ackers, C. Smith and P. Smith (eds), *The New Workplace and Trade Unionism*, London: Routledge, pp. 77-109.

Kelly, J. (2005), 'Social Partnership agreements in Britain', in M. Stuart and M. Martinez Lucio (eds), *Partnership and Modernisation in Employment Relations*, London: Routledge, pp. 188-209.

Kersley, B., C. Alpin, J. Forth, A. Bryson, H. Bewley, G. Dix and S. Oxenbridge (2005), *Inside the Workplace: First Findings from the 2004 Workplace Employment Relations Survey*, London: DTI.

Kochan, T.A. and P. Osterman (1994), *The Mutual Gains Enterprise: Forging a Winning Partnership Among Labour, Management and Government*, Boston: Harvard University Press.

Leadbetter, C. (2003), *Up the Down Escalator: Why Global Pessimists are Wrong*, London: Viking Penguin.

Lehmbruch, G. (1984), 'Concertation and the structure of corporatist networks', in J.E. Goldthorpe (ed.), *Order and Conflict in Contemporary Capitalism*, Oxford: Oxford University Press.

Marks, A., P. Findlay, J. Hine and P. Thompson (1998), 'The politics of partnership? Innovation in employment relations in the Scottish spirits industry', *British Journal of Industrial Relations*, **36** (2), 277-89.

Martinez Lucio, M. and M. Stuart (2002a), 'Assessing partnership: the prospects for and challenges of modernisation', *Employee Relations*, **24** (3), 252-261.

Martinez Lucio, M. and M. Stuart (2002b), 'Assessing the principles of partnership: workplace trade union representatives' attitudes and experiences', *Employee Relations*, **24** (3), 305-20.

Martinez Lucio, M. and M. Stuart (2004), 'Swimming against the tide: social partnership, mutual gains and the revival of "tired" HRM', *International Journal of Human Resource Management*, **15** (2), 404-418.

Martinez Lucio, M. and M. Stuart (2005) '"Partnership" and new industrial relations in a risk society: an age of shotgun weddings and marriages of convenience', *Work, Employment and Society*, **19** (4), 797-817.

Oxenbridge, S. and W. Brown (2002), 'The two faces of partnership? An assessment of partnership and co-operative employer/trade union relationships', *Employee Relations*, **24** (3), 277-89.

Oxenbridge, S. and W. Brown (2005), 'Developing partnership relationships: A case of leveraging power', in M. Stuart and M. Martinez Lucio (eds), *Partnership and Modernisation in Employment Relations*, London: Routledge, pp. 83-100.

Rainbird, H. (2005), 'Assessing Partnership Approaches to Lifelong Learning: "A New and Modern Role for Trade Unions"?', in M. Stuart, and M. Martinez Lucio (eds), *Partnership and Modernisation in Employment Relations*, London: Routledge, pp. 46-62.

Ramsay, H. (1977), 'Cycles of control', *Sociology*, **11** (3), 481-506.

Regini, M. (1995), *Uncertain Boundaries*, Cambridge: Cambridge University Press.

Richardson, M., P. Stewart, A. Danford, S. Tailby and M. Upchurch (2005), 'Employees' experiences of workplace partnership in the private and public sector', in M. Stuart and M. Martinez Lucio (eds), *Partnership and Modernisation in Employment Relations*, London: Routledge, pp. 210-225.

Roche, W.K. and J.F. Geary (2005), 'Workplace Partnership and the Search for Dual Commitment', in M. Stuart and M. Martinez Lucio (eds), *Partnership and Modernisation in Employment Relations*, London: Routledge, pp. 226-250.

Samuel, P. (2005), 'Partnership working and the cultivated activist', *Industrial Relations Journal*, **36** (1), 59-76.

Sisson, K. (1999), 'The "new" European social model: the end of the search for an orthodoxy or another false dawn?', *Employee Relations*, **21** (4 and 5), 445-462.

Stuart, M. and M. Martinez Lucio (2000), 'Renewing the model employer: changing employment relations and partnership in the health and private sectors', *Journal of Management in Medicine*, **14** (5 and 6), 310-325.

Stuart, M. and M. Martinez Lucio (eds) (2005a), *Partnership and Modernisation in Employment Relations*, London: Routledge, pp. 101-119.

Stuart, M. and M. Martinez Lucio (2005b), 'Trade union representatives' attitudes and experiences of the principles and practices of partnership', in M. Stuart and M. Martinez Lucio (eds), *Partnership and Modernisation in Employment Relations*, London: Routledge.

Suff, R. and S. Williams (2004), 'The myth of mutuality? Employee perceptions of partnership at Borg Warner', *Employee Relations*, **26** (1), 30-43.

Taylor, P. and H. Ramsay (1998), 'Unions, partnership and HRM: sleeping with the enemy?', *International Journal of Employment Studies*, **6** (2), 115-43.

Terry, M. (2003), 'Can "partnership" reverse the decline of British trade unions?', *Work, Employment and Society*, **17** (3), 459-472.

Terry, M. and J. Smith (2003), 'Evaluation of the Partnership at Work Fund', Employment Relations Research Series No 17, Department of Trade and Industry.

TUC Partnership Institute (2001), *Partners for Progress: Winning at Work*, London: TUC.

8. The Only Game in Town? British Trade Unions and the European Union

Erin van der Maas

'The only card game in town is in a town called Brussels and it is a game of poker where we have got to learn the rules and learn them fast' (Ron Todd, TUC, 1988).

INTRODUCTION

During the 1980s and 1990s the European Economic Community (EEC) transformed itself from a 'common market' into a more coherent single market (EC) and then into the European Union (EU) with the establishment of Economic and Monetary Union (EMU) and deeper political cooperation. Interpretations of this change process vary widely both in terms of the conceptualization of the dynamics underlying the process of change (European integration) and the subsequent implications for national actors (Europeanization), such as trade unions.[1]

The literature on trade union Europeanization and European integration has mainly focused on European-level processes, institutions and developments; European Industry Federations; the company level/European Works Councils in transnational corporations (Hancké 2000); and the European Trades Union Confederation (ETUC) (Dølvik 1997). These European-level studies have been complemented by cross-national comparative studies of different trade union organizations (Bieler 2003; Foster and Scott 2003). This chapter seeks to fill this gap in the current literature by providing an overview of the responses to European integration by trade union organizations within one national context.

As Turner (1995) points out, the institution building at the EU level, with regard to industrial relations and social dialogue processes, has preceded rather than flowed from trade union activity and mobilization, 'structure before action'. An important question is: can institution building at the European level draw trade unions into bottom-up activity or will EU institutions and processes remain primarily a channel for top-down political strategies, hollow 'formal structures' for elite activity (Dølvik 1997)? Studies that concentrate at the EU-level miss the extent to which domestic-level actors engage with and react to European developments.

The literature on British trade unions and European integration predominantly focuses on the TUC and especially the policy reorientation towards EU engagement from 1988 onwards. The TUC is the sole peak-level labour organization in the UK; trade unions are not differentiated into separate confessional or political (con) federations. In addition, the TUC has very limited authority over its affiliates, unlike peak labour organizations in a (neo-) corporatist context, and has no formal role in collective bargaining in the UK. Authority over its affiliates is mainly limited to rules and regulations concerning inter-union organizing issues and certainly does not extend to wider policy positions. Therefore, individual affiliates can develop independent and divergent policies with regard to European integration.

Throughout the 1980s and 1990s, the Conservative government in the UK adopted a radical neo-liberal agenda that excluded trade unions from the political agenda. The TUC was particularly hard hit by the refusal of the Conservatives to deal with the union movement and the dismantling of the various tripartite bodies, as these functions represented the core activities of the TUC. Intuitively the reorientation of the TUC towards the EU from the 1988 Congress onwards has been explained by the rational pursuit of organizational and material goals impossible to realize in the union-hostile UK environment (Strange 2002; Rosamond 1993). The journey into Europe began at a time when the TUC's domestic role was being seriously eroded. Can the same logic be applied to the TUC affiliates?

The main argument of this chapter is that approaches to trade union Europeanization that solely rely on external incentives to explain policy orientation, are insufficient, especially when divergent case studies are found within one national context. To understand how and why trade unions have responded to EU developments, internal factors must be considered. Internal institutions for decision making constrain or enable particular constituencies (trade groups, regions) or actors (leadership) within the trade union to participate in and influence policy formation. Aside from the official constitutional rules, informal groups (factions) also potentially have influential roles in union decision making.

The case studies were chosen to include trade unions that organize workers in the sheltered sector of the labour market (UNISON), the exposed sector (GPMU) and two general unions that have a mix of members in both exposed and sheltered sectors (TGWU and GMB). Case studies are based on official union material (policy documents, conference motions, press releases) and semi-structured interviews of 17 trade union representatives and officials from the four organizations. The trade union officials/representatives interviewed were all situated in the national office of their respective union organizations and comprise research officers, European officers, national industry officers and general secretaries.

The chapter will be organized as follows. The first section of this paper outlines some of the various ways in which European integration and Europeanization have been interpreted before proceeding to analyse the diverse policy responses of the four case study trade union organizations and how the internal processes and actors have influenced policy positions and engagement with the EU. The particular policy under scrutiny is Economic and Monetary Union (EMU).

EUROPEAN INTEGRATION

Initially the Treaty of Rome (1957) was ambiguous as to how improved conditions and living standards of workers were to be achieved, it states they, '. . . will ensue not only from the functioning of the common market, which will favour the harmonisation of social systems, but also from the procedures provided for in this Treaty and from the approximation of provisions laid down by law, regulation or administrative action' (Article 117).

Article 117 therefore gives credence to both interventionist and liberal strategies at the same time. However, the social dimension of the European Community was not a priority probably given the relative economic homogeneity of the six founding Member States in terms of their economic development.

The re-launch of the integration process in the mid-1980s, with its focus on the completion of the internal European market, brought with it fears that market integration and the ensuing restructuring would likely result in social dumping. To offset these fears, to garner support for further integration from employers and trade unions and to circumvent the neo-liberal and nationalist perspective of the UK Conservative government (Thatcher/Major, 1979-1997) and its vehement opposition and blocking of EU social policy, the Commission began a process of social dialogue at Val Duchesse on 31 January 1985. This subsequently led to Article 118B (now Articles 138 and 139) entrusting the Commission with the task of developing dialogue between management and labour at European level.

The subsequent Agreement on Social Policy (Maastricht) was annexed (due to UK opt out) to the Protocol on Social Policy of the Treaty on European Union. This agreement of 31 October 1991 proposed a radical change in the Community legislative process in the sphere of social policy allowing for a constitutionally recognized role for the social partners in the Community legislative process. In 1997, the Maastricht Social Agreement was incorporated into the Treaty under the Social Chapter (Treaty of Amsterdam of June 1997). These developments in EU economic and social integration present trade unions with a complex picture to respond to.

The Single European Act 1986 and the subsequent rounds of intergovernmental conferences have deepened market integration within the EU by removing both tariff and non-tariff barriers to the free movement of goods, services and workers. Market making, the removal of obstacles to free trade, or negative integration (Scharpf 1996), has been facilitated by allowing decision making in this limited field to require only a qualified majority vote (QMV) in the Council of Ministers. Previously, decision making required unanimity and so the opposition of just one Member State in the Council could halt the progress of an initiative. In this new European market place, previously nationally-bounded companies have become Euro-companies with corporate governance, in addition to macroeconomic and financial governance, shifting to the European level.

Market correcting policies at the European level, at least in the field of labour law and industrial relations are only partially subject to QMV. Positive integration, the creation of labour laws rather than the removal of market impediments (Scharpf 1996), is much more difficult to achieve. The situation is complicated by the limited application of the Maastricht Social Chapter (MSA) procedure; if an issue is not within the prescribed remit of the MSA, then any initiative is subject to unanimity in the Council of Ministers and therefore it is unlikely to be adopted.[2]

Therefore European integration has implicitly constrained the national role in economic management (exchange rates and interest rates) and shifted economic competence to the European level for those countries in the Euro-zone. Increased competitive pressures within the internal market means governments, who can no longer utilize exchange/interest rate adjustments to redress problems of competitiveness, have to rely more on utilizing the labour market and public spending to meet the convergence criteria set by EMU. This dilemma is compounded for trade unions as economic integration has not been accompanied by an equal upward shift in European social/labour market policy competence. Political governance over market dynamics has therefore been eroded at national level and thus far not replaced adequately at the EU-level. The integration process is asymmetric.

Trade unions find themselves in a new terrain of industrial relations, where the targets of their activity (the locus of power-employer, economic/political decision making) have shifted. Accordingly this situation pushes trade unions, who no longer find allies or rewards in the national context of industrial relations, to pursue cooperation across national borders (Visser 1998).[3] The Maastricht Social Agreement (MSA), associated with the aspiration for a social dimension to the EU, has provided, on paper, an institutional framework to address the asymmetry of EU governance by enabling the social partners at Euro-level to construct a social edifice to the single market. This opportunity structure of the EU pulls or draws trade unions (national elites?) into European engagement. A 'logic of influence' is at work (Dølvik 1997), however, it must be stressed that the pull is an opportunity to construct an EU social model and is by no means a certainty to reproduce trade union aims and objectives.

The above very brief overview of the EU presents trade unions with a complex set of opportunities and threats. The optimists point to recent developments, especially with regard to institution building and substantive Directives (industrial democracy, health and safety, working time, etc.), as indicators that outcomes can surpass expectations of a simple structural analysis. For instance, Pierson and Leibfried (1995) argue that institutional dynamics and the complexities of multi-tiered governance systems create unpredictable outcomes and recent developments illustrate this point, especially when important actors can mobilize support for initiatives. The process establishing the MSA itself is a manifestation of these dynamics.

The 'pessimists' view the MSA as a decisive defeat for the aspiration for a comprehensive social dimension to European integration. Streeck (1995) specifically points out the obstacles; the asymmetry and multi-layered governance structure, likely to result in logjams in decision making in the social sphere (Scharpf 1988), lack of real support for initiatives from either the employers or a strong central government at the EU level and the diversity of ETUC affiliates making a common agenda difficult to aggregate. How might British trade unions make sense of the combination of opportunities and threats posed by the European integration process?

EUROPEANIZATION

Studies in Europeanization, broadly defined as domestic responses/adaptation to European integration, generally aim to understand how and why responses to the EU are divergent. In many cases actors and/or policy responses in various Member States are compared. Research of this type generally finds that the 'national situation' is the explanatory variable. For instance, Geyer (1997) examined the responses of UK and Norwegian Social Democrats in order to ascertain why the British were much more pro-EU than the Norwegians. His conclusion was that the well functioning social democratic system in Norway meant there was little or no incentive for social democrats to join the EU, the push and pull factors were minimal. For the British the erosion of social democracy throughout the 1980s and 1990s meant that what was on offer at the EU level was much more appealing than the domestic situation.

Strange (2002) found that the trade union response in Britain (TUC) was a rational response to the exertion of the push and pull factors, however, the research did not examine why diversity persists among TUC affiliates. The 'national situation' is not a sufficient explanation in this case; it does not help to explain why different trade union organizations within one national context have adopted divergent responses to the EU.

Bieler (2003) utilizes a neo-Gramscian perspective, taking the sphere of production as the starting point it distinguishes between the social forces manifest in different parts of the labour market. Using this approach, the diversity of policy response to EMU can be explained by where a trade union's members are located, different trade unions within one country have alternate 'national situations'. If membership is primarily based in the internationally exposed sectors of the economy they will be more likely to support EMU.

'Partly because they may support their companies, on which their own well-being depends, which benefit from a stable monetary environment and institutionalized free trade within the EU. Partly because they realize that they have lost control over capital at the national level' (Bieler 2003, p. 29).

Unions that organize in the sheltered part of the economy are more likely to oppose EMU because it restricts national policy autonomy upon which they rely. Given the confusing array of trade union organizations in the UK and the recent mergers, many trade unions in the UK organize workers from both the exposed and sheltered parts of the labour market. Therefore we might expect the aggregation of interest based on sector or trade group to be internally contested.

The above Europeanization perspectives are too deterministic emphasizing external factors and do not take account of the internal governance structures and politics within a union organization. Internal organizational and political factors have a bearing on policy formation. Which groups (informal/formal) have influence over policy formation within a union, trade groups, national and/or regional leaderships and political factions?

BRITISH TRADE UNION RESPONSES

In order to illustrate the various policy approaches to the EMU and to identify how they relate to wider processes of European integration and globalization I will categorize policy positions within Dyson's (2002, p. 14) discourse framework. This allows a comparison of policy positions with regard to EMU, globalization and European integration.[4] In addition, the case studies will provide an overview of wider organizational and policy responses in order to contextualize a particular EMU position within a wider EU strategy. The four discourses identified by Dyson are:

1. EMU as a mechanism to neo-liberalize the EU in line with 'globalization'.
2. EMU as a mechanism to erode national sovereignty.
3. EMU as a means to preserve the European Social Model against globalizing neo-liberalism (US Model).
4. EMU as a mechanism to harmonize the European model with globalization.

Dyson (2002) associates the first discourse with the Blair government's approach that tends to welcome globalizing neo-liberalism and resist attempts to strengthen social and/or labour market policy at the EU level (inflexibilities). The second discourse is more closely associated with the Conservative Party's approach to European integration; even if EMU is in line with their economic priorities it conflicts with their nationalistic perspective and erodes national sovereignty. Discourse 3 contextualizes EMU within wider efforts to build a Social Dimension to the EU; EMU is supported if accompanied by a comprehensive social dimension, an alternative social model to dominant neo-liberalism. Dyson (2002) associates this with the Franco-German left. The final discourse accepts globalization as inevitable and views EMU as a means of gradually reforming the European social model to globalization by managing capitalism through social dialogue; it is distinguished from discourse 1 by the reforming tone rather than shock treatment of neo-liberalism.

Table 8.1 Trade Union policy discourse EMU

Discourse 1	Discourse 2	Discourse 3	Discourse 4
UNISON	TGWU	GMB	AEEU
TGWU	RMT	TUC	GPMU
RMT	ASLEF	GPMU	GMB
ASLEF	NATFHE	MSF	
		PCS	

Table 8.1 illustrates the diversity of policy positions among the TUC affiliates.[5] At first glance it appears to confirm Bieler's (2003) claims that those unions in the sheltered sector of the economy will resist EMU and visa versa. The opponents of EMU are made up of railway workers, higher

education workers and other public-sector workers. The supporters are drawn from the exposed manufacturing sector.

However, there are some interesting variations. The PCS trade union organizes civil servants in Britain and has come out in support although with the qualification that support for membership be underscored with a guarantee not to cut public expenditure. The Communication Workers Union (CWU) organizes workers in the post office and the telecoms industry and has been unable to aggregate a clear policy on EMU given the sector divide among its members. Britain's two 'general' unions also make interesting case studies with one coming out in favour (GMB) and one against (TGWU).

The following section outlines the various responses to EMU from four major TUC affiliates. The trade union organizations are UNISON, the Graphical Print and Media Union (GPMU), the Transport and General Workers Union (TGWU) and another 'general' union, the GMB. These organizations represent workers located in a number of industrial sectors, in both the exposed and sheltered parts of the economy.

UNISON

UNISON was formed in 1993 by the amalgamation of the National Association of Local Government Officers (NALGO, 759 735 members), the National Union of Public Employees (NUPE, 551 165 members) and the Confederation of Health Service Employees (COHSE, 201 993 members). This produced Britain's largest trade union organization with over one and a half million members. Before merger, NALGO, on the one hand, and COHSE and NUPE on the other had very different organizational features and cultures. NALGO has been characterized as a member-led organization insisting on 'lay control at all levels' (Terry 1996, p. 94) in the merger talks. NUPE placed much more emphasis on full-time officers and has been termed an 'officer-led' trade union (Undy, Ellis, McCarthy and Halmos 1981, p. 80). For NUPE it was important to secure representation for low-paid workers on the various decision making bodies, otherwise they feared that 'its blue-collar members would be overawed, or numerically swamped, by NALGO's more articulate and better educated membership' (Undy 1999, p. 454). The 'fair representation' agreement combined the principles of 'lay control' with representation for the low-paid, regions, service groups and women.

Prior to merger, at the TUC 1993 debate on the Maastricht Treaty, NUPE and NALGO had divergent policy positions. The 'officer-led' union (NUPE) in support of the Treaty on European Union and the 'membership-led' union (NALGO) opposed. The merger therefore brought together two organizations with divergent ideological approaches to European integration. Two departments within UNISON initially vied for competence with regard to EU matters. The research department eventually took policy competence on EU matters with the international department dealing with inter-union relations, although it was initially a confusing picture.

Interviews with officials reveal that EU matters were not a high priority in the aftermath of the merger, especially given the domestic agenda of public-sector restructuring. Within the research department, ex-NALGO and ex-NUPE officers had divergent views on the EU. Policy coherence across the department also proved difficult at first, given the divergent ideological approaches of ex-NUPE and ex-NALGO officials.

The NALGO position (1993) was independent of Labour Party influence given that they were not an affiliated union, although their policy approach did bear remarkable similarities to the Alternative Economic Strategy (AES), Labour Party policy, before the major policy review under Neil Kinnock (1987). The Labour Party was anti-EU prior to 1987. The AES viewed the restrictions on national sovereignty, especially with regard to economic policy, as incompatible with the aspiration for a socialist Britain. This 'old Labour' policy position was popular with both NALGO's officials and lay-activists.

NUPE, on the other hand, was affiliated to the Labour Party and therefore subject to policy influence from this affiliation. The General Secretary and full-time officials were seen as Labour loyalists (Undy 1999) and so it is no surprise that their EMU policy matched the current Labour Party's pro-EMU position, especially given the fact that the officials dominated the decision making structures of NUPE. Officials were impressed with the Delors address to the TUC in 1988 that stressed the importance of constructing a robust social dimension to the EU.

The clash of ideological perspectives led eventually to the senior ex-NALGO research officer leaving UNISON. However, the emphasis on 'lay control' at all levels meant that the head of research and the UNISON General Secretary (both ex-NUPE) were not able to influence the policy positions of UNISON as effectively as they were in NUPE. The strong anti-EMU sentiment within the NALGO National Executive Committee (NEC) was inherited by UNISON. Conference decisions also supported this anti-EMU position. Official policy limits objections to EMU to economic terms framing opposition policy with regard to the specific Maastricht convergence criteria and the impact on domestic public-sector spending. UNISON policy highlights the neo-liberal core of the EMU convergence criteria and concludes that public spending, on which their members' jobs rely, will be reduced if Britain were to join the single currency under present conditions (discourse 1).

This policy position does not address the political implications of EMU. Officially UNISON politically supports the integration project and to this end plays a very influential role in the public services industry federation at European level. The single currency is not ruled out per se. This position hides an underlying political hostility to EMU among many members especially those organized by the influential 'broad left' faction.

UNISON have been supportive of the developing EU social legislation, the Transfer of Undertakings Directive, working time and other directives on industrial democracy and atypical work all provide benefits especially for UNISON members working for the 'contracted out' part of the public sector. In official literature, UNISON are at pains to put across the message 'EU yes, EMU no', in order to differentiate their policy position from the nationalistic positions adopted by both left and right in Britain. Response to the various EU directives has tended to be in a receiving mode, producing materials both educational and informational on the provisions of new legislation for their members. UNISON tends to project their policy via the industry federation and do not generally undertake direct representation of its interests to the EU institutions. However, individuals within the research department have from time to time been engaged in directly lobbying MEPs; 'UNISON dip in and out' (Interview MEP).

Whilst UNISON's EMU policy position fits well with Bieler's (2003) approach, it does not help explain why NUPE was previously pro-EMU. Internal governance factors, especially factionalism and the insistence on 'lay control at all levels' have ensured that the NALGO position was adopted by UNISON.

THE GRAPHICAL PRINT AND MEDIA UNION

The GPMU was formed by a merger between a craft-based and semi-skilled print union (SOGAT and the NGA) to form an industrial union. The merger brought together two different union typologies 'popular bossdom' and 'exclusive democracy' (Undy 1999). The autonomy (financial/bargaining) of branch and chapel had been closely guarded in the craft tradition; in a similar way the political activities of the GPMU are under the jurisdiction of the national office. A long serving representative (NGA and GPMU) described the governance structure of the GPMU as comparable to the old feudal system in pre-industrial times (interview). Branch, chapel and regional officials are autonomous to run their own fiefdoms but at the same time the national office expected support, as the King might from his barons, for national issues or action. National policy had to be underpinned by the support of the Executive Council (regional representation) and the Biennial Delegate Conference (branch representation).

The leadership have been able to turn an anti-common market trade union into a pro-EU organization. This transformation of ideology with regard to European integration has been top-down and strategic. The election of Tony Dubbins as NGA General Secretary in 1985, subsequently to assume this position in the GPMU, appears to be the initial catalyst for change. He was determined to play an influential role in developing a more positive approach to European integration within the union, the industry and in the wider labour movement, both the TUC and Labour Party.

In 1989 the GPMU established, together with the British Printing Industries Federation, a Joint European Action Group 'to examine the implications of the Single European Market for the printing industry' (GPMU 1993). A bilateral officer exchange programme was developed with the German print union IG Medien, funded by the European Commission.

Initially an internal information and educational approach was adopted from the top down, involving initially national officers, the GPMU's International Committee, the Women's Committee (both including lay members) and branch/chapel officials especially from the larger multinational companies. In 1992, chapel officials participated in 35 seminars funded by the EU, covering issues around the major multinational companies in media and print. National officials and the International Committee travelled to Brussels to meet key Commission personnel, MEPs, ETUC and TUC officials again funded by the EU Commission. Specific MEPs had a 'watching brief' on matters relevant to GPMU members. Education courses were run in conjunction with these developments at the GPMU Bedford headquarters. As one key GPMU official put it:

> Printers are generally smart guys, they read a lot. Education and information were all you needed to persuade the comrades of the merits of the case . . . We were getting nothing from the Tory government. Once you showed 'em what were happening and what were coming out in terms of legislation, they were understanding of the potential benefits of it all (Interview 2006).

In the mid-1990s the GPMU also rented office space from the GMB union in Brussels and stationed an official there. The office has enabled the GPMU to build a higher profile at the EU level and closely follow developments. They have developed close links with a number of MEPs to both monitor and influence developments. The office in Brussels also allowed the GPMU to keep an eye on developments within the European Graphical Federation, especially after the 1994 Budapest Conference fall out with the other influential player, the German printing union IG Medien.

The leadership of the NGA became convinced of the need to engage with the EU for two main reasons. The first was that after a decade or more of Thatcherism the paucity of domestic opportunities to advance worker interests was more than apparent. In addition, the threat of increasing competition inevitable in the new single European market seemed to be partially offset by certain Treaty developments. Article 118A of the EEC Treaty allowed qualified majority voting (QMV) for all matters relating to health and safety. This obscure legal provision was picked up by the GPMU leadership and was deemed especially significant given the expansive definition of health and safety provided by the European Court of Justice. These developments were closely followed by the Social Charter 1989 and then the Maastricht Social Agreement, all indicators for the GPMU leadership that the EU was now an important arena for pursuing trade union objectives; a pragmatic assessment of EU developments.

EMU will prove beneficial to the printing industry and GPMU members (GPMU 2001, p. 113). Exchange rate stability is cited as beneficial to the export side of the industry and for potential inward investment. Support for EMU is, however, contingent on the concurrent development of the EU social dimension. EMU and further market integration are only acceptable if accompanied by a social programme that ameliorates the worst effects of these restructuring processes (discourse 3 and 4). The US model has too many 'dire social consequences . . . Europe must do better' (TUFE 2002, p. 14). In addition, the social dimension is seen as crucial to persuading working people in Britain to support European integration. The social dimension is essential if, 'Europe is to be a people's Europe – not just a business Europe' (Dubbins, GPMU 2001, p. 113).

In contrast to UNISON the leadership of the GPMU have been able and willing to pursue an explicit agenda espousing a pragmatic but positive EU agenda. The absence of national-level factionalism or other organized informal opposition groupings enabled the leadership to undertake a transformative EU agenda. An attempt by the 'broad left' to organize in the early 1990s was met with stiff resistance from the leadership, all GPMU officials were barred from participating in the attempted development of a political faction (Undy 1999), an indication that the disciplined craft approach of the NGA had won over the SOGAT perspective on factions. In the absence of organized opposition, numerous pro-EMU motions have been passed at the Biennial Delegate Conference.

Although Bieler's (2003) perspective of sectoral differentiation holds for these two unions studied above, internal governance factors, especially the political and democratic rationalities of each union organization, have constrained and/or enabled the leaderships of the unions. In both organizations the leaderships have wanted to pursue a supportive EU policy.

For UNISON the influence of formal groups (lay control in NEC) and informal factions (broad left) have organized significant opposition to developing such a policy. In the case of the GPMU, the absence of such restrictions on de facto leadership autonomy enabled the leadership to undertake a strategy of transformation both in terms of policy positions and organizational engagement with the EU.

THE GMB

The GMB is a general union and has over 700 000 members from a number of different sectors in both the exposed and sheltered parts of the economy. The union has an unusual regional structure, with each of the ten regions guaranteed places on the Central Executive Council (CEC) dependent on their respective membership levels. The National Office (General Secretary) has jurisdiction over international policy and decision making is subject to CEC approval.

The GMB is a highly regionalized trade union organization. Until the 1960s, it had no trade group representation and a single channel for decision making on bargaining and non-bargaining issues. Significant responsibilities are decentralized to the regions with the regional secretaries often described as 'Barons'. It was not until the mergers with the Boilermakers in 1982 and especially APEX in 1989 that trade groups acquired formal representation status within the Central Executive Committee (CEC). However, the regional influence still dominates. The majority of the CEC officials are elected via the regions, including trade group representatives, and the CEC operates under the watchful eyes of the Barons.

In general, the organizational response of the GMB to the EU has been internally innovative and externally engaging. The overall strategy to Europe has been termed 'going over and under', referring to bypassing the UK government preferring to cooperate with local, regional and European tiers of government. The GMB leadership made important domestic organizational changes that enhanced their capacity to receive and aggregate interests before projecting a coherent response to EU initiatives. The Brussels Office ensure co-ordination of political representation across the various trade groups of the GMB.

A European Steering Group was established to provide an informal forum for senior officials (national trade groups and regional officials) and representatives of the GMB to meet, put together the information they had gleaned and exchange experiences. As it stood, the European Steering group did not have any direct authority to direct matters and had an unclear relationship with the CEC's International Committee. Subsequently the

International Committee of the CEC became the European and International Committee, absorbing the European Steering Group. Half of all meetings were to be EU-related and the Brussels-based official also regularly attends.

Research has indicated that the General Secretary is able to lead on matters European. Political factions do not feature at the national level as constraints on discretionary decision making. 'To be quite honest I think the General Secretary had an easy run on matters European, there was never any strong opposition to the union's formal stance' (GMB official).

In addition, the regional secretaries did not prove as significant a constraint as their de jure position might indicate. Regional secretaries 'were prepared to let the General Secretary take the lead on matters European providing he would leave them more or less alone to run their regions' (GMB official).

The GMB opened a Brussels office even before the TUC in the early 1990s and in the political area have been the most engaged British trade union in Brussels. A monthly European News Bulletin is produced by the office, outlining the major news from Brussels. The monthly bulletin is sent out to relevant GMB officials and activists (reception), but also it is disseminated to the network of contacts and lobby targets established by the office since the early 1990s (projection). The information disseminated from the Brussels office is presented to GMB officials, activists and members in a user friendly format, translating 'Brussels speak' into a more accessible language. Interviews with regional officials indicate that this is a much valued resource, as it clearly and concisely sets out EU-developments and their implications for the GMB.

One of the major reasons, outside of perceived cost, of other trade union organizations not locating an office in Brussels is that the perceived benefits are hard to quantify. In addition to informing their membership and raising their profile (local, regional and European), can a tangible benefit be discerned from the permanent presence in terms of the contents of EU legislation? One MEP certainly thinks so: 'Some 60 per cent of the amendments, which we have adopted in this field, have been incorporated in the finished legislation. That means in reality that much of the content of these laws has come from Nigel's pen or the pen of other trade unionists' (Simon Hughes MEP, GMB 1993, p. 425).

The GMB arguments for full participation in EMU are economic and political. Pointing to job losses from the high value of Sterling and its damage to UK industry, in the manufacturing, textiles and engineering sectors specifically, the GMB regard full membership of the Euro-zone as providing a degree of certainty for inward investors unattainable if the UK remains on the periphery (GMB 2001; Guardian 2003).

The GMB dismiss analysis emanating especially from the public-sector unions that membership of EMU threatens current levels of public spending in the UK. The examples of greater social spending per capita in Germany, France and the Benelux Countries demonstrate that membership of the Euro-zone does not necessarily mean lower public spending, just lower debt to income ratios.

The EU is a whole package and cannot be viewed as a menu to pick and choose from if British credibility as a Euro-player is to be maintained. Together with the GPMU (and other unions), the GMB started the Trade Unionists for Europe (Tufe) group with the express aims of supporting EMU in the context of further developing the EU social dimension (discourse 3 and 4). The gradual development of the EU social dimension is viewed as an alternative to the traditional UK model of industrial relations. Social dialogue, industrial democracy and other features of 'continental' industrial relations are viewed not as threats to the British model but as a means to reinvigorate it. Without EMU at its core it is unlikely that further development of the EU social dimension will occur, essential to counter the worst effects of globalization. 'The EU can be a bulwark against the worst effects of globalization and is more capable than the nation state at defending and promoting a European Social Model' (Interview GMB Official).

EU market reform must be linked to a strong social agenda that enables the protection of workers from the worst effects of structural change. One cannot occur without the other (GMB 2001). If the GMB, and the UK more generally, are to retain their current influence in Brussels on the decision making processes, its partners must view them as credible. An approach that asks for the benefits of the social dimension without also supporting Euro membership is not a credible strategy. The UK must be part of the inner-core of economic policymaking and this means joining the Euro.

'To date the UK has not borne the brunt of exclusion as our partners in Europe are giving us the benefit of the doubt and expect us to join sometime in the future. The longer uncertainty remains the more isolated the UK will become' (GMB 2001).

The supportive and engaging EU response by the GMB leadership has been possible due to the absence of de facto internal constraints in the development of this strategy, both formal and informal groups (trade groups/factions). The GMB has adapted its organization and expanded its organizational capacity with regard to the EU. Although the mix of exposed and sheltered workers in its membership constituency could have proved problematic, the predominance of regional over trade group representation in the CEC has in effect circumventive sectoral differentiation.

THE TRANSPORT AND GENERAL WORKERS UNION

The TGWU is a general union and represents over 900 000 members and organizes in a number of industrial sectors, it has a higher percentage of members in the manufacturing sector than does the GMB. The TGWU is much more factionalized (at all levels) than the GMB. In addition to the influence of informal groups (faction), representation on the NEC is dominated by the trade groups. Conflict between trade groups in the National Executive Committee is traditionally resolved by consensus; if no consensus is reached, no national office position is adopted. Factionalism and trade group influence have brought to the fore economic and political arguments against EMU (discourse 1 and 2).

In general, the organizational approach of the TGWU to the EU has been adaptive rather than inventive. Initially, taking 1988 as a starting point, the Todd leadership appointed a European co-ordinator. The responsibilities of the role were to monitor developments at the EU level, to disseminate this to relevant TGWU personnel (reception) and to engage with lobbying the various EU institutions (projection). The TGWU official travelled periodically to Brussels but was based in London. Contacts were made with officials from the EU Commission, representatives from the European Parliament (MEPs) and the Economic and Social Committee. In addition, Ron Todd, along with David Lea (TUC) was instrumental in inviting Jacques Delors to the Bournemouth TUC in 1988.

Under the leadership of Bill Morris, the position of European co-ordinator was made redundant. This is emblematic of the TGWU retreat from the pragmatic political engagement begun by Todd. The Morris period of leadership is characterized by a disengagement from EU issues and inertia in the political sphere of EU activity. Contacts with the various officials from the EU institutions dissolved. The relationship with TGWU 'sponsored' MEPs became sketchy. In a period when the development of a coherent organizational response should have accelerated given the increasing importance of labour market legislation emanating from Brussels, there was a lack of central political co-ordination. This disengagement with EU political representation has coincided with the election of New Labour.

Organizational inertia questions the efficacy of the TGWU political response to the EU. By failing to co-ordinate (non-sector) EU responsibilities and removing the position of European co-ordinator, the organizational capacity of the TGWU to monitor, respond and intervene in EU policymaking diminished. The failure to maintain contacts with the EU institutions and especially the Commission mean that in the drafting of the social dimension Directives the TGWU perspective is absent. The TGWU have relied on representing their interests via the various trade groups and industry federations. TGWU 'sponsored' MEPs have had a hard time identifying individuals within the TGWU who have policy responsibilities for EU affairs (Interview with MEP).

The policy response to EMU by the TGWU is not easy to summarize. A cursory reading of press releases and newspaper articles written on behalf of the TGWU leadership (TGWU 2001, 2003a, 2003b) suggests that the emphasis is on the Chancellor's five economic tests being met and ensuring a favourable Sterling/Euro exchange rate on joining. It would seem that the timing of entry is the most important issue for the TGWU and it is the economic tests that determine the criteria of entry. However, closer examination of the official policy position opens up caveats illustrating both the sectoral influence of the trade groups and the political influence of the 'broad left' faction.

The official policy explicitly refers to both manufacturing and public sectors as having different interests with regard to EMU. Far from there being a perceived divide between manufacturing and public sector interests with regard to EMU (Bieler 2003), the composite motion frames EMU as a threat to both manufacturing and public-sector spending. For the exposed sectors, the deflationary bias of the European Central Bank's (ECB) rules (can act when inflation is high, but not in periods of stagnation) compounded by the 'one fits all' exchange rate, are a potential for recessionary disaster with no space for democratic intervention. The TGWU argue that membership of the Euro under the current EMU framework jeopardizes manufacturing employment across the EU given the lack of provision for and inability to exert political control and implement policy in times of recession (Morris 1998). In addition EMU is also framed as posing a huge threat to public-service provision (discourse 1).

> Conference notes that the evidence of the potential negative impact on public services can be clearly seen in France, Portugal and the Republic of Ireland, where the need to meet the inflexible criteria and strict budget limits of the Euro's Stability and Growth Pact is putting public expenditure and government commitments to improved services in these Eurozone countries under the severest pressure (TGWU Composite Motion 24, 2003).

TGWU policy is implicitly seeking reform of the ECB and a revision of the EMU convergence criteria. In addition to root and branch reform of EMU, the political dimension of the project presents problems for the TGWU; problems that mean they will be unlikely to support UK entry even if the Chancellor's five economic tests are met (discourse 2).

'Conference acknowledges that membership of the Euro has a political dimension, as it raises crucial fundamentally important questions about political sovereignty, democratic accountability and national governance of macroeconomic policies' (TGWU Composite Motion 24, 2003).

The objections to European integration articulated above (discourse 1 and 2) clearly indicate that the TGWU are economically, politically and democratically opposed to EMU. The formal (trade groups) and informal groups (factions) influential at the national level of the TGWU have all left their mark on the official policy position. In policy terms, the leadership is constrained by the democratic and political rationality of the TGWU. In addition the election of Labour and the shift toward deregulatory neo-liberal policymaking in the Commission has altered the external environment upon which the pragmatic acceptance of the EU was premised. Ron Todd famously referred to the EU as 'the only game in town' in his address to the TUC in 1988. With Delors departed and domestically a Labour government elected, for the TGWU, Brussels is no longer the 'only game in town'.

CONCLUSION

In terms of the overall response to European integration two of the case study trade unions are what might be termed positively pragmatic (GMB and GPMU). Their responses, in terms of policies and especially their political engagement with EU institutions, seek to push for a rebalancing of the integration project. This includes supporting further economic and market integration if it is likely to result in further developments to the social dimension. The impetus for this reorientation derives from the inability (and unwillingness) of domestic institutions and actors to engage and deliver trade union aims and objectives, but also from an acknowledgement that the EU is currently the best option for the pursuit of international solutions and regulation in an increasingly globalized world.

UNISON's response is more neutrally pragmatic; support for the social dimension of the EU is tempered by its opposition to EMU, although opposition is focused on the particular aspects of the Stability and Growth Pact. Engagement with the EU directly, outside of the industry federations it is affiliated to, is limited and piecemeal. The TGWU are politically hostile to the integration project, due to the dominance of the broad left faction. The leadership has made efforts to disguise this by emphasizing the Chancellor's five economic tests. In addition, engagement with EU institutions is minimal, normally through the various trade groups and rarely in support of an EU Directive. UNISON or the TGWU have not made great strides to influence decision making with non-sector specific Directives; both trade unions focus more on the domestic transposition stage. Quite clearly these two case studies illustrate that not only is the EU not the 'only game in town' but it is a game that can be partially played or not played at all. The irony is that it was the General Secretary (Ron Todd) of the TGWU who advocated an engaged pragmatism nearly 20 years ago at the TUC.

The case studies illustrate that theoretical approaches overlooking internal factors are insufficient in explaining trade union Europeanization. In addition, the election of a 'New' Labour government and a shift to the right in the composition of the Commission means the premise upon which trade unions sought EU solutions in the 1980s and 1990s has shifted. Bieler's (2003) approach to EMU policy positions generally holds, but again the case studies illustrate how internal politics and institutions can skew policy positions. The GMB, with more public-sector members than the TGWU, is supportive of EMU and the TGWU hostile. Although with the exception of the PCS, most trade unions in Britain with members either exclusively in the sheltered or exposed sectors of the labour market do adhere to Bieler's sectoral differentiation.

Trends towards trade union mergers since the 1960s have confused the picture somewhat, making the application of Bieler's approach much more problematic. The proposed merger between the two general unions (GMB and TGWU) and Amicus will compound this. Amicus will be then composed of a mixed membership constituency (exposed and sheltered) and bring together affiliate unions with divergent ideological approaches to the EU and EMU. Future policy positions of this new 'super' union will be determined on the confluence of both internal and external factors. The new union governance model established for Amicus and the self-organization of members into informal groupings (factions) will prove crucial to the determination of future policy. Union governance sets the parameters for the influence of industrial sectors (trade groups) in decision making (de jure); political factions, depending on the extent of their penetration, can skew policy determination (de facto).

Theories ignoring the internal factors of union organization are helpful in identifying the pressures for change but are ultimately insufficient for explaining both diversity and how change has happened. Trade unions are political and social institutions and as such each possess their own political, democratic and administrative rationality (Undy et al. 1981). Attempting to prejudge political responses solely by analyses of external factors and the environment in which they operate overlooks this.

NOTES

1. In the field of European Studies the term European integration generally applies to the study of the dynamics underlying the integration process, whereas Europeanization

normally refers to subsequent adaptations to the integration process in the Member States. Separating these processes often referred to as 'bottom-up' (European integration) and 'top-down' (Europeanization) is a messy business. For instance one type of Europeanization response to integration from a national actor could conceivably entail attempts to amend the integration process at the EU level – so at one and the same time Europeanization is European integration! In addition, the process of Europeanization can also be horizontal; the cross-transfer of practices and/or policies between Member States without reference to the EU institutions.

2. Important areas, such as social security, remuneration, the right of association and the right to strike or lock out, are not addressed at Community level.

3. The push and pull factors relate to the idea that trade union organization (if it is to remain effective) must be congruent to the geographical size of the market in which they operate (Commons 1909).

4. See Foster & Scott (2003) for an application of this discourse analysis to public service unions across the EU.

5. RMT, National Union of Rail, Maritime and Transport Workers; ASLEF, Associated Society of Locomotive Engineers and Firemen; NATFHE, The University & College Lecturers' Union; MSF, Manufacturing, Science and Finance Union (now Amicus); PCS, Public and Commercial Services Union; AEEU, Amalgamated Engineering and Electrical Union (now Amicus).

REFERENCES

Bieler, A. (2003), 'Labour, Neo-liberalism and the conflict over monetary union', *German Politics*, **12** (2), 24-44.

Commons, J.R. (1909), 'American Shoemakers, 1648-1895: A Sketch of Industrial Evolution', *The Quarterly Journal of Economics*, **24** (1), reprinted in S. Larson and B. Nissen (1987), *Theories of the Labor Movement*, Detroit: Wayne State University Press, pp. 140-155.

Dølvik, J.E. (1997), *Redrawing the Boundaries of Solidarity: ETUC, social dialogue and the Europeanisation of trade unions in the 1990s*, Oslo: ARENA.

Dyson, K. (ed.) (2002), *European states and the Euro: Europeanization, variation and convergence*, Oxford: Oxford University Press.

Foster, D. and P. Scott (2003), 'EMU and public service trade unionism: between states and markets', *Transfer*, **9** (4), 688-702.

Geyer, R. (1997), *The Uncertain Union: British and Norwegian Social Democrats in an Integrating Europe*, Aldershot: Avebury.

GMB (1993), *Jobs and Recovery: Report of Congress.*

GMB (2001), *European Union: CEU Statement to GMB Congress 2001*, 2-5 June.

GPMU (1993), *The IG Medien/Graphical Paper and Media Union Officer Exchange Programme: An independent evaluation for the European Commission*, GPMU, IG Medien, European Graphical Federation and European Commission.

GPMU (2001), *Report of the 2001 Biennial Delegate Conference*, Bedford: GPMU.

Guardian (2003), 'Union leader says delay would put Euro in a coma', January.

Hancké, B. (2000), 'European Work Councils and Industrial Restructuring in the European Motor Industry', *European Journal of Industrial Relations*, **6** (1), 35-39.

Morris, W. (1998), 'EMU & the Democratic Deficit', in B. Moss and J. Michie, *The Single European Currency in National Perspective: A Community in Crisis?*, Basingstoke: Macmillan Press, pp. 181-91.

Pierson, P. and S. Leibfried (1995), *European Social Policy: Between Fragmentation and Integration*, Washington, DC: The Brookings Institute.

Rosamond, B. (1993), 'National Labour Organizations and European Integration: British Trade Unions and 1992', *Political Studies*, **XLI**, 412-434.

Scharpf, F. (1988), 'The joint-decision trap: Lessons from German Federalism and European integration', *Public Administration*, **66**, 239-278.

Scharpf, F. (1996), 'Negative and Positive Integration in the Political Economy of European Welfare State', in G. Marks (ed.), *Governance in the European Union*, London: Sage, pp. 15-39.

Strange, G. (2002), 'British Trade Unions and European Integration in the 1990s: Politics versus Political Economy', *Political Studies*, **50**, 332-353.

Streeck, W. (1995), 'From Market Making to State Building? Reflections on the Political Economy of European Social Policy', in P. Pierson and S. Leibfried (eds), *European Social Policy: Between Fragmentation and Integration*, Washington, DC: The Brookings Institute, pp. 389-431.

Terry, M. (1996), 'Negotiating the Government of UNISON: Union Democracy in Theory and Practice', *British Journal of Industrial Relations*, **34** (1), 87-111.

TGWU (2001), 'Let's make 2002 a fight for jobs, not the euro', Press Release PR02/001, 30 December.

TGWU (2003a), 'Bill Morris calls on government to lead the Euro debate not divide the country', Press release, PR03/167, 21 May.

TGWU (2003b), 'Morris on euro: Time for certainty not just hope', Press release PR03/0180, 9 June.

Trade Unionists For Europe (2002), A *Trade Union Agenda for Europe*.

Turner, L. (1995), 'The Europeanization of Labor: Structure before action', *European Journal of Industrial Relations*, **2** (3), 325-344.

Undy, R. (1999), 'Negotiating Amalgamations: Territorial and Political Consolidation and Administrative Reform in Public-Sector Unions in the UK', *British Journal of Industrial Relations*, **37** (3), 445-463.

Undy, R., V. Ellis, W.E.J. McCarthy and A.M. Halmos (1981), *Change in Trade Unions: The development of UK unions since the 1960s*, London: Hutchinson.

Visser, J. (1998), 'Learning to Play: The Europeanisation of Trade Unions', in P. Pasture and J. Verberckmoes (eds), *Working-Class Internationalism and the Appeal of National Identity: Historical Debates and Current Perspectives*, Oxford: Berg, pp. 231-253.

PART II

The Impact of Public Management Reform
Ideas in Europe on Public Sector Industrial
Relations

9. The End of an Era: Structural Changes in German Public Sector Collective Bargaining

Heiner Dribbusch and Thorsten Schulten

INTRODUCTION

Since the mid-1990s, industrial relations in Germany have shown strong tendencies towards decentralization and fragmentation of collective bargaining (Bispinck and Schulten 2003). At first sight collective bargaining in the public sector seems to have been an important exception to this development, showing a considerable degree of stability and continuity. Until 2005 there existed a rather centralized system, with national collective agreements covering all public service employees at federal, federal states and local level. This collective bargaining system centred around the idea of equal standards of pay and working conditions for all employees in the public sector. It was accompanied by an established culture of social partnership and an overall non-adversarial bargaining culture illustrated by the fact that there have been only two national strikes in the public sector since 1949.

As in other European countries, however, the German public sector has been confronted with various challenges, such as increasing budget restraints, privatization and liberalization of public services or the introduction of New Public Management concepts. Enforced by the completion of the European Single Market, during the 1990s neo-liberal policies were successful in giving the public sector the reputation of being inefficient and out of fashion. Consequently, the mainstream policies have called for a 'modernization' of public services, which basically meant to make them function as private companies either by privatization or by internal restructuring.

Until today there has been comparatively little research into the consequences of these developments on labour relations and collective bargaining in the public sector.[1] We therefore ask how the established system of collective bargaining has been affected by the structural and political changes in the German public sector. In contrast to the first impression of continuity and stability we argue that public sector collective bargaining has been destabilized by major changes since the mid-1990s. First of all, many operations and sub-sectors such as local transport, refuse disposal and utilities have been moved outside the scope of the national public services agreements. Furthermore, the employers' bargaining association which so far combined public employers at all levels has eroded and finally broken down. Finally, in 2005 trade unions and employers agreed to replace the old collective framework agreements for the public sector by entirely new ones which, however, open the door to further decentralization and differentiation of collective bargaining. The era of the old collective bargaining system in the German public sector has come to an end.

TRADITIONAL STRUCTURE OF LABOUR RELATIONS IN GERMAN PUBLIC SECTOR

The state has always been by far the largest employer in Germany. In 2003 nearly six million employees were hired in the public sector which corresponded to about 17 per cent of all German employees (see Table 9.1). Around 4.8 million employees or nearly 14 per cent of the entire German workforce were working in public services. Another 1.1 million were employed in companies under private law in which the state holds the majority of the shares.

The organizational structure of public services reflects the German political constitution as a federalist state, whereby the political power is divided among three main levels of governance and administration: the federal level, the level of the 16 federal states (*Länder*) and the local level. The largest number of about 45 per cent of all public services employees are hired by the federal states, which mirrors their far-reaching political competencies (e.g. for schools and universities or for the police). Around 30 per cent of public services employees work at local level and another 10 per cent at federal level. Finally, around 12 per cent are employed by public organizations and agencies which are not under the direct control of public administration.

The employees in German public services are divided into two major status groups: public civil servants (*Beamte*) and public employees including white- and blue-collar workers. In 2003, civil servants accounted for around 35 per cent of all employees in public services. White-collar workers were by far the largest group at 48 per cent, while blue-collar workers represented only 13 per cent.

Table 9.1 Number and composition of employees in German public sector (2003)

Public Services		
Federal level	491 115	10.3%
Federal states level	2 155 281	45.1%
Local level	1 409 592	29,5%
Others	128 286	2.7%
Organizations under public law	595 130	12.5%
Blue-collar workers	601 106	12.6%
White-collar workers	2 301 493	48.2%
Civil servants (including judges)	1 689 916	35.4%
Military personnel (permanent and fixed-term)	186 889	3.9%
Women	2 476 766	51.8%
Men	2 302 638	48.2%
Full-time	3 438 974	72.0%
Part-time	1 340 430	28.0%
Total number of employees in public services	**4 779 404**	**100.0%**
Public Sector		
Total number of employees in public services	4 779 404	81.4%
Companies under private law in which public holds majority of shares	1 094 945	18.6%
Total number of employees in public sector	**5 874 349**	**100.0%**

Source: Statistisches Bundesamt (2005), own calculations.

The distinction between civil servants and public employees, which is covered by different legal statuses, has led to the emergence of two sub-systems of labour relations in public services (see Figure 9.1). Public civil servants enjoy lifelong job security, but have neither the right to bargain collectively nor to go on strike. Instead, wages and working conditions are determined by law through the German Parliament. Although there are no negotiations on pay and working conditions, the government used to consult the peak organizations of trade unions and professional associations in advance of new legal initiatives. Until recently, pay increases for civil servants were mostly oriented to what has been concluded for blue- and white-collar workers (BMI 2002, p. 94).

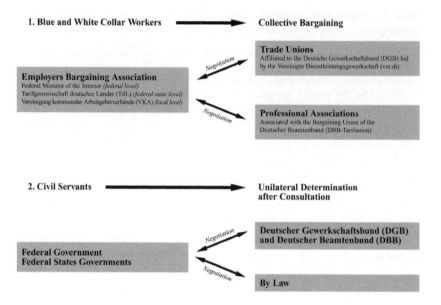

1. **Blue and White Collar Workers** ➡️ **Collective Bargaining**

Trade Unions
Affiliated to the Deutsche Gewerkschaftsbund (DGB) led by the Vereinigte Dienstleistungsgewerkschaft (ver.di)

Negotiation

Employers Bargaining Association
Federal Minister of the Interior *(federal level)*
Tarifgemeinschaft deutscher Länder (TdL.) *(federal state level)*
Vereinigung kommunaler Arbeitgeberverbände (VKA) *(local level)*

Negotiation

Professional Associations
Associated with the Bargaining Union of the Deutscher Beamtenbund (DBB-Tarifunion)

2. **Civil Servants** ➡️ **Unilateral Determination after Consultation**

Negotiation

Deutscher Gewerkschaftsbund (DGB) and Deutscher Beamtenbund (DBB)

**Federal Government
Federal States Governments**

Negotiation

By Law

Figure 9.1 Traditional systems of wage determination in German public services

Unlike civil servants, all other public employees fall under the regulations of the Collective Agreements Act (*Tarifvertragsgesetz*) and have the same rights regarding collective bargaining and industrial action as their counterparts in the private sector. As in most other west-European countries, the collective bargaining system in German public services used to be rather centralized (Bordogna and Winchester 2001). Joint negotiations between employers and trade unions covering all blue- and white-collar workers in public services at federal, federal states and local level at the same time were the norm. Until 2003 public employers formed a collective bargaining association which was composed of:

- the federal government represented by the Federal Minister of the Interior;
- the federal states governments represented by the Bargaining Association of German Federal States (Tarifgemeinschaft deutscher Länder, TdL); and
- the municipalities represented by the Municipal Employers' Association (Vereinigung kommunaler Arbeitgeberverbände, VKA).

On the employees' side most employees in public services who are trade union members are organized in trade unions affiliated to the Confederation of German Trade Unions (*Deutscher Gewerkschaftsbund*, DGB). The biggest trade union is the United Services Union (*Vereinte Dienstleistungsgewerkschaft*, ver.di) which had in 2003 about 500 000 members in the public sector.[2] The bulk of its membership are blue- and white-collar workers. Other DGB affiliates which organize some public employees are the German Police Union (*Gewerkschaft der Polizei*, GdP), the German Union of Education *(Gewerkschaft Erziehung Wissenschaft*, GEW) and TRANSNET (Rail Workers Union). Usually the DGB affiliates create a bargaining association headed by ver.di.

Moreover, there are a lot of employees in the public sector who are not organized in a DGB affiliated trade union but in one of the numerous professional associations. The most important one is the German Civil Servants' Association (*Deutscher Beamtenbund*, DBB) which mainly organizes civil servants but also has members among blue- and white-collar workers.[3] Together with around 40 mostly rather small professional associations the DBB has created a bargaining union (*DBB-Tarifunion*) which also negotiates collective agreements for public employees claiming to represent about 360 000 employees. Traditionally, public employers hold parallel separate negotiations with both groups, but conclude the agreements first with the DGB-affiliates. The agreements are then almost completely taken over by the *DBB-Tarifunion*.

Up to 2005, pay and conditions for public employees were mainly regulated by three national collective framework agreements as follows:

1. the Federal Collective Agreement for White-Collar Workers in the Public Sector (*Bundes-Angestelltentarifvertrag*, BAT);
2. the Federal Framework Collective Agreement for Blue-Collar Workers in the Public Service at Federal and Federal State Level (*Manteltarifvertrag für Arbeiterinnen und Arbeiter des Bundes und der Länder*, MTArb); and
3. the Federal Framework Collective Agreement for Blue-Collar Workers at Local Level (*Bundesmanteltarifvertrag für Arbeiter gemeindlicher Verwaltungen und Betriebe*, BMT G II).

Traditionally, labour relations in the German public sector have always been highly cooperative and based on a strong culture of social partnership. It has been not unusual for trade union representatives to switch during their career on the employers' side to become managers in public companies or administration. The bargaining associations on both the employers' and the trade unions' side have guaranteed a high degree of centralization in collective bargaining and therewith helped to minimize industrial conflicts. It was usually at municipal level where trade unions could develop the greatest pressure and where threats of industrial action were most effective, not least because the workers in refuse disposal and local transport were at the core of public sector unionization (Keller 1993). The public sector did not add significantly to the low German strike rates. Since 1949 there have been only two national strikes in the public sector with four and 11 strike days respectively. Much of the stability of labour relations in the public service arose also from the fact that, although pay levels have been on average below those paid in core industries of the private sector, public workers have enjoyed greater job security.

GERMAN PUBLIC SECTOR IN THE 1990S: STRUCTURAL CHANGES AND DEVELOPMENTS

The development of the German public sector in the 1990s was influenced by three main factors which had more or less far-reaching consequences for the established systems of labour relations and collective bargaining and caused a substantial reduction of public employment: 1) the persistently high public deficit, 2) the privatization and liberalization of public services, and 3) the introduction of New Public Management concepts.

Between 1991 and 2003 the overall public debt in Germany increased by more than 120 per cent to a total sum of 1 326 billion Euro which was equivalent to 64.2 per cent of Germany's GDP in 2003 (Statistisches Bundesamt 2004). During the 1990s the total public budget always showed a strong deficit which has become even more dramatic since 2001, after which Germany has continuously failed the 3 per cent deficit criteria of the European Stability Pact. The reasons for the enduring crisis of public finances are manifold: it is partly caused by German unification as well as by a relatively weak economic performance, persisting high unemployment and increasing social welfare payments during the 1990s. Moreover, it is also caused by a certain fiscal and tax policy which favours tax cuts in particular for companies and groups with higher incomes (Truger 2004).

Since personnel costs count for a significant proportion of the public budget, there has continuously been strong pressure to reduce the number of public employees and to decrease the costs for the remaining staff. In 2000, the state spent altogether around 160 billion Euro for personnel, which was equivalent to 15.7 per cent of the total state budget. Considering their specific labour intensive responsibilities, the expenditures for personnel were particularly high at the level of the federal states where they counted for around 38 per cent of total expenditure in 2000. In comparison, the share of personnel costs of total expenditure was 27 per cent at local level and only about 11 per cent at federal level in the same year. During the 1990s the share of personnel expenditure showed a slight but continuing decline (BMI 2002, p. 99).

The large public debts and budgets deficits were also a driving force behind the policy of privatization. In addition to that, privatization became further encouraged by the deregulation of former public monopolies in areas such as telecommunication, railways, public transport, energy etc., which was enforced by the European Single Market project. During the 1990s the two most important initiatives at federal level were the privatization of the German Federal Post Service and the German Federal Rail Service, which were both split up and transformed into various private companies. At federal state and local level privatization took place in sectors such as public transport, waste disposal, street cleaning, energy supply, health and care companies. Remaining public activities were often reorganized as independent companies under public or private law or were transformed into public-private partnerships (Schneider 2002). Following the political liberalization of formerly protected sectors, more and more public companies had to deal with private competitors.

Both the persisting crises of public finances and the restructuring of public services encouraged by liberalization policies have also demanded a more cost saving organization of the sector itself. In order to make the public sector behave less like a bureaucracy and more like private companies, so-called New Public Management concepts became widely debated and implemented in Germany (Keller 1999, pp. 68-70). According to these concepts the internal organization of the public sector should no longer be guided primarily by principles of hierarchy and administrative rules, but more by market principles such as efficiency and competition. The implementation of New Public Management concepts should go along with a far-reaching decentralization in the organization of public services whereby each organizational unit should take its own financial responsibility in order to compete with other units or companies.

Finally, the considered tendencies of change and restructuring in the German public sector have had serious consequences for the development of public sector employment (Ahlers 2004, Figure 9.2). Until the late 1980s there was permanent growth in the number of public services employees increasing from around 3 million in 1960 to nearly 4.7 million in 1989. With the unification in 1990, the number of public services employees expanded rapidly to 6.7 million. Since then public employment has shown permanent decline. Between 1991 and 2003 the total number of public services employees decreased by more than 28 per cent and has now almost reached the pre-unification level. Moreover, the total numbers of hours worked in public services have become even more reduced, since the number of part-time employees had shown a sharp increase in the same period (Statistisches Bundesamt 2005).

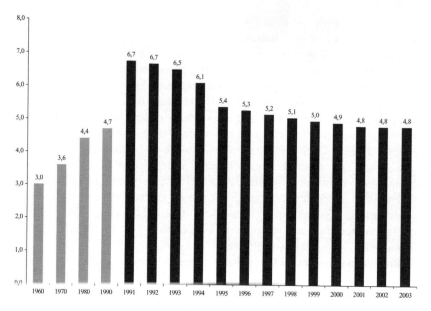

*   Data for 1960-1990: West-Germany

Sources: Statliches Bundesamt (2005) and Keller (1993: 36).

Figure 9.2 Total number of employees in German public services (in Mio.)*

Summarizing the reasons for the overall decline of employment in German public services between 1991 and 2002, more than half of the reduction (56 per cent) was a result of privatization of German Federal Post and Rail Services (see Figure 9.3). Nearly 30 per cent was further caused by a reduction of employees in eastern Germany which had a much larger public sector before unification. Finally, the reduction of public services employees in western Germany contributed only 10 per cent to the overall decline in public employment.

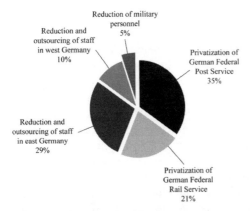

Source: Koufen (2002: 914).

Figure 9.3 Reasons for the reduction of German public services employment between 1991 and 2002

THE DECENTRALIZATION OF COLLECTIVE BARGAINING IN THE 1990S

At the beginning of the new millennium a first glance at the collective bargaining system in the German public sector gave the impression of remaining stable. The most important collective framework agreements such as the BAT, the BMT and the MTArb were continued and collective bargaining was still highly centralized. Below the surface, however, the traditional bargaining system had already begun to crumble and public-sector collective bargaining had become much more conflictual.

The Shifting Balance of Power

During the 1990s the economic and structural setting which framed collective bargaining in the public sector changed fundamentally. Following the liberalization policies since 1992, the public service has tended to fall into two main parts. One is the ever shrinking public service in the strict sense of the meaning, that is: all those public services which remain exclusively financed by taxes. The second part of what once used to be the public sector is formed by all those services which have to compete with private companies (Wendl 2003). This growing division, together with a financial crisis in the area of public budgeting, effectively changed the system of public sector bargaining – not least because it helped to shift the balance of power between trade unions and public employers.

The first major change was triggered at federal level following the privatization of the Federal Post Service and the Federal Rail Service. As a result, telecommunication, the postal service and rail effectively ceased to be part of the central collective bargaining rounds in the public sector.[4] Furthermore many of the new competitors entering the privatized telecommunication and the rail transport market were neither members of an employers' association nor signatory to any collective agreement.

Less highlighted, but not less influential for the future development of collective bargaining, was the process of privatization and liberalization of public services at local level. Many local authorities started either to establish new service companies or to transfer former municipal services into companies under private law which remained publicly owned but were no longer covered by the main collective agreements in the sector. This process occurred subsequent to the establishment of the single European market and affected public utilities and public local transport in particular. The central problem was not that those sectors would no longer be covered by any collective agreements. In general, new collective agreements for the outsourced companies were concluded and at least for the existing staff, pay and conditions did not change. As in the case of the former post service and the railways, however, outsourcing helped public employers to move public services outside the scope of the public sector collective agreements and offered the opportunity to realize substantial savings in personnel costs – not least as a consequence of massive job cuts which usually followed the outsourcing.[5]

These developments subsequently affected the balance of power within the remaining public sector. The traditional strength of public-sector trade unionism was largely based on the structural and associational power (Silver 2003) of blue-collar workers in public transport, utilities and refuse disposal. White-collar employees in public administration for example have always had a much weaker tradition of involvement in industrial action or trade union organization. Here, contrary to those sectors with a high proportion of blue-collar workers, labour relations are strongly influenced by the absence of conflictual collective bargaining and a mix of high job security, and sense of duty and loyalty to the employer which characterizes the officialdom of German career civil servants.

Now these bastions of public-sector trade unionism were increasingly dropping out of the scope of the central collective bargaining round in the public service due to privatization. This undermined the bargaining strength of the unions in the remaining public service as it became increasingly difficult to stage industrial action in those sectors remaining under the cover of the national framework collective agreements. At the same time every outsourced job helped public employers to be confident that the scenario of a nation-wide strike in the public sector as in 1992 was unlikely to be repeated.

Another side effect of the financial crisis of public budgets was that it influenced the public discourse to the detriment of the trade unions. This became more apparent the longer the financial crisis lasted and the deeper it became. During the 1992 strike the trade unions could count on considerable sympathy amongst the public because many people agreed with the unions' argument that nurses, fire fighters or bus drivers deserved at least the same pay increases as those in the private sector. Since the mid-1990s the public debate focused increasingly on the necessity for tight restrictions on public expenditure. This implied that trade unions were expected not only to limit their demands but also to accept what public employers claimed to be painful but necessary: cuts in public employment and pay. All these developments led to a fundamental shift in the power relations to the disadvantage of the unions.

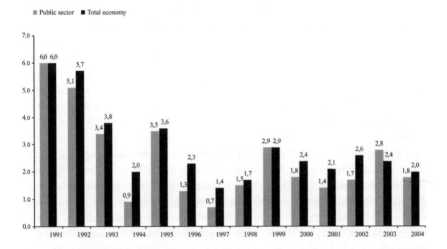

■ Public sector ■ Total economy

* Annual average pay increase in %

Source: WSI Collective Agreements Archive 2005.

Figure 9.4 Collectively agreed pay increases in the German public sector and the total economy (1991-2004)

As one major result of this, during the 1990s public sector pay increases clearly lagged behind the increases in the total economy (see Figure 9.4).

Between 1991 and 2004 collectively agreed pay in the public sector was below pay increases in the total economy in 11 out of 14 years. In total, overall collectively agreed pay increases grew on average by 50 per cent compared with only 41 per cent in the public sector.

It is against this background that the decentralization of collective bargaining took place. This process had many facets, but two major elements can be distinguished. One was the decentralization of collective bargaining by way of opening clauses and the other was a growing diversification and fragmentation within public sector collective bargaining, which led to new collective agreements for specific sectors within public services.

Decentralization by Way of Opening Clauses: The Case of Eastern Germany

In eastern Germany, following the frictions resulting from the integration of the eastern German public services into the western economic and industrial relations framework, the tradition that employees in the public sector were covered by the same federal collective agreements received its first major blow. It soon became apparent that following the collapse of much of the east German economy, the eastern German federal states and municipalities were running into major financial problems and that many jobs were under threat during the restructuring process of the eastern public service. In 1994 the bargaining parties therefore agreed to include in the central collective agreements for eastern Germany provisions on the so-called 'social distribution of working time'. With the aim of securing employment in the public sector, these provisions allowed for regional and local collective agreements to be concluded in order to reduce weekly working time to 32 hours a week with only partial pay compensation. The level of this partial pay compensation was not fixed, but remained open to regional and local negotiations. This relocated the dispute from the central to the regional and local level (Rosdücher 1998). In 1998 the provisions concerning the 'social distribution of working time' were continued, but this time allowing a reduction of the weekly working time down to as little as 30 hours. In 2004 such agreements in eastern Germany were almost common place.

Diversification and Fragmentation: The Case of Public Transport

In 1994 ver.di's predecessor, the Public Sector and Transport Workers Union (ÖTV) held a special congress at which the organization debated the future of collective bargaining in the public sector. Well aware that the national framework agreements were under threat, the trade union developed the idea of a new system of collective agreements consisting of a uniform collective framework agreement for white- and blue-collar employees which would fix the broad terms and conditions and a number of specific collective agreements regulating pay and conditions for specific sectors within the public service. It would take until 2003, however, before the bargaining parties even agreed on a procedure of how to negotiate a new system of collective agreements.

In the meantime, however, the discussion over specific collective agreements for certain sub-sectors within public services continued and focused on public local transport (Wendl 1998). Within the process of liberalization of public transport, the traditional municipal public transport organizations found it difficult to compete with private coach companies offering their services based on a low-cost structure, usually resulting from much lower pay rates and longer working times for their staff according to collective agreements, which had also been concluded by ÖTV but always reflected the weak position of trade unionism in the highly fragmented private transport industry.

In the biggest German federal state of North-Rhine-Westphalia, public employers finally cancelled the regional grading system for blue-collar workers in the public sector in 1994. The dispute which followed resulted in 1995 in a new two-tier agreement according to which on the one hand the existing standards were guaranteed and on the other hand specific agreements were allowed which diverged from the framework agreement of the public sector.

As the wage levels of the 1995 collective agreement were still about 12 per cent above the pay levels applying to private bus companies, the idea to move municipal transport companies completely outside the scope of the public-sector collective agreements did not lose its attraction. Some municipalities even managed to convince the local staff council and the representatives of the employees on the supervising boards that the existing standards of pay and conditions could best be guaranteed for all staff in employment if the municipality could save additional costs by lowering the standards at least for new recruits by establishing new transport companies under private law.

With regard to this situation, the trade union developed a new strategy which aimed at negotiating so-called 'branch-level collective agreements' (*Spartentarifverträge*). The idea was to conclude framework agreements for the local transport sector covering both public and private companies. Negotiations took place in various federal states and one of the first branch-level agreements was finally agreed in North-Rhine-Westphalia in 2001, the so-called TV-N (*Tarifvertrag Nahverkehr*, collective agreement for local transport). The collective agreement introduced a uniform pay system for white- and blue-collar employees with pay rates and bonus payments well below the standards of the old framework but above those rates effectively paid by many private companies. A special clause secured the pay level of those who had been employed under the old collective agreements for the public sector. The application of those agreements remained to be negotiated at local level.

In the light of the new sector collective agreement in local transport ver.di no longer wanted to be confronted with the low rates of some collective agreements for private bus and coach companies and decided not to continue those collective agreements any longer as they were. At that point in time however, a fairly unimportant trade union the so-called Trade Union for the Public Service (*Gewerkschaft Öffentlicher Dienst und Dienstleistungen*, GÖD) which is affiliated to the Christian Confederation of Trade Unions (*Christlicher Gewerkschaftsbund*, CGB), jumped into the gap and concluded a collective agreement in North-Rhine-Westphalia together with the employers' association concerned which continued the tradition of low pay and conditions in this sector.[6] According to trade union estimates, in 2004 about 21 000 employees in public transport in North-Rhine-Westphalia were covered by the sectoral collective agreement TV-N. Only about 6 000 employees were still covered by the old BMT-G and probably another 6 000 were covered by collective agreements signed by the GÖD.

Also in 1999, the unions had concluded a package of agreements with the municipal employers' association VKA which covered about 110 000 employees in approximately 1 600 public utilities establishments. This agreement too included cuts in bonuses and other payments and diverging provisions on promotion for new employees, but it also abolished the distinction between blue-collar workers and salaried employees and created a uniform grading and pay system. This represented a novelty for public sector labour relations. This collective agreement, called TV-V (*Tarifvertrag Versorgung*), was regarded by the union in many aspects as a pilot agreement.

Nevertheless, all these kind of collective agreements were highly contentious within the ranks of the unions. First of all it was argued that these 'branch collective agreements' would increase the fragmentation of what used to be a central bargaining system in the public sector which covered almost all sectors of the public service. The second major argument against these kind of agreements was that they would erode levels of pay and standards of working conditions.

The trade union saw itself in a dilemma which is illustrated by the situation in local transport. Many employees who work for private bus companies and who are right now outside the scope of the collective agreement of the public sector, receive considerably lower pay and work longer hours. In many conflicts and even long-lasting strikes those workers struggle hard to win at least a collective agreement which approaches pay and conditions to the achieved standards of the public sector, even if it does not match them. These workers therefore have something to gain from a new branch-level collective agreement, even if it includes decreased levels of pay compared to the established standard in the public sector. From the point of view of trade union activists, however, the new agreement threatens existing pay and conditions in the long run. A possible solution to this dilemma, aimed at winning the same high standards as in the public sector agreement for all employees has so far never been successful.

To sum up: during the 1990s, collective bargaining in the public sector had become more decentralized and deviations from the once achieved standards of pay and conditions had become more frequent. It became more and more obvious that the days of the old system of collective agreements were numbered. Against this background, the unions strongly pushed for the conclusion of a new framework agreement in the public sector which they saw as an opportunity to stabilize a relatively centralized bargaining structure.

THE BREAKDOWN OF THE EMPLOYERS' BARGAINING ASSOCIATION

The highly contentious 2002 bargaining round in the public sector ended in January 2003. The bargaining parties settled on general wage increases and the final adjustment of eastern German wages. In exchange for the wage increases, ver.di agreed to a number of concessions concerning working time and modes of payment (for details see Behrens 2003). Furthermore, the bargaining parties agreed to a procedure to overhaul the whole system of collective agreements and to replace it by a new framework agreement which would cover both white- and blue-collar employees.

Even before the public employers decided to agree to the settlement, there was massive criticism among their members. One day before the final settlement, the city state of Berlin resigned from the employers' associations concerned in order not to be bound by the final agreement and the wage increases involved. Berlin argued that it could not afford any increases but instead insisted that any settlement had to lead to major savings in effective labour costs. The situation ver.di was confronted with was rather uncomfortable. It did not much help that the city state was governed by a centre-left coalition composed of the Social Democratic Party (SPD) and the Party of Democratic Socialism (PDS) which has its roots in the former ruling party of eastern Germany. On the contrary, it only highlighted the growing alienation between the SPD and the trade union, which had begun with the privatization of the public sector.

To enter into a dispute was particularly complicated as the move of the state of Berlin affected only those 70 000 public service employees in administration, child care etc., who were directly employed by the city of Berlin. The trade union therefore had to enter into a dispute without support from those groups of employees in garbage removal and local transport who had proved in the past that they were able to take industrial action. But they were not affected because these services already operated in Berlin as separate agencies under private law. The dispute in Berlin finally ended in August 2003 with further concessions being made by ver.di which added up to a decrease in individual income in exchange for a promise by the state that forced redundancies would be excluded until 2009 (Ver.di 2003).

Even before the Berlin agreement was finally signed in summer 2003 the 'joint bargaining association' (*Tarifgemeinschaft*) for the public sector had officially collapsed (Dribbusch 2003). The TdL declared that it would no longer accept the traditional role of the federal government as leader of the negotiations in public-sector collective bargaining. How fragile the bargaining association of public employers had become was highlighted when the state of Hesse announced that it would join Berlin and leave the TdL with effect from April 2004. Other states threatened to follow this example.

Furthermore, being discontent with the results of the 2003 agreement, a number of federal states sought ways to further cut back their labour costs. In doing so they first focused on the working time of civil servants, a promising way – as federal or state governments can always change their pay and conditions without having to enter into negotiations with trade unions or staff associations. Finally all federal states regardless of the political affiliation of the governments extended the weekly working time for their civil servants from 38.5 to 40 hours and the federal government decided at the end of 2003 to follow this example. A number of states, however, did not stop there and declared that the weekly working time of civil servants would be extended to 41 or even 42 hours in 2004 (Keller 2005).

Having done this, the federal states in western Germany demanded (on grounds of equal treatment) that public employees who were still covered by the collectively agreed working time of 38.5 hours should also work longer. They finally cancelled the collective agreements on working time for white- and blue-collar employees with effect from April 2004. According to the German Collective Agreements Act (*Tarifvertragsgesetz*) this has the effect that as long as there will be no new collective agreement on working time, all those who are already employed will keep the 38.5 hour week but that all those who were employed after May 2004 effectively face longer working times of up to 42 hours. Ver.di regarded this as a breach of the procedural agreement of January 2003 to achieve a new framework agreement and declared it would only continue negotiations on this issue with the Federal Government and the Municipal Employers' Association (VKA).

A NEW FRAMEWORK AGREEMENT

During the negotiations on a new framework agreement, the unions were confronted with ongoing threats of further breakaways in the employers' camp and the trade union leadership feared a collapse of the negotiations leading to a fragmented and unmanageable bargaining landscape. Critics from within ver.di (Sauerborn 2005) acknowledged the complexity of the issue at stake and the trade union's interest in achieving a new framework agreement, but doubted whether the union leadership's decision for a consensual negotiation strategy and against a major mobilization of members was the appropriate way to deal with the difficult situation.

The negotiations finally ended with a compromise on 9 February 2005, when ver.di agreed with representatives of the federal government and the VKA on a new general framework collective agreement (*Tarifvertrag öffentlicher Dienst*, TVöD) for about 2.1 million employees in the federal and municipal public sector. The settlement which included substantial concessions of the trade unions concerning pay increases, was also accepted by the other DGB-affiliates and the DBB. TdL rejected the agreement on behalf of the federal states demanding further concessions on the part of the trade unions, in particular regarding further working time extension and further cuts in annual bonuses.

The new public sector framework agreement TVöD, which came into force on 1 October 2005, replaces the old collective framework agreements that had existed for 45 years. The new framework is designed alongside similar agreements in the private sector (Keller 2005; Wendl 2005). The TVöD introduces a new uniform grading system that applies to both blue- and white-collar workers. It comprises 15 scales, ranging from simple repetitive work that does not require much training (scale 1) to work requiring a university degree, several years of work experience and a supervisory position (scale 15). Ver.di conceded that the basic pay rate of scale 1 will undercut the lowest rate of the old collective agreements. The new low pay rate is intended to help stop the process of outsourcing of certain service jobs, for example in canteens and cleaning. New provisions on promotion and performance-related pay are to be introduced and certain allowances which linked pay to age, marital status and number of children will be abandoned for future employees. The provision that public employees in western Germany cannot be dismissed after 15 years of continuous employment, except in cases of gross misconduct, is continued but was not extended to eastern Germany.

Part of the compromise was that the standard weekly working time for public employees at federal level will be 39 hours a week. Previously the standard working week was set at 38.5 hours in western Germany and 40 hours in eastern Germany. For municipal employees, the current standard weekly working time will remain unchanged in principle. However, the bargaining parties agreed to a so-called opening clause that allows for negotiation of new working time arrangements for municipal employees which may allow working time of up to 40 hours provided these new arrangements cover all municipalities of a given federal state.

Immediately after the new TVöD came into force in October 2005 the municipal employers' associations of the federal states of Hamburg, Lower Saxony and Baden-Württemberg made use of this opening-clause and demanded an extension of working time to 40 hours a week. The unions rejected these demands and following the breakdown of negotiations called for industrial action in February 2006. The strikes which followed lasted up to nine weeks and ended in compromises which included on average an extension of weekly working time by 30 minutes.

In May 2006 following fourteen weeks of strike action ver.di also reached an agreement with TdL covering about 780 000 public employees in all federal states except Hesse and Berlin. This new collective agreement (Tarifvertrag für den öffentlichen Dienst der Länder, TV-L) replaces all previous collective and wage agreements. In many parts (e.g. the pay structure) the new TV-L took over the provisions of the TVöD. Regarding the highly controversial question of working time the new agreement provides that each federal state will have its own average weekly working time ranging between 38.7 in Schleswig-Holstein and 39.73 hours in Bavaria (Bispinck 2006). As a further step towards the decentralization of public sector collective bargaining the federal states obtained the right to bargain in future individually with the union on working time issues.

Two large sectors, the utilities and public local transport retain their distinctive collective agreements. The one for the utilities provides on average better pay levels than the TVöD. In the local transport sectors a variety of collective agreements are maintained which vary in their pay levels with some local agreements offering better and some offering worse pay levels compared to the TVöD.

Finally, some groups of employees also believe that they were better off with the old agreement. The organization of hospital doctors, the Marburger Bund, which traditionally cooperated with ver.di in collective bargaining revoked its signature under the new agreement and entered into a dispute with public hospital employers and finally reached a separate agreement for doctors only. This move might show the potential for a further fragmentation of collective bargaining whereby groups of employees who see themselves in a strong bargaining position try to establish their own collective agreements (Wendl 2005).

CONCLUSIONS: THE END OF AN ERA

The German public sector has undergone a fundamental structural change since the 1990s which has not been without consequences for the established system of collective bargaining. Privatization and liberalization have effectively undermined the bargaining power of the unions based on high trade union densities in some key sectors of the public sector. The successive removal of such sectors as public transport, utilities and refuse disposal from the scope of the general framework agreement has revealed the traditional weakness of trade unionism amongst white-collar employees, especially in public administration.

The developments in public-sector collective bargaining since the 1990s give weight to the argument that we are currently observing the end of an era. Important sectors have been finally moved outside the scope of public sector collective bargaining and others are likely to follow. The process of privatization and liberalization of public services and utilities will continue and has already affected other sectors such as health services and education.

It is questionable whether the decentralization of collective bargaining can be characterized as 'controlled decentralization' (Keller 2005). As far as the trade union is concerned, the decentralization happened in an uncontrolled way and beyond the trade unions' strategic planning (Wendl 2004). The trade union has basically been reactive in its attempts to catch up with events. It has ended up by often only fixing those points into new collective agreements which had already been accepted by local trade union and staff representatives – who had been confronted with the combination of public debts and the threat of outsourcing.

The growing internal division of the employers' side does not really help ver.di. Whereas the employers might be more comfortable with a divided and fragmented workforce and with decentralized bargaining, for the trade union things become complicated if it has to negotiate a great number of agreements instead of one. This was the rationale behind the concessions ver.di made in order to secure a new federal framework agreement at least for the federal and local level. The trade union is now confronted with the fact that for some public employers sector-level collective bargaining is no longer the only option. The new framework agreement itself includes various possibilities for a further decentralization and differentiation of collective bargaining via the use of opening clauses. Moreover, the logic of liberalization and privatization of public services will continue to put financial and competitive pressure on public employers making it rather unlikely that the public sector will regain the stability of collective bargaining for which it was known in the past.

NOTES

1. An important exception has been the studies by Keller (1983, 1993) which give a comprehensive insight into the development of German public sector labour relations. For a more recent overview in English see: Keller (1999) and BMI (2002).
2. Ver.di was created in 2001 by a merger of five trade unions including the former Public Sector and Transport Workers Union (*Gewerkschaft Öffentliche Dienste, Transport und Verkehr*, ÖTV), which that time was by far the largest trade union in the public sector.
3. The DBB declares to have around 1.3 million members in 2005, of whom nearly 920 000 are civil servants. Among the latter it is therefore the largest organization. In comparison to that, ver.di organizes only about 227 000 civil servants.
4. Until privatization the German postworkers union (*Deutsche Post Gewerkschaft*) and the German rail workers union (*Gewerkschaft der Eisenbahner Deutschlands*, GdED), while following their own specific strategies, had closely cooperated with the ÖTV during the central bargaining rounds in the public sector (Keller 1999).
5. For example, after the privatization of *Deutsche Telekom AG* the number of employees was reduced from 223 000 in 1994 to 123 000 in 2002 (Sauerland, Lorenz and Gregor 2004, p. 69).
6. The 'trade unions' affiliated to the CGB are notorious for undercutting existing collective agreements. As they often do not even have members in the sectors for which they negotiate, DGB-affiliated trade unions question whether they can be regarded as trade unions in the legal sense.

REFERENCES

Ahlers, Elke (2004), 'Beschäftigungskrise im öffentlichen Dienst?', *WSI-Mitteilungen*, **57** (2), 78-83.

Behrens, Martin (2003), 'Germany: New Agreement signed in Public Sector', *EIROnline*, www.eiro.eurofound.eu.int/2003/01/feature/de0301204f.html.

Bispinck, Reinhard and Thorsten Schulten (2003), 'Decentralisation of German Collective Bargaining: Current Trends and Assessments from a Works and Staff Council Perspective', *WSI-Mitteilungen*, **56**, Special English Issue, 24-33.

Bispinck, Reinhard (2006), 'Nur ein Streik um 18 Minuten? - Die Tarifauseinandersetzungen im öffentlichen Dienst 2006', *WSI-Mitteilungen*, **59** (7), 374-381.

BMI (Bundesministerium des Inneren) (2002), 'The Public Service in Germany', Berlin: BMI, second edition.

Bordogna, Lorenzo and David Winchester (2001), 'Collective Bargaining in Western Europe', in Carlo Dell'Aringa, Giuseppe Della Rocca and Berndt Keller (eds),

Strategic Choices in Reforming Public Service Employment, Houndmills: Palgrave, pp. 48-70.

Dribbusch, Heiner (2003), 'Germany: Public Sector Employers' Bargaining Association collapses', *EIROnline*, http://www.eiro.eurofound.eu.int/2003/06/inbrief/de0306202n.html.

Keller, Berndt (1983), *Arbeitsbeziehungen im öffentlichen Dienst: Tarifpolitik der Gewerkschaften und Interessenpolitik der Beamtenverbände*, Frankfurt/New York: Campus.

Keller, Berndt (1993), *Arbeitspolitik des öffentlichen Sektors*, Baden-Baden: Nomos.

Keller, Berndt (1999), 'Germany: Negotiated Change, Modernisation and the Challenge of Unification', in Stephen Bach, Lorenzo Bordogna, Giuseppe Della Rocca and David Winchester (eds), *Public Service Employment Relations in Europe*, London: Routledge, pp. 56-93.

Keller, Berndt (2005), 'Aktuelle Entwicklungen der Beschäftigungsbeziehungen im öffentlichen Dienst', mimeo.

Koufen, Sebastian (2003), 'Beschäftigte der öffentlichen Arbeitgeber am 30. Juni 2002', *Wirtschaft und Statistik*, **10**, 912-921.

Rosdücher, Jörg (1998), 'Beschäftigungssicherung im öffentlichen Dienst der neuen Länder', in Ulrich von Alemann and Josef Schmid (eds), *Die Gewerkschaft ÖTV: Reformen im Dickicht gewerkschaftlicher Organisationspolitik*, Baden-Baden: Nomos, pp. 225-240.

Sauerborn, Werner (2005), 'Stellvertreterpolitik, aber gute', *Express*, Zeitung für sozialistisches Betriebs- und Gewerkschaftsarbeit, **43** (3), 1-4.

Sauerland, Frank, Frank Lorenz and Wilbert Gregor (2004), 'Privatisierung und Liberalisierung am Beispiel der Deutschen Telekom AG', in Frank Lorenz and Günther Schneider (eds), *Wenn öffentliche Dienste privatisiert werden*, Hamburg: VSA, pp. 65-75.

Schneider, Karsten (2002), *Arbeitspolitik im 'Konzern Stadt': Zwischen der Erosion des Zusammenhalts im kommunalen Sektor und den effizienzfördernden Wirkungen organisatorischer Dezentralisierung*, Baden-Baden: Nomos.

Silver, Beverly (2003), *Forces of Labour*, Cambridge: University Press.

Statistisches Bundesamt (2004), *Finanzen und Steuern, Schulden der öffentlichen Haushalte 2003*, Fachserie 14, Reihe 4, Wiesbaden: Statistisches Bundesamt.

Statistisches Bundesamt (2005), *Finanzen und Steuern, Personal des Öffentlichen Dienstes 2003*, Fachserie 14, Reihe 6, Wiesbaden: Statistisches Bundesamt.

Truger, Achim (2004), 'Rot-grüne Steuerreformen, Finanzpolitik und makroökonomische Performance - was ist schief gelaufen?', in Arne Heise, Eckhard Hein and Achim Truger (eds), *Finanzpolitik in der Kontroverse*, Marburg: Metropolis, pp. 169-208.

Ver.di (2003), *Der Berliner Tarifvertrag: Sichere Arbeitsplätze bis 2009 und kein tarifpolitisches Abseits*, edited by Ver.di Landesbezirk, Berlin-Brandenburg, Berlin: ver.di.

Wendl, Michael (1998), 'Konkurrenz erzwingt Absenkung: Die Erosion der Flächentarifverträge des öffentlichen Dienstes am Beispiel des Personennahverkehrs', in Otto König, Sybille Stamm and Michael Wendl (eds), *Erosion oder Erneuerung? Krise und Reform des Flächentarifvertrags*, Hamburg: VSA, pp. 100-115.

Wendl, Michael (2003), 'Der öffentliche Dienst im tarifpolitischen Umbruch', in Vereinte Dienstleistungsgewerkschaft (ed.), *Hat der Flächentarifvertrag noch eine Zukunft?*, Berlin: ver.di, pp. 48-60.

Wendl, Michael (2004), 'Brüning light: Tarifpolitik im Öffentlichen Dienst', *Sozialismus*, **31** (1), 27-31.

Wendl, Michael (2005), 'Öffentlicher Dienst: Abschied vom einheitlichen Entgeltniveau?', *Sozialismus*, **32** (10), 40-43.

10. Reforming Employment Relations in the French Administration Services: Is the Status of Civil Servants an Obstacle to Efficient HRM?

Olivier Mériaux

INTRODUCTION

The wave of New Public Management (NPM) that has hit all OECD countries during the two last decades has led to major changes in the inner workings of public administrations. Strongly supported and widely diffused by international institutions and private experts alike, the New Public Management's central credo is that reforms should aim to manage public service organizations on the basis of objectives and targets, rather than observance of rules and precedents as postulated in the classic Weberian '*Idealtype*' of bureaucracy.

However, if 'the ideas of "New Public Management" have become in essence a Zeitgest for reforming public sector management' (Hogwood and Peters 2000, p. 4), their actual impact on employment relations seems to vary dramatically across countries. The literature on public sector reform clearly shows that the 'paradigm shift' towards a more business-like approach to public management has been more rapid and intense in certain countries, especially the Anglo-American democracies, than in others (Peters 1997). In their efforts to account for these national variations – or to point their fingers at those who are lagging behind – proponents of NPM are quick to denounce the specificity and excessive rigidity of the legal-institutional frameworks that define public employment relations. Indeed, in many European countries, the employment conditions of civil servants are governed by a set of statutory rules laid down by the State, as opposed to the employment contract model that governs employment relations in the private sector.

In this respect, the case of France – often described as one of the most 'resistant' to the adoption of the managerialist culture – is particularly interesting, not only because the Status of civil servants has its origins in the French doctrine of public law, but also because the belief in an incompatibility between *le statut des fonctionnaires* and the requirements of public management has been quite popular of late. In comparison with most other European countries, where the question of efficiency has often been directly addressed, the debate on public employment and how to invigorate a more dynamic Human Resources Management has, in France, remained largely focused on a juridical approach of 'administrative modernization'. This became a major strand of public policy in the late 1980s, at the beginning of François Mitterrand's second presidential mandate, by 'giving political endorsement to a body of "new public management" ideas that were already in good currency within the rank of some segments of the higher civil service' (Clark 1998, p. 104).

Since then, the various initiatives around the theme of administrative reform have been characterized by broad continuity rather than by partisan differences between governments of the Left and the Right (Bouckaert and Pollitt 2000). Nevertheless, there is at least one major point where the two 'approaches' were clearly diverging: reforms conducted under left-wing governments were negotiated with, and largely endorsed by, the trade unions – mainly because they were presented as securing additional flexibility and initiatives without threatening the rights and guarantees associated with *le statut des fonctionnaires*. Conversely, the reforms led by the right-wing Juppé government in 1996 were conceived of as a prelude to a sound reform of the Status, seen as an obstacle to adapting public administration to the requirements of an open economy and consequently faced fierce opposition from the united trade unions.

The question I want to address here, namely, is that the Status of civil servants appropriate to the challenges faced by a modern public administration, is thus the subject of contrasting and often impassioned views. However, as so often happens in the public debate in France, antagonistic views are above all expressing ideological preferences, rather than being based on empirical analysis. This way of setting out political controversies not only makes collectively agreed solutions more difficult to reach, it also impedes attempts to identify the crucial issues that underlie the conventional discourses: how can the professional ethics and practices built into a derogation-based legal framework accommodate the requirements of public management; how can one reconcile the logic of a bureaucracy based on the principles of rule observance and impersonality with the logic of performance; and to what extent can public management be implemented where derogatory rules regulate employment relations?

Clearly, the way that French social and political actors focus on the juridical aspects when tackling the issue of public employment reform shows at least a naive belief in the effectiveness of law. However, it also reflects the crucial importance of the civil service and of the concept of public service in the genesis of the French State (Section I). The symbolic and political function of the Status and of the *corps* systems, and the ideological battles in which they have been joined, have often led to losing sight of the effective management practices that actors have developed within them and which sometimes go against the juridical framework (Section II).

I. THE JURIDICAL FOUNDATIONS OF PUBLIC EMPLOYMENT RELATIONS

In France, more than in any other European country, public law has been of crucial importance in setting the juridical framework for public employment relations. Public servants are governed by two sets of legal provisions: the 'General Status' that defines the main guarantees, obligations and principles governing their employment and career (*le statut général des fonctionnaires*) and the regulatory provisions that specify the implementation of the General Status applicable to each *corps* of public servants. Resulting from a long historical process and expressing a very peculiar State tradition, the Status and the *corps* system have a political and sociological dimension which makes them the central institutions of French public service.

Civil Service as Statutory Employment

Contemporary debates on the Status of civil servants and how to reform public employment cannot be properly understood without giving attention to the historical background in which this issue is embedded. The institutional framework of public employment relations is deeply rooted in the history of the French State and its interventionist and *dirigiste* tradition.

The republican model of public administration, which dates back to the revolutionary era, is a 'legal model' which conceives the state administration as inhabiting an autonomous domain that 'overhangs' civil society (Chevallier 1996). This model in many ways opposes the Anglo-Saxon tradition, in which the very notion of law refers to the system of rules by which civil society regulates itself, outside of State intervention and very often against it. Conversely, the French law tradition conceives social regulation as being achieved in the first instance through the political law of the State, in accordance with the revolutionary doctrine of Rousseauist popular sovereignty. The effects of this dogma on the politics of interests and state-society relationships are well understood by historians, who have shown that the French state has always aimed to guide and enlighten civil society, rather than seeking compromises with autonomous, organized interests (Rosanvallon 1990, 1998).

Nevertheless, by the 19th century, the doctrine of sovereignty had become the object of growing dissatisfaction among legal theorists, as the legitimacy of the State became increasingly challenged by the industrial revolution and the political and trade union struggles which ensued (Laborde 1996). One of the most radical critics of state sovereignty, Léon Duguit, a self-proclaimed Durkheimian law professor, turned to the principle of solidarity to establish a new theory of the state, based on the idea of public service.

Originally conceived as a principle of political theory, aiming to replace the notion of *puissance publique* (what the German lawyers called *Herrschaft*), the idea of public service would enjoy an exceptional fate by founding French administrative law through the *Conseil d'Etat* jurisprudence, giving the State the juridical base for expanding its interventions and taking charge of its citizens' welfare. But Duguit's doctrine and its transcription into public law, also had important implications for framing the relations between the State and its agents. At the very beginning of the 20th century, the issue of civil servant unionism became a subject of harsh debates; unionists claimed that the State was a manager, like any other, and its agents should hold the same rights (including the rights to unionize and to go on strike) as private sector workers. For Duguit, and for the public law doctrine he inspired, the specificity and superiority of the State made civil servants a special class of citizens with special rights and obligations and this ruled out the possibility of contractualizing the relations between the State and its agents: 'Therefore, to the privatist notion of contract, Duguit opposed the *publiciste* notion of status' (Laborde 1996, p. 236).

If the very idea of 'Status' has its origin in France, the importance of administrative law in regulating many crucial aspects of public employment, such as recruitment, promotion, discipline and remuneration, is a characteristic shared with many other European countries. All of them have at least some of their civil servants governed by a set of rules of public law, unilaterally granted by the State, but in no other country is the coverage of the Status among public sector agents wider than in France.[1] Conceived, in Duguit's doctrine, as 'the proud symbol of the distinctiveness of public law, of the superior end pursued by the State' (Laborde 1996, p. 237) the Status of civil servants also has an important unifying function.

From this point of view, the elaboration of the first general Status in 1946 marked considerable progress, in contrast with the previous situation of a mosaic of inconsistent rules. A second legislation, very similar to the first, was adopted in 1959. Its replacement by the laws of 1983, 1984 and 1986, which form the current Status, was motivated by the need to adapt the legal framework to a more decentralized political system, while reasserting the unity surrounding the plurality of public services. Indeed, the French public administration is currently divided into three civil service branches governed by common basic legal principles: the State civil service (i.e. all the administrative civil servants working for the central State – whatever their hierarchical level); the 'local' civil service, serving under the authority of 22 regions, 100 departments and about 36 000 municipalities; and the public hospital civil service.

Paying particular attention to this historical context is crucial in avoiding the ideological bad old ways. Firstly, Status has not been conceived to exclusively benefit civil servants, it also provides public authorities with guarantees against a misuse of power which could threaten their legitimacy (such as favouritism and nepotism in recruiting or promoting civil servants). Secondly, one has to remember that Status is in many ways a relic of an era in which public administrations were totally free of any legal concerns regarding their own performance. Throughout history, the standard of 'good administration' almost exclusively referred to the observance of rules and it was only in the mid-1980s that it began to integrate the New Public Management mottos of efficiency and performance.

The reasons for the growing concern about the employment status of civil servants are fundamentally linked to the changes that have affected the political issues that were dominant at the time those rules were established. It is not only a matter of protecting civil servants against political hazards while ensuring their neutrality towards the policy options of public authorities, it is now simultaneously a matter of promoting the involvement of each civil servant so as to achieve results that can demonstrate the efficacy of public policies. However, this results in divergent, not to say antagonistic, perspectives: between the Weberian paradigm of bureaucracy, of which *le statut* is a legal expression – aiming to deprive civil servants of their 'personal' characteristics in order to efficiently attain the organization's goals – and the managerial rationality that, on the contrary, calls for developing and monitoring individual performances and abilities.

Corporatism Within the State: The Corps System

The symbolic function of this Status seems all the more important when closer examination reveals the variety of rules that govern the major elements of the public employment relationship. Behind the sham unity of the 'General Status' lies a multitude of specific provisions which relate the general rules to the particular situation of each *corps* of civil servants (Caillosse 2003). Indeed, the French civil service has the peculiarity – and one can speak here of a real French specificity – of being structured into a mosaic of some 1 700 different *corps* spread across three occupational categories defined by the level of diploma required for entry.

Although central to the effective Human Resources Management practices, this notion of *corps* remains very vaguely defined by law.[2] The current legislation only mentions that 'civil servants belong to *corps* which include one or several ranks . . . the *corps* groups civil servants placed under the same particular Status and that have an aptitude for the same ranks'.[3] One would be pushed to be more elliptic and a historical detour is certainly more instructive than a reading of the laws. Indeed, the civil service *corps* appears to be the most obvious institutional inheritance of the Ancient Regime's corporatist organization style. At the very least they have kept their main characteristics intact: an organized profession, endowed with a stable position guaranteed by the State, governed by rules, whose members are recruited according to known modalities and, on a more sociological level, have developed a strong feeling of collective identity and share the same professional culture.

Historically, the first sets of rules defining the employment conditions for particular categories of civil servants were established at the beginning of the 18th century for the State's civil (*'Ponts et Chaussées'*) and mining engineers. This technical elite was thus the original core of the *grands corps* system in which a very limited fringe of civil servants, recruited from *grandes écoles* (*Ecole Nationale d'Administration, Ecole Polytechnique,* etc.) and reputed to hold the highest level of technical, financial and legal expertise, fills all the top executive positions within public administration and also in the private sector.

While the French *grands corps* have often received a great deal of attention from public administration experts, mainly because of their central role in policymaking and economic governance, the general phenomenon of the *corps* is critical when it comes to the issue of 'modernizing' public employment. Indeed, the French public service is no more than a set of *corps* and it is no exaggeration to say that civil servants see themselves as belonging to their *corps* before considering themselves members of the public administration.

Indeed, from the promulgation of the 1946 General Status onwards, *corps* have multiplied in a largely uncontrolled manner under the influence of two powerful and convergent interests: that of the civil servants, who push for the creation of 'interconnected channels of *corps*', guaranteeing long career perspectives and that of each segment within public administration, who sees the creation of its 'own' *corps* as a means to assert its power and autonomy. The result of this process has been an extreme fragmentation of the rules and institutions governing public employment; each *corps* is endowed with a particular Status, adapting or complementing the rules of the General Status, and has an established joint administrative committee (*Commission Administrative Paritaire*) in which the civil servants' union representatives and their employers monitor individual careers. While nearly 80 per cent of all civil servants belong to one of 25 *corps* (the largest covering secondary school teachers with more than 220 000 members), many of them have a ridiculously small number of members.[4]

II. IS THE LEGAL FRAMEWORK OF PUBLIC EMPLOYMENT AN OBSTACLE TO EFFICIENT HUMAN RESOURCES MANAGEMENT?

As mentioned above, there are only a few political issues in France that are more subject to ideological controversy than the question of how to modernize public administration and the legal framework surrounding public employment. The liberal credo regards this Status as the last bastion of an obsolete bureaucratic model of society, unable to evolve and thus endangering the nation's competitiveness. While only a few politicians and officials advocate an entire repeal of this Status, most of them see the legal situation of civil servants as an impediment to improving public administration efficiency. Inspired by the experience of neighbouring countries, such as Italy,[5] they recommend reducing the statutory system's application field, or at least introducing the principles of New Public Management into the body of statutory rules. On the other hand, for a majority of unions, the statutory rules guarantee the impartiality of public service and equal access to public utilities and any attempt made to change them is nothing less than the demolition of the last bastion that protects France against the hegemonic Anglo-Saxon liberal model.

Such controversial discourses, in my view, are very much inclined to overestimate the specificity of the rules governing public employment relations. They tend to refer to a 'golden age' of French public administration and one that no longer exists, at least if one closely examines positive law. The progressive subservience of national law to European laws and regulations, the global trend towards the 'contractualization' of norms in every field of social regulation and, maybe more importantly, the erosion and depreciation of public law, which has been the cornerstone of public employment regulation, all have converged to progressively reduce the specificity of the rules governing public employment relations (Caillosse and Hardy 2000). Moreover, it is not necessary to hold liberal views to observe that the law applicable to employment relations in the public sector is often used as a shield against attempts to promote 'individual management' civil servants. Conversely, there is no need to be a unionist, defending the advantages of Status, to claim that the promoters of management reforms, dependent as they so often are on the liberal dogma of the superiority of free contracts over status, frequently ignore opportunities offered within the current civil service employment system.

Rigidities and Potentialities of the Status of Public Servants for Managing Human Resources

Are the statuses of the various *corps*, and more generally the legal provisions of public law, an obstacle to efficient Human Resource Management (HRM), as so often claimed by the promoters of modernization in public administration? In a recent report, the State's Council, which is the highest administrative court and the government's legal expert over policymaking, has tried to balance the inconveniences and the advantages of the current system within a perspective of a more dynamic approach to public management (Conseil d'Etat 2003).

For the authors of this report, the current statutory organization by *corps* has at least one quality: it provides a stable and clear managerial framework, since the major part of the managerial activity is determined by statutory provisions. This is advantageous both for civil servants, in terms for instance of career prospects, and for managers, in terms of comfort.

However, this 'good' aspect of the bureaucratic routine is immediately opposed by a long list of rigidities inherent in the 'career principle' which gives civil servants a lifelong guarantee of employment and the right, some would say certainty, to be promoted within their *corps*, irrespective of their professional abilities. The existence of hundreds of different individual *corps* statuses is depicted as a formidable obstacle to the application of functional management in any organizational unit. The *corps* logic, in which the statutory situation of civil servants prevails over the specificities of their day-to-day work, is considered as contradictory to any rigorous approach to job requirements and skills, producing huge wastes in terms of job matching and training. Moreover, the *corps* organization is seen as preventing mobility, by establishing partitions between the same classes of jobs (from a functional point of view) and multiplying constraining procedures because any assignment outside one's own *corps* requires a 'cross-examination' by all the existing consultative bodies. The report claims to have found a reluctance by these bodies to accept external 'ascendant mobility', as any promotion of a 'newcomer' restricts the possibilities of promoting a *corps* member. Indeed, the particular Status of each *corps* establishes the frontier between the various ranks, according to the *corps'* total strength or to the size of the immediately inferior rank. This pyramidal approach, originally designed to control the budgetary impact of civil service wages, leaves virtually no room to manoeuvre in terms of HRM and, in a less favourable demographic context, may lead to progressively fewer promotion opportunities.

All the points made in the State's Council report are correct, and none of them should have come as a surprise for any connoisseur of French public administration. It is indeed a very frequent criticism, albeit a somewhat lazy one, to point out the inertia of this combination of career model and the French-specific organizational approach by *corps*. However, many other elements of the Status seem at least to be potentially able to retain a certain degree of flexibility within the career system and to allow for some mobility between the *corps* (Eymeri 2000). Here, one can mention at least some of these mechanisms.

The most important one is the fundamental principle of the separation of rank from employment (here meaning: assignment). In the French system, a civil servant belongs to a *corps*, in which he holds a clear rank which cannot be taken away without very serious misconduct. However, a civil servant's assignment is always within the competence of the hierarchical authority. If the principle of 'participation' is to be respected, by submitting managerial decisions to due consultative procedures, then the legal texts give public employers effective leeway in reassigning civil servants, geographically or functionally for their organizational needs. This legal dissociation between the rank and the assignment also allows for considerable lateral mobility: civil servants can be indefinitely 'loaned' or 'detached' to another administrative entity, while retaining their career track and promotion rights. There are no less than 80 000 civil servants working under such a detachment, with the mechanism widely used as a tool of flexibility. French public administrations, just like French firms, are also frequent users of external flexibility and this is very often harshly criticized by both unions and public employment experts. Great use is made of 'contract' personnel, placed under public law but outside the *corps* and career system, and thus very often in precarious situations. In the State civil service, about 10 per cent of workers are untenured personnel and 24 per cent in the territorial civil service (source: *Observatoire de la fonction publique* 2002). Another statutory resource for achieving mobility of civil servants between the *corps* is the dual system of examination: besides the entry examination (the 'external'), open to young candidates according to their diploma level, there is the 'internal' way, reserved for civil servants already in position, whatever their diplomas. Coupled with the public education system, these internal examinations have been one of the major instruments of the 'republican' model of social promotion. Nevertheless, it is widely acknowledged that these 'social elevator' mechanisms have become less effective since the 1980s. The huge rise of unemployment plus the expansion of higher education has led to an enormous growth in the number of candidates wanting to enter the civil service, greater selectivity and 'over-qualification' of the youngest entrants, thus making it harder for internal candidates to progress.

Overall, it would certainly be a mistake to see the legal principles regulating public employment and the *corps* system as no more than a set of archaic rigidities that should be swept away by the 'wave' of New Public Management. Given the symbolic and political function of the General Status within the civil service, and the sociological embeddedness of the *corps*, such an evolution in any case seems highly unlikely. Further, as we will see, it is very probable that the best results in terms of modernizing HRM will be achieved through a reform strategy which takes into account the sociological reality of employment relations, rather than one that focuses on the relevance of their juridical framework.

Human Resources Management in Practice

For those who want to see it, a very clear point emerges from the huge number of official reports which have recently been dedicated to surveying and developing HRM in the French civil service:[6] despite most of the efforts and reflections having been focused on organizations and on the legal framework of public employment, 'bureaucratic' HRM practices are only partially dependent on this structural context. In other words: Status by itself is not an obstacle to reform; it is much more the way in which it has been used by the civil service's 'social partners' that has reinforced its potential for rigidity.

There is almost no disputing the fact that HRM within French public organizations remains highly centered around the 'impersonal' application of existing norms and procedures, to the detriment of the personal capabilities and ambitions of civil servants. In public administrations, 'managing human resources' means above all implementing norms and directives, applying 'automatic' rules for promotion, following a strict pattern of consultative procedures. Despite all the criticisms made, the hegemonic HRM tendency in the public sector is still to apply the same treatment to all civil servants, whatever their effective involvement at work. The influence of this egalitarian management is particularly apparent when it comes to evaluation, wages and career development. The evaluation of civil servants monopolizes the time and energy of hierarchical officials for months, for a result that is inevitably a mark slightly above the one of the previous year and a written appreciation in which one would be hard pushed to discern any hint of criticism. Such practices reveal the difficulty of transforming an instrument originally conceived to guarantee equal treatment of all civil servants through a management tool able to assess the professional qualities of individuals.

According to statutory provisions, one's 'professional value', expressed by the mark and the appreciation of the department head, has to be taken into account in the same way as seniority in grade promotion. Theoretically, 'meritorious' civil servants can be promoted by selection and more rapidly reach higher grades. In practice, union representatives who sit on joint administrative bodies have always showed a great distrust of promotion on merit, for doctrinal reasons – it infringes the pivotal republican value of equality – but certainly also to maintain a certain degree of cohesion among civil servants from the perspective of organizing collective action. Moreover, the institution itself has incorporated this norm, with the implicit objective of avoiding conflicts. In the ministerial departments where the unions' influence has been the strongest (such as Education), upgradings are based on a global scale and a system of equalization that forbids officials from 'rewarding' civil servants beyond a certain level.

The same kind of 'pragmatic arrangements' exist between the actors in social dialogue as regards mobility. A modern HRM approach would include an appointment system which places a priority on matching the candidate's profile to the needs of the administrative unit. In reality, joint administrative commissions almost systematically apply the rule of seniority in the appointment process; the most senior rank makes its choice, and the others follow in decreasing order of seniority. Domestic situations can counterbalance the first criterion (seniority), but this one remains dominant. It is worth noting that the Status provisions regarding positions which imply geographical mobility, do not give any priority to seniority. Moreover, it is perfectly possible to interpret the Status provisions in a sense that would give priority to the most qualified candidates in regard to the 'proper functioning of the service' (Caillosse and Hardy 2000).

Thus, it appears that the deficiencies in HRM in public service are largely due to implementation failures and only marginally to the legal provisions regarding employment relations. In fact, statutory rules give great importance to the 'professional value' of civil servants and offer many possibilities to reward individual merit or to sanction incapacity.[7] Clearly, the reluctance of managers to fully exert their prerogatives is a major factor in perpetuating egalitarian management routines in which the individual interests of civil servants often take precedence over the public interest. Structures and actors in social dialogue certainly bear a great deal of responsibility for this situation; social dialogue is largely a place of implicit consensus, where the unions can claim to be defending equality while securing their institutional positions, and where the hierarchy can easily buy social peace.

In this context, it is doubtful whether any reforms that focus only on the juridical framework of civil service management will have an impact on the effectiveness of HRM practices. It seems, for instance, quite unlikely that the decree issued in April 2002 on the evaluation of civil servants (with the explicit aim of reinforcing links between evaluation and promotion) will change well-established habits. The same goes for the recent official announcement on the extension to merit pay; nothing in the current legal provisions stands in the way of this governmental project, the real problem is the lack of will shown by both managers and unions alike to implement the existing texts.

These observations lead to new interpretations of the meaning of the notion of 'civil service Status'. Beyond the set of legal rules constituted by the 'General Status' and a host of enforcement measures (including the particular Status of each *corps*), lies a set of sociological regulations born from the constant interactions between authorities and unions within consultative bodies that occur in an institutional sphere largely isolated from where the effective issues of management arise. Given this situation, studying industrial relations in the public sector is a major interest in order to develop a more complete understanding of the type of inertia that modern management has to face.

CONCLUSIONS

After decades of a somewhat ideological controversy, the sociological dimension of public employment regulation in France seems today to be more widely acknowledged. At least it now seems beyond dispute that overcoming the rigidities of HRM is more than just a matter of changing or improving statutory rules and requires action on both social dialogue and on management methods.

On the first axis – social dialogue – the major evolution in the past decade has seen a wider use of negotiated agreements. In establishing a second channel for social dialogue, beside the traditional and rather hidebound consultative bodies, the objective of the hierarchical authorities was to break with the permanent collusion, not to say co-management, between unions and local officials. Despite a very restrictive legal basis, this pseudo-collective bargaining has been progressively extended to include a wide range of topics, including training (1989, 1992, 1996), anticipated retirement (1996) and the re-absorption of precarious employment (1996, 2000). However, in 2001, a failure in the negotiations on working time reduction at the national level (for the three branches of the civil service) has stopped this dynamic and no major agreement has been signed since. While the budgetary context is now less favourable, it is clear that the bargaining procedures also need to be clarified and the agreements endowed with an effective juridical force since, according to Article 8 of the law of 11 July 1983, only wages can be the subject of a negotiated agreement. On other topics related to working conditions and work organization, unions and governmental authorities can only 'discuss'. However, it is also apparent that even a more favourable institutional framework will not resolve the problems linked to the role of unionism in the public sector.

The development of social dialogue is of great importance in providing a vehicle for negotiated HRM policies that are based on employment and competencies' planning. For a long time, such policies were only experimented with on a limited scale. However, since 2000, all ministries are supposed to have been engaged in a process aimed at assessing their future needs in terms of skills as a step towards developing a 'functional management'. Each managerial unit has to identify the professional knowledge and know-how needed for civil servants to adequately perform their duty, as well as their likely evolutions in the near future. This should lead, theoretically, to an enhanced convergence between organizational needs and individual careers.

Taking 'professional' requirements into consideration instead of the formal definition of the *corps* is a cultural revolution for the French civil service. The preliminary step in any new managerial approach to human resources, which is to map the 'real' skills and know-how of each profession, represents here a considerable task for which the public managers are not well-equipped. Thus it is hardly surprising that, according to the *'Observatoire de la fonction publique'* 2002 report, only six ministries – and not the largest ones – have consolidated their strategy into a prospective HRM plan. The pace of modernization is slow, but the fastest roads to reform are not always the most secure.

NOTES

1. In this respect, the French model is distinct from both the British model, where the title of civil servant is much more restrictively granted, and from the German model, which makes a hierarchical distinction between *Beamten*, in charge of public authority duties, and the subordinate staff governed by contractual law.
2. And the notion is also impossible to translate. The *corps* is such a typically French institution that the military notion of *'esprit de corps'* has not translated into several European languages (including English).
3. *Article 29, 1er alinéa de la loi n° 84-16 du 11 janvier 1984 portant dispositions statutaires relatives à la Fonction publique de l'Etat, in Statut général des fonctionnaires, Paris, Les éditions des Journaux officiels, n° 1571, 1999, p. 27.*
4. A recent report from the State's Council enumerates some of these 'micro-*corps*': the 68 sailor syndics, the 42 storemen at the Court of Accounts' archives, the 36 teachers of the *Légion d'Honneur*, the 24 secretaries of the information and communication system at the Minister of Foreign Affairs and the two foremen of the Government Printing Office. Cf. *Rapport public du Conseil d'Etat, 'Perspectives pour la fonction publique', Etudes et documents n°54, La documentation Française, 2003.*

5. In 1993, the Italian government introduced a comprehensive reform by replacing the legal status of civil servants with a 'standard' contractual system for establishing terms of employment for most employees. Managerial reforms were also developed for applying performance-related pay. In 1997, a second reform step extended the 1993 regime to new categories and temporary contracts were introduced for top managers in public sector industries and services.
6. Amongst the most recent: Commissariat général du Plan (2000), *Fonctions publiques: enjeux et stratégie pour le renouvellement*, sous la direction de Bernard Cieutat, Paris: La Documentation française; Cour des comptes, *La fonction publique de l'État, rapports publics particuliers, décembre 1999 et avril 2001*, Paris: Les éditions des Journaux officials; Roché, J. (1999), *Le temps de travail dans les trois fonctions publiques*, Paris: La Documentation française; Vallemont, S. (1999), *Gestion des ressources humaines dans l'administration, rapport au ministre chargé de la Fonction publique*, Paris: La Documentation française; Vallemont, S. (2000) (ed.), *Gestion dynamique de la fonction publique: une méthode*, Paris: Commissariat général du Plan.
7. Sanctioning a civil servant seems to be even more difficult than to recognize merit: there are less than 3 500 first-level disciplinary sanctions each year, and in 2001 there were only 24 forced dismissals for reasons such as indiscipline or serious offences (Source: *Observatoire de la fonction publique, rapport annuel* 2002).

REFERENCES

Bouckaert, G. and C. Pollitt (2000), *Public management reform: A comparative analysis*, Oxford: Oxford University Press.

Caillosse, J. (2003), 'La conscience professionnelle de l'agent public entre rappels à l'ordre statutaire et exigences manageriales', *Revue administrative*, **334**, 350-361.

Caillosse, J. and J. Hardy (2000), *Droit et modernisation administrative*, Paris: La Documentation Française.

Chevallier, J. (1996), 'Public administration in statist France', *Public administration review*, **56** (1), 67-74.

Clark, D. (1998), 'The modernization of the French civil service: crisis, change and continuity', *Public administration*, **76**, 97-115.

Conseil d'Etat (2003), *Perspectives pour la fonction publique*, Etudes et documents du Conseil d'Etat n°54, Paris: La documentation Française.

Eymeri, J.M. (2000), 'De la souplesse dans la rigidité: les corps administratifs à la française', *Eipascope*, **2**, 6-17.

Hogwood, B.W. and B.G. Peters (2000), 'Diffuse or diverse? Explaining patterns of public employment', paper for the American Political Science Association annual meeting, Washington, DC, 31 August-3 September.

Laborde, C. (1996), 'Pluralism, syndicalism and corporatism: Léon Duguit and the crisis of the state (1900-25)', *History of European Ideas*, **22** (3), 227-244.

Peters B.G. (1997), 'Policy transfers between governments: the case of administrative reforms', *European Journal of Political Research*, **4**, 247-289.

Rosanvallon, P. (1990), *L'Etat en France, de 1789 à nos jours*, Paris: Gallimard.

Rosanvallon, P. (1998), *Le peuple introuvable: Histoire de la représentation démocratique en France*, Paris: Gallimard.

11. Staff Participation in the Administrative Reform of the Flemish Community

Christophe Pelgrims, Trui Steen and Nick Thijs [1]

INTRODUCTION

Administrative reforms are introduced in a range of public services across Europe (Pollitt and Bouckaert 2004). This tendency to reform is also present in the Flemish Community, one of the regional entities in Belgium.[2] In 1999 the Flemish government launched a new reform project called '*Beter Bestuurlijk Beleid*' ('Better Administrative Policy'). This project aims at a reorganization of the core civil service – the Ministry of the Flemish Community – the agencies or 'Flemish Public Institutions' and the advisory boards. In this chapter we examine the extent to which staff has been able to participate, either directly of indirectly – via trade union representation – in this reform. First we define staff and their unions as major stakeholders in public management reform. After describing the context and content of the reforms in the Flemish Community, we look at the different forms of participation which can be distinguished in the reform and examine the effect of this participation on the process and content of reform. Finally, we try to establish whether reform, in turn, had lasting effects on staff participation and social dialogue in the public sector in Flanders.

STAFF AND UNIONS AS STAKEHOLDERS

When analysing staff participation, the scale of the reform prove to be an important variable (Halligan 2001). Comprehensive reforms introduce a range of reforms that affect most aspects of the public sector. These reforms may consist of different specialized and sectoral reforms. Comprehensive reforms typically start from a well-developed framework for action, encompass different aspects of the functioning of public services and are applied on a large scale. In comprehensive reforms there is little room for a bottom-up approach. These reforms require a top-down and a directive approach, while a bottom-up approach seems to be more likely in applied reforms at micro- or organizational level. Since most of the recent New Public Management (NPM) reforms are comprehensive, Halligan is sceptic about the role of staff participation in these reforms. 'Initially, then, reform is likely to be implemented from top down, using a directive approach. Over time, however, as individual agencies become responsible for implementation and seek to institutionalize reform at the middle and lower levels, bottom-up or hybrid elements will probably become more common' (Halligan 2001, p. 81). Halligan's conclusion has been confirmed by comparative empirical research. Pollitt and Bouckaert state that NPM reforms are elite-driven processes. In the centre of their model of public management reform stands the concept of elite-decision making. Executive politicians and top civil servants are defined as key actors in reform processes (Pollitt and Bouckaert 2004).

Although Pollitt and Bouckaert do not exclude influences and pressures from actors other than executive politicians and top civil servants, they hardly focus on these actors (Hondeghem, Horton and Steen 2005). However, a stakeholder approach may offer a richer analysis of administrative reforms. Hondeghem et al. (2005) define politicians, senior civil servants, staff and staff unions, citizens and external advisers as 'primary' stakeholders in public management reform. A stakeholder is defined as 'any group or individual who can affect or is affected by the achievement of the organization's objectives' (Freeman 1984, p. 46). Primary stakeholders are groups or individuals without whose continuing participation the organization cannot survive. Staff and trade unions clearly meet these definitions of being major stakeholders in reforms (Hondeghem et al. 2005). Reform affects the interest of staff and their unions, while they in turn shape organizations. The organization will, in the end, depend on their cooperation to implement the reform. It is thus hard to deny that staff and their representatives affect and are affected by reforms.

In stakeholder theory we notice three streams: a descriptive stream, an instrumental stream and a normative stream. The descriptive stream classifies stakeholders according to different variables (Mitchell, Agle and Wood 1997; Murdock 2004; Johnson and Scholes 1999). Stakeholders possess at least one of the following attributes: the power to influence the organization, the legitimacy of the stakeholder's relationship with the organization and the urgency of the stakeholder's claim on the organization (Mitchell, Agle and Wood 1997). The instrumental stream focuses on the relation between stakeholder management and performance. According to this line of reasoning, participation should lead towards a better implementation of reforms (Donaldson and Preston 1995). The instrumental stakeholder stream fits in the classic formula of Maier ($E = K * A$) in which he states that the effectiveness of reforms (E) is equal to the quality of the reform (K) multiplied by the acceptation of the involved stakeholders (A) (Maier 1967). The last stream, the normative one, concentrates on the ethical aspects of the involvement of stakeholders in reform (Donaldson and Preston 1995). Involving stakeholders in reform processes is seen as morally obliged, since these stakeholders are affected by the reforms.

Staff participation may be defined in two ways: direct staff participation and indirect staff participation. Direct participation refers to personal contributions of employees to the organization. Farnham and Parys (2005, p. 54) classify direct staff participation as a management-driven practice: 'aimed at individual employees or workgroups in the workplace covering operational issues so as to gain their commitment and contribution to organisational goals, improved performance and better customer service'. Indirect participation refers to 'represented' participation of employees in the organizational decision making (Dachler and Wilpert 1978). Distinct from the management-driven practice, indirect staff participation is defined by power-based arrangements (Farnham and Parys 2005). Farnham and Parys (2005) distinguish three forms of indirect staff participation: collective bargaining, partnership and consultation. Collective bargaining is a joint decision making process, based on power relations between employers and employees and aiming at facilitating compromises between possible conflicting interests. Collective bargaining can be characterized as a zero-sum game, with conflict and low trust. Partnership substitutes the adversarial tensions for a cooperative approach. Therefore it is characterized as a positive-sum game, with high trust and cooperation. Consultation provides forums where decision makers/managers take employee views into account. Decisions might be influenced before they are actually taken. This does not mean that consultation is equal to negotiation. Decision makers/managers are still responsible for the final decision.

Gill and Krieger (2000) note that whilst in earlier days the emphasis was on indirect (or representative) participation, since the beginning of the 1990s there has been a focus on direct forms of participation. This shift has gone hand in hand with a rediscovery of the human factor in work organizations, which can be seen as a response to the increasing competitive pressures facing enterprises and the growth of Human Resource Management (Parys 2002). Therefore analysing staff participation in reform processes should focus both on direct and indirect staff participation.

The first element of our research question – to what extent staff has been able to participate in reform – can now be operationalized into questioning whether we notice direct participation as well as the above described threefold of indirect participation (consultation, bargaining, partnership) in the reforms of the Flemish administration, the so called '*Beter Bestuurlijk Beleid*' reform ('Better Administrative Policy'). The question then moves to discussing the relationship between staff participation and reform: what has been the effect of these different forms of participation on the reform and, vice versa, has the reform shifted staff involvement and employment relationships in the Flemish public sector? We noted that stakeholder theory defines stakeholders as those groups or individuals that can affect or are affected by reform. As such, our research into the impact of staff and unions on reform and the impact of reform on the positioning of staff and unions, tests the notion of staff and unions being primary stakeholders in public management reform.

CONTEXT AND CONTENT OF THE FLEMISH REFORMS

The Flemish government, which took office in 1999, had the explicit ambition to transform the Flemish administration into one of the best performing administrations in the OECD. We can distinguish three main reasons. Firstly, the so called 'gap between government and citizen' was considered to be one of the main causes of the growing anti-political sentiments (Maesschalck, Hondeghem and Pelgrims 2002). Secondly, the perception was that government did not fulfil the expectations of citizens, who demand a transparent, high level service from their government. Thirdly, a disturbed political relationship created a trigger for change. Due to the elections in 1999 the Christian-Democrat and Socialist government lost office to 'a Purple-Green' government. Christian-Democrats ended up in opposition after 40 years in power.

Two principles underpin the proposed reforms. The first one is the 'restoration of the primacy of politics'.[3] Initially, the concept referred to the power balance between politics on the one hand and the trade unions and other interest groups on the other (Stouthuysen 2002). In the years after its introduction, the meaning of the concept 'primacy of politics' gradually evolved. Increasingly it referred to politico-administrative relations and the necessarily dominant role for politics. A second core aim of the reforms was to downsize the ministerial cabinets and to strengthen the policy capacities of the administration. In Flanders, as in the Belgian federal and other regional governments, most of the policy formulation and design is done in ministerial cabinets (Dewachter 1995). As such, the administration is left with implementation only (Hondeghem 1996). In the Flemish government agreement of 1999, the government explicitly acknowledged that downsizing the ministerial cabinets is a necessary condition to strengthen the policy capacities of the administration (Vlaamse Regering 2002a; Pelgrims, Steen and Hondeghem 2003).

The reform aims at establishing homogeneous policy domains around departments and agencies. A 'homogeneous policy domain' is defined as a cluster of policy fields that create a coherent entity both from the perspective of politics and from the perspective of the client (Victor and Stroobants 2000). For every policy domain a ministry will be created, consisting of a core department and agencies. The department will be responsible for policy formulation, monitoring and evaluation. The agencies' primary task will be implementation. The reform wants to establish a 'one-to-one' relationship between the minister and his/her department and agencies.[4] The reforms were embedded judicially in the so called 'framework decree' approved by the Flemish Parliament on 9 July 2003 (declared 18 July 2003).

Besides these structural reforms, *'Beter Bestuurlijk Beleid'* has intentions to reshape the Human Resource Management. In contrast with previous reform programmes, the *'Beter Bestuurlijk Beleid'* reform targets the Flemish administration as a whole; not only the Flemish ministry, but also semi-governmental bodies are included. Next to the administrative entities, the advisory structure is also a focus of the reforms. Some gave binding advice, which is in contradiction with the idea of the primacy of politics. Therefore a new decree on advisory boards will regulate the advisory structure in Flanders.

The integration of all these different reform proposals in one major project allows us to conclude *'Beter Bestuurlijk Beleid'* is a comprehensive reform including different aspects of sectoral and specialization reforms. On the basis of our earlier theoretical framework, we may expect a top-down and directive reform with less room for direct and indirect participation.

DIRECT PARTICIPATION IN THE REFORM PROCESS?

In its Coalition Agreement of 1999, the Flemish government explicitly agreed to reform the administration (Vlaamse Regering 2002a). That same year, the Flemish government presented a far-reaching reform plan, further elaborated in the Leuven Agreement (19 February 2000). Two senior civil servants, so called Special Commissioners were appointed to develop the actual plans and to prepare the process of administrative reform. The Flemish government and the two senior civil servants remained the most central actors during the first years of the reforms.

In 2002 new actors showed up: the change managers (Vlaamse Regering, 2002b). They had an advisory role and reported straight to the minister concerning the transformation of the policy field concerned. The change manager could decide to involve the line management, but this was not obligatory. The Steering Committee, staffed by members of the ministerial cabinets and the two Special Commissioners, would present the ultimate proposal concerning the different policy domains to the Flemish government (Pelgrims et al. 2003).

The second task of the change managers was to create a basis for change in their policy domain by supplying information to the civil servants in general. In spite of the major consequences of the reform for the civil servants in the Flemish public service, there was little communication about the reform. As a consequence, many civil servants were kept in the dark about the planned changes in the Flemish public service and about their own future (Pelgrims et al. 2003). The communication touched only upon decisions made by the Flemish government and was considered as being very vague. These initiatives focused on informing the civil servants and had no intention of letting them participate or give their opinion about the reform.

After the elections of June 2004, a new government was installed. Christian-Democrats and Flemish Nationalists formed a government together with Socialists and Liberals. The government agreement stated that the reform plans would be continued in consultation with civil servants (Vlaamse Regering 2004b).[5]

To strengthen implementation of the reforms, government agreement creates a ministerial committee[6] and a committee of civil servants. Besides the 'decisional' ministerial committee, an advisory board was also created. The members of this boards are all top civil servants appointed by Flemish government (Vlaamse Regering 2004a). This board advises the ministerial committee on concrete issues of the reorganization. This instrument may broaden support for the reform at the top of the organization. In line with 'the primacy of politics' the final decision is taken by the ministerial committee. The new government decided to nominate a co-ordinator for each policy domain. The co-ordinator should be the first spokesperson and initiator in his/her policy domain (Vlaamse Regering 2004c).

In general, the civil servants were not offered much chance to participate (Pelgrims et al. 2003). Only a few civil servants had the opportunity to participate in the reform process.

THE ORGANIZATION OF INDIRECT STAFF PARTICIPATION IN THE BELGIAN PUBLIC SECTOR

Besides discussing the level of direct participation during the '*Beter Bestuurlijk Beleid*' reform process, the interaction between government and the trade unions during the ongoing reform is analysed. First, however, we look at the way indirect participation is organized in the Belgian public sector.

Like in most European countries, social dialogue is a legally required step in Belgium (Bossaert, Demmke and Nomden 2001). Dialogue with the trade unions is an obligatory step before measures can be taken by government, especially with regards to employment conditions. Van Gyes, de Witte and van der Hallen (2000) stress the strong trade union presence in Belgium. Trade union coverage for wage earners is estimated at 53 per cent, whereas the European average is 30 per cent (Martens 2002; European Commission: Employment & social affairs 2000). This relatively high figure is still increasing (Martens 2002). Belgian unionism reflects the major dividing lines of Belgian society. The separate confederations exist for each of the three dominant ideologies in Belgium: catholic, socialist and liberal. Each is affiliated to a political party (Parys and Hondeghem 2005). The largest union confederations are the catholic General Christian Trade Union Confederation (53 per cent) and the socialist General Belgian Trade Union Federation (40 per cent). The General Confederation of Liberal Trade Unions in Belgium is rather small (seven per cent) (Martens 2002). Belgian trade unions are known for their pragmatism. The differences between the three trade unions today tend to concern manners of acting and defending workers' rights, rather than the causes being championed (Van Gyes et al. 2000). The same three unions are also the ones officially represented in the public sector: the Christian-inspired CCOD, the socialist ACOD and the liberal VSOA.

> Within the socialist union some 23 per cent of the members belong to the Public Services Central (ACOD). This is the socialist confederation's second largest unit. The comparable figure for the Christian union (CCOD) is 11 per cent. The socialist union has a very strong presence in the public sector in general, where it organizes two-thirds of the members of the two main unions (Parys and Hondeghem 2005, p. 103).

Belgium's nation-wide, rather detailed trade union statute is unique. It provides for procedures in public service labour relations. The statute consists of a framework that was set up in 1973 to organize 'relations between public authorities and the unions of officials' and a royal decree of 1984 implementing this framework (Parys and Hondeghem 2005). The law of 1974 imposes an obligation on every government that wishes to enact measures relating to labour regulations in its administration to negotiate and consult with the representative unions beforehand (Bossaert et al. 2001). The procedures provided in the trade union statute involve a multitude of negotiation and consultation committees.

A distinction is made between 'negotiation' and 'consultation'. 'Negotiation' involves a procedure by which the representative trade unions are informed in advance of important measures government is planning with regard to the labour regulations affecting staff (Janvier and Humblet 1998). The results of the negotiations are recorded in a so-called 'protocol'. 'Consultation' on the other hand is a procedure by which there is a dialogue between government and representative trade unions. This procedure is necessary before government takes decisions on less important measures relating to the labour regulations affecting staff. The results of the dialogue are recorded in a 'motivated advice'.

Both concepts only include the obligation for government to talk with the representative employee organizations, preceding the unilateral imposition of certain measures impacting on staff (Janvier and Humblet 1998). The legal obligation for social dialogue is very clear. The infringement of negotiation and consultation procedures affects the legality of the measure thus adopted. Infringement of these procedures may therefore lead to intervention by the supervisory authority (Council of State), annulment proceedings by ordinary courts and tribunals (Bossaert et al. 2001). The agreements themselves are not formally binding and government can unilaterally impose the measures it wants. However, when negotiations result in an agreement between government and representative trade unions, the agreement is seen as a political commitment and as such it is morally binding on government.

The structure of social dialogue is very hierarchical, with important elements being discussed at a central level. As regards negotiation, the following committees are put in place:

- the committee for all public services (Committee A);
- the committee for federal, community and regional public services (Committee B);
- the committee for provincial and local public services (Committee C);
- eighteen sector committees for federal, community and regional public services; and
- the special committees (one per local administration: i.e. one per province, one per municipality, etc.).

Every two years, negotiations take place in Committee A on intersectoral social planning. Committee A has sole competency for negotiation proposals concerning measures in fields such as rules for unions or social security for the entire public sector. Specific measures are dealt with in separate committees for the different government tiers. For the Flemish administration this is the sector committee XVIII. In this committee all official negotiations have to be handled. Parallel with the negotiation structure, a dialogue structure is created.

There are separate dialogue commissions under each sector committee and the structure of each of these dialogue committees is also pyramid-like, with the higher dialogue committee at the top. There is also a distinction made between basic discussion committees, intermediate discussion committees and special discussion committees (Janvier and Humblet 1998). In the new structure of the administration each policy domain will have an intermediate discussion committee and several basic discussion committees per department or agency.

The Belgian public sector unions prove to hold a specific position when compared to unions in other European countries. Their strong presence is linked with a relatively high coverage for public sector workers, as well as an institutional embeddedness in the political and economic system of 'pillarization'. While social dialogue is legally required in most Member States of the European Union, Belgium is unique in having a nation-wide legislation detailing procedures for public sector labour relations.

Another interesting aspect in the social dialogue is the centralization/decentralization approach diverging in different states. The most far-reaching form of centralization exists when the social dialogue takes place for the civil service as a whole. In practice, in no EU Member State is the social dialogue in public administration either completely centralized or decentralized. Elements of both are mostly present. Three groups of countries can be distinguished. The first group comprises those countries with an accent on decentralized social dialogue, where essential elements like remuneration are dealt with by individual departments/ministries and agencies. The second group includes countries with partially decentralized social dialogue and the third group contains those in which the social dialogue incorporates a lot of centralized elements and in which decentralization is more limited (Bossaert et al. 2001). Belgium clearly belongs to those countries with a generally centralized social dialogue. This also led to a very hierarchical structure of social dialogue.

The unions often get criticized for taking up a rather conservative stance towards administrative reform. Protecting the employees' 'achieved advantages' often is one of their main goals. This also ensures that unions use Europeanization only to a limited extent to legitimate their own reform agenda: they fear negative results of Europeanization for the social model as implemented in Flanders. However, when European policy or international comparisons show opportunities to enhance the working conditions – e.g. the increased attention given to training – the unions use this information in the social dialogue. The unions also try to influence the European policy-agenda, e.g. via participation in international demonstrations and lobby work, the Belgian unions support the introduction of a European social dialogue for the public sector.

THE INVOLVEMENT OF TRADE UNIONS IN THE FLEMISH REFORM

Before we can answer the question whether and how the reforms fit into the threefold of indirect participation of consultation, bargaining and partnership (Farnham and Parys 2005), we will discuss the involvement of trade unions in the Flemish reform. The so-called framework decree, which the Flemish Parliament approved of in 2003, contains the framework for the organizational structure of the Flemish administration and the basic principles of the new personnel policy. Separate resolutions and decrees, however, were needed to operationalize the elements of this framework. This chapter focuses on the involvement of trade unions with the operationalization of the resolutions and decrees concerning the new personnel statute and the management code linked to this statute, the remuneration policy, the organizational structure, the migration of personnel and, finally, the statute of top civil servants.

Initially, the labour unions were not consulted during the preparation of the reform plans. The unions were involved for the first time, when the negotiations on the framework decree started (Sectorcomite XVIII 2002). The elements of the framework decree had to be operationalized by the Flemish Government and Parliament in separate resolutions and decrees. The unions' involvement however, was limited to those topics for which social dialogue was legally and formally obliged (articles concerning the personnel matters).

The New Personnel Statute

The first element taken care of was the personnel statute. On 15 July 2002 the Flemish Government agreed on 'the general principles of a framework personnel statute'. On the basis of these general principles a new personnel statute is to be designed. Before, three separated personnel statutes existed in the Flemish administration: firstly, the statute for the personnel of the core administration; secondly, a statute for the personnel of the Flemish agencies;

and thirdly, a separated statute for the personnel of the Flemish scientific institutions.

The new personnel statute aims at creating one general statute for all personnel. This general statute will present itself in a generic framework, rather than detailed legislation for the personnel policy. The spirit of this new statute is one of deregulation, giving responsibility to the line managers and making them accountable for 'their' personnel policy.

During negotiations, which started in the second half of 2002, the Government decided to carry out research on the possibilities of introducing job classification and job weighting. This research was carried out by the Hay Group. Rumours spread about the abolishment of the functional career system. The unions were not consulted and informed of the research, although it deals with a main point of interest to them. This resulted in the negotiations ending prematurely. Government considered the personnel statute to be a political important issue and wanted to continue working on it. Since the statute was to include the controversial topic of a new remuneration policy, the negotiations promised to be long and difficult. On 19 March 2003 the Flemish Minister-President met the representatives of the different unions on this issue and they agreed that before the elections (mid 2004) the new statute had to be operational. In order to reach this goal, the pillar of the new remuneration policy was left out of the statute and was to be negotiated elsewhere (see infra on new remuneration policy). This agreement was a compromise between government and the unions.

On 4 July 2003 the Flemish Government approved the statute for the first time. A major aim of the statute was deregulation. The unions focused on the legal security and guarantees for the employees in the statute during the negotiations. These negotiations resulted in a protocol of partial agreement. Two unions agreed (ACOD and VSOA), while the CCOD did not sign the protocol of agreement, arguing that time procedures were not respected (CCOD 2004). Actually, the CCOD wanted to make a principal statement of its disagreement with the way negotiations were handled. Specifically, the CCOD stated that the time period in which the negotiations had to be finished (before the elections) was too short. The Flemish government approved the statute for the second time on 4 June 2004. However, the new statute is not yet operationalized, since the new elected Flemish Government has to approve the statute before it can be approved by the Flemish Parliament.

The Management Code

The new personnel statute only stipulates a generic framework. Top managers are given the autonomy and responsibility to set up their own personnel management and lay their own accents. To support these managers and prevent abuses of managerial freedom, the management code was constructed and approved by the Flemish Government in 2002. This code proclaims 12 general principles of good and decent HRM. It also contains the results that managers have to obtain in regard to the management of their personnel. The code is not juridical binding, but the political authority has to supervise compliance with it. The negotiations with the unions started in the second half of 2003. Unions were not consulted concerning the formulation of the general principles. Their major concern for the unions is the lack of juridical binding power of the code. The final negotiations on the management code have to be finished in the second half of 2005.

The Remuneration Policy

With the agreement on 'the general principles of a framework personnel statute' (15 July 2002), the Flemish Government launched the idea of a new remuneration policy. The basis for this new policy is formed by job classification and performance-related payment. To support the introduction of the remuneration policy the Flemish Government installed a 'strategic cell'. This cell had to do some international comparative research on remuneration policies and performance-related payment.

The negotiations concerning the remuneration policy were decoupled from the personnel statute due to the specific concerns the unions had about the remuneration policy. Before the official negotiations on the remuneration policy started, an advising committee was created to prepare these negotiations and to establish an agreement on the basic principles of the remuneration policy. This advising committee was composed of representatives of the Flemish core administrations, the agencies, the scientific institutions and representatives of the three unions. In this committee no official decisions were taken, its single task was to search for consensus concerning proposals on the remuneration policy (Claeys 2004). In May 2004 the advising committee laid down some policy proposals for the new Flemish government (Kenniscel Beloningsbeleid 2004). The unions are in favour of this way of working, although it is not that easy to carry out a policy preparation role. The government decided in July 2004 to introduce the new remuneration policy and to continue the work of the advising committee. Until now no resolution is agreed on by the government and the official negotiations have not started yet.

Decree on the Organizational Structure

The framework decree of 18 July 2003 stipulated that the Flemish government has to create homogeneous policy domains (article 2). For each policy domain one ministry has to be created, consisting of a core department and several agencies (article 3). The core departments are responsible for policy preparation and the agencies are responsible for policy implementation (article 5). The different articles have to be concretized by a decree on the organizational structure. The resolution of 3 June 2005 creates the organizational structure for the 13 homogeneous policy domains. Negotiations with the unions are not legally obliged for this topic and the unions only receive information on the decisions taken.

Decree on the Migration of Personnel

According to the new organizational structure, as defined in the framework decree, criteria have to be formulated in detail as to which entity the personnel members belong. The negotiations on this topic were concluded in June 2004 with a partial protocol of agreement, signed by the ACOD and VSOA. Again, the CCOD did not sign, stating that time procedures had not been respected. Again this was a principal statement reacting against the way negotiations had taken place. After taking into account adjustment proposals of the Advisory Board and the Ministerial Committee, the Flemish government agreed on the resolution on 20 May 2005.

Basically it is decided that employees will keep their function as much as possible. If in the future, his/her task will be handled by another department or agency, the employee shifts to that entity. For this movement an ad hoc commission is installed, chaired by the Minister of Civil Service and a representative of each policy domain. The final decision on a person's migration is taken by the policy board of the policy domain concerned.

Decree on the Statute of Top Civil Servants

The procedure for the appointment of managers was included in the framework decree. It was formulated as a principle that top managers will be appointed by mandate. However, since a separate resolution had to be made on this issue, it was not elaborated as an integral point of the personnel statute. On 4 June 2004 the Flemish Government took a principal decision about the appointment procedure and the conditions of employment. On 17 June 2005 concluding a year of discussions on the conditions of employment, the Flemish Government took a decision on this issue. The negotiations with committee XVIII have recently started.

EXTENT OF INDIRECT PARTICIPATION

How and where do we notice the threefold of consultation, bargaining and partnership in the indirect participation in the Flemish reform process?

In Belgium, a unique trade union statute provides detailed procedures for public service labour relations. This makes it obligatory to set up formal negotiations and consultation with the trade unions on the organizational-administrative reforms planned in the Flemish Community. Most steps related to indirect participation of the reform process described above focus on bargaining. Table 11.1 points out the different steps taken in relation to the threefold.

Table 11.1: Consultation, bargaining and partnerships in the indirect participation in the Flemish reform process

	Consultation	Bargaining	Partnership
Preparation reform plans			
Framework decree	X	X	
New personnel statute		X	
Management code		X	
Remuneration policy			X
Organizational structure			
Migration of personnel		X	
Statute top civil servants		X	

It is important of course to know how much influence these negotiation and consultation rounds exert on decision making (Dachler and Wilpert 1978). One could state that formally the trade union statute makes sure that the trade unions, as a representation of (unionized) employees, receive information about the reform plans and can give their opinion on the matter. As noted before, the government is not legally obliged to take these opinions into account. However, the historical context and the strong position of unions in the public sector, as well as the fact that union participation has a permanent character, rather than being ad hoc (De Leede and Looise 1994), show that in practice, government can not easily overrule all comments made by the unions.

Although a protocol of non-agreement does not oblige the government to change its reform plans, we may denote important changes in the reform process imposed by the trade unions. An example is the decision not to include the new remuneration policy as a part of the new personnel statute. The topic of remuneration was known to be a controversial one. In order to be able to get the statute operational in the short term, remuneration was discussed separately in an advising committee composed of representatives of the administration and of the unions. The committee is to look for a consensus before official negotiations start.

In the past it was often the case that a number of informal meetings between government representatives – senior civil servants and members of the political cabinets – and union representatives were held, in order to discuss reform plans. After an agreement was reached during these informal meetings, the meetings were stopped. The same happened whenever it became clear that no consent was possible. Then, a concluding formal meeting was set up in order to fulfil the legally imposed obligations as to the bargaining process. This practice, however, has diminished. According to a union representative, informal negotiations seldom take place (Interview CCOD representative, Brussels, 19 July 2005). Instead we notice that for the initial preparation of the reform plans and in the development of the decree on organizational structure no indirect participation has taken place, or at least no participation that can be categorized as either consultation, bargaining or partnership. The unions only got information on the decisions or the plans. Therefore we would extend the threefold with a fourth category of 'information'.

This question of indirect participation being limited to receiving information only, should also be seen against the background of the content of the decision. De Leede and Looise (1994) mention three categories: 1) job content; 2) personnel concerns, namely working conditions, conditions of employment and industrial relations; and 3) overall policy or long term policy with a more strategic character. Traditionally, unions focus on the second category and the negotiations related to the administrative reform in the Flemish community do not seem to make an exception to this.

A last dimension on which to describe the extent of participation, is the timing of the participation (Hermel 1998; Cressey and Williams 1990). This is important in determining the influence of employees (or representatives) on organizational change. Research shows that (the intensity of) participation varies according to the phase of the change process. Participation seems to be less applied in the phase of development (Kanter 1983; Cressey and Williams 1990). The phase of decision making shows little participation happening. The possibilities of participation increase in later phases. By then, however, the most important decisions have already been taken. This is often called the participation paradox (Cressey and Williams 1990).

This general trend is confirmed in our specific case. Indirect participation only starts after government has presented the principles underlying the plan to reform the administration and after an actual reform plan has been published. Only after this, bargaining starts. This may account for the paradox that on the one hand the unions are criticized for being conservative – in a sense of opposing changes – and for focusing on remuneration and other aspects of employment conditions only, while on the other hand it is not clear how much opportunity unions actually get to discuss long-term strategic plans for the administration. This tendency is further enhanced by the fact that, although for instance the redesigning of the organizational structure holds many repercussions, this is one of the topics government legally is not obliged to discuss with the unions.

CONCLUSION

In this chapter we examined the extent to which staff has been able to participate, either directly of indirectly – via trade union representation – in the reform of the Flemish Community. An analysis of the '*Beter Bestuurlijk Beleid*' reform process shows that it may be considered an elitist reform. While staff is a major stakeholder in public management reform, there has been little opportunity for civil servants to participate in the reform process. The basic principles and the general framework of the reform were decided on by the political level. Only a few senior civil servants were allowed to participate in the reform. Two top-level civil servants were appointed to develop the actual plans and prepare the process of administrative reform. Change managers, specifically appointed to implement the reform, had an important task as to the operationalization of the reform within the different policy domains established around departments and agencies. In general, however, the civil servant was not offered a chance to participate. As such the impact of direct participation on the reform is limited, or even nil. Yet, when the process will take a step from elaborating reform plans and writing the legal framework for reform to the actual implementation of reform, the sympathy of civil servants at the organization's work floor towards the changes can be expected to become a crucial factor for success.

The extent to which staff has been able to participate in reform, however, does not relate to direct participation only. We also questioned whether indirect participation took place and, if so, which form it has taken. In line with the legal provisions as to negotiation and consultation, the reforms of the Flemish administration are characterized by bargaining relationships between government and unions on a high number of regulations. Only with regard to the remuneration policy, an item which is of major interest to the unions, can we denote partnership. The remuneration was a rather controversial issue, which endangered a smooth formulation of the new personnel statute. Therefore, the governments and the unions collaboratively decided to decouple the remuneration policy from the statute and to create an advising committee to prepare negotiations on this aspect. It is the functioning of this advising committee of mixed composition that comes most closely to what we can call partnership. Although in this committee no official decisions are taken, its search for consensus concerning policy proposals provide a major role for unions in policy preparation.

Overall, we conclude that, while unions have not been actively involved in the preparation of reform plans and can only negotiate on specific regulations, they still hold a strong position influencing reforms. This position is linked with the unions' history in Belgium: traditionally high numbers of civil servants are union members and unions are being seen as having a legitimate interest in public sector reform. The 1974 trade union statute details the procedures by which social dialogue should take place, and as such gives trade unions' position a legal base. Through informal and formal processes of negotiation and consultation, the unions tried to influence the impact of reform on employees' working conditions, and indeed the unions could exercise some real influence on the reform. The unions are being criticized for being too conservative, opposing changes and focusing on remuneration and other aspects of employment conditions only. However, it is also true that they were involved only after the major principles and outlines of the reform plan were already established and debate focused on how to translate these in concrete measures to be implemented.

The question then remains if we can expect patterns of staff participation in public sector reform to shift due to recent reform experiences. The historically based position of unions is not expected to be influenced much by recent reforms. However, if the involvement of unions during the policy preparation phase on a crucial issue such as remuneration policy can make for a smoother decision making process and implementation of reforms, these experiences may set an example for future relations evolving towards greater partnership. Finally, in contrast to the practice of indirect participation, there is no tradition of direct participation within the public sector in Flanders and recent reforms do not seem to distract from this historical path.

NOTES

1. Christophe Pelgrims and Nick Thijs are both researchers at the Public Management Institute (Katholieke Universiteit Leuven, Belgium). Dr Trui Steen is Assistant Professor at the Department of Public Administration (Leiden University, The Netherlands).
2. During the last three decades, Belgium changed from a unitary to a genuinely federal state through a four step state reform process (1970, 1980, 1988, 1993). The federation is composed of three communities and three regions, each with legislative powers and thus

with their own parliament, government and administration: the Flemish, Walloon and the Brussels regions on the one hand and the Dutch-speaking, French-speaking and German-speaking communities on the other. The Flemish government combines the competences of both the Flemish region and the Dutch-speaking community. Apart from the political level, it comprises the Ministry of the Flemish Community (core civil service) and a number of 'Flemish Public Institutions' (agencies).

3. The role of the concepts 'New Political Culture' and 'primacy of politics' in the agenda setting process of administrative and political reform has been described in Maesschalck, Hondeghem and Pelgrims (2002).
4. This precludes that more than one minister will bear responsibility over one department or one agency.
5. The new Flemish government decided to reshuffle the policy domains and the one-to-one relationship. The intention to slim down ministerial cabinets was not implemented by the previous government. For the new government, the issue was not worth a discussion. Ministerial cabinets turned out to be too important for ministers in a Flemish context.
6. The ministerial committee is responsible for the co-ordination between different ministers, steering and monitoring of the reform, keeping an eye on the budgetary neutrality of the reforms and taking care of horizontal portfolios (Vlaamse Regering 2004a).

REFERENCES

Bossaert, D., C. Demmke and K. Nomden (2001), *Civil services in the Europe of Fifteen: Trends and New Developments,* Maastricht: EIPA.

CCOD (2004), *Protocol Sectorcomité XVIII bij het Besluit van de Vlaamse regering van 15 juli 2002 houdende organisatie van het Ministerie van de Vlaamse Gemeenschap en de regeling van de rechtspositie van het personeel.*

Claeys, J. (2004), 'Duidelijkheid over het beloningsbeleid', *Goedendag,* Maart, p. 46.

Cressey, P. and R. Williams (1990), *Participation in change; new technology and the role of employee involvement,* Dublin: European Foundation for the Improvement of the Living and Working Conditions.

Dachler, P. and B. Wilpert (1978), 'Conceptual Dimensions and Boundaries of Participation in Organizations: a critical evaluation', *Administrative Science Quarterly,* **23**, 1-37.

De Leede, J. and J. Looise (1994), *Participatie en organisatie; HRM Thema Cahiers XXIV,* Deventer: Kluwer Bedrijfswetenschappen.

Dewachter, W. (1995), *Besluitvorming in Politiek België,* Leuven: Acco.

Donaldson, T. and L. Preston (1995), 'The stakeholder theory of the corporation: concepts, evidence and implications', *Academy of Management Review,* **20** (1), 65-91.

European Commission: Employment & social affairs (2000), *Industrial relations in Europe.*

Farnham, D. and M. Parys (2005), 'Staff participation in the public service', in D. Farnham, A. Hondeghem and S. Horton (eds), *Staff participation and public management reform: some international comparisons,* Basingstoke: Palgrave, pp. 54-82.

Freeman, R. (1984), *Strategic management, a stakeholder approach,* Boston: Pitman.

Gill, C. and H. Krieger (2000), 'Recent Survey Evidence on Participation in Europe: Towards a European Model?', *European Journal of Industrial Relations,* **6** (1), 109-32.

Halligan, J. (2001), 'The process of reform in the era of public sector transformation', in T. Christensen and P. Laegreid (eds), *New public management; The transformation of ideas and practice*, Aldershot: Ashgate, pp. 73-89.

Hermel, P. (1998), *Le management participatif: sens, réalités, actions*, Paris: Les Editions d'Organisation.

Hondeghem, A. (1996), 'De politieke en ambtelijke component in het openbaar bestuur', in R. Maes and K. Jochmans (eds), *Inleiding tot de Bestuurskunde*, Brussel: STOHO, pp. 45-72.

Hondeghem, A., S. Horton and T. Steen (2005), 'Trajectories, institutions and stakeholders in public management reform', in D. Farnham, A. Hondeghem and S. Horton (eds), *Staff participation and public management reform: some international comparisons*, Basingstoke: Palgrave, pp. 27-53.

Janvier, R. and P. Humblet (1998), *Ambtenarenrecht 1: Vakbondsstatuut: collectieve arbeidsverhoudingen in de publieke sector in rechte en in de feiten*, Brugge: Die Keure.

Johnson, G. and K. Scholes (1999), *Exploring corporate strategy*, Harlow: Pearson Education.

Kanter, R. (1983), *The Change Managers: Innovation and Entrepreneurship in the American Corporation*, New York: Simon and Schuster.

Kenniscel Beloningsbeleid (2004), *Synthesenota Beloningsbeleid.*

Maesschalck, J., A. Hondeghem and C. Pelgrims (2002), 'De evolutie naar Nieuwe Politieke Cultuur in België: een beleidswetenschappelijke analyse', *Beleidswetenschap*, **16** (4), 295-317.

Maier, N. (1967), 'Assets and liabilities in group problem solving: the need for an integrative function', *Psychological Review*, **74**, 239-49.

Martens, A. (2002), 'Een snelle introductie tot het Belgisch syndicalisme', in A. Martens, G. van Gyes and P. van der Hallen (eds), *De vakbond naar de 21ste eeuw*, Leuven: HIVA, pp. 1-12.

Mitchell, R., B. Agle and D. Wood (1997), 'Toward a theory of stakeholder identification and salience: defining the principle of who and what really counts', *Academy of Management Review*, **22** (4), 853-86.

Murdock, A. (2004), 'Stakeholder theory, partnerships and alliances in the health care sector of the UK and Scotland', *International Public Management Review*, **5** (1), 21-40.

Parys, M. (2002), 'Staff participation and involvement in the public sector reform of the Belgian federal government: the case of the Artemis-enquiry', paper presented to the annual meeting of the European Group of Public Administration, Potsdam, Germany.

Parys, M. and A. Hondeghem (2005), 'Belgium: Staff participation in the Copernic reform', in D. Farnham, A. Hondeghem and S. Horton (eds), *Staff participation and public management reform: some international comparisons*, Basingstoke: Palgrave, pp. 100-13.

Pelgrims, C., T. Steen and A. Hondeghem (2003), *Coördinatie van beleid binnen een veranderende politieke ambtelijke verhouding*, Leuven: SBOV.

Pollitt, C. and G. Bouckaert (2004), *Public management reform: A comparative analysis*, Oxford: Oxford University Press.

Sectorcomite XVIII (2002), *Protocol houdende de conclusies van de onderhandelingen van 16 en 23 april 2002 die gevoerd werden in het sectorcomite XVIII Vlaamse gemeenschap en Vlaams Gewest, Protocol nr. 177 533.*

Stouthuysen, P. (2002), 'Het primaat van de politiek. Een situering van het Vlaamse debat', *Bestuurskunde*, **11** (2), 69-78.

Van Gyes, G., H. de Witte and P. van der hallen (2000), 'Belgian trade unions in the 1990s: does strong today mean strong tomorrow?', in J. Waddington and R. Hoffman (eds), *Trade unions in Europe: facing challenges and searching for solutions*, Brussels: ETUI, pp. 105-41.

Victor, L. and E. Stroobants (2000), *Beter Bestuur: Een visie op een transparant organisatiemodel voor de Vlaamse administratie*, Brussel: Vlaamse administratie.

Vlaamse Regering (2002a), *Vlaams regeerakkoord*, Brussel.

Vlaamse Regering (2002b), *Beter Bestuurlijk Beleid: Aanstelling van dertien veranderingsmanagers*, Brussel.

Vlaamse Regering (2004a), *Beter Bestuurlijk Beleid: Oprichting van het ministerieel comité en een college van ambtenaren-generaal voor de invoering van de bestuurlijke hervorming*, Brussel.

Vlaamse Regering (2004b), *Regeerakkoord 2004*, Brussel.

Vlaamse Regering (2004c), *Bijdrage Vlaamse administratie aan het regeerprogramma van de aantredende Vlaamse regering, 21 december*, Brussel.

12. Public Management Reform and Employee Voice in UK Public Services

Geoff White, Paul Dennison, David Farnham and Sylvia Horton

INTRODUCTION

The election of a Labour government in 1997, following an 18 year period of Conservative Party rule in the UK, promised a major change in governmental industrial relations policy. The new government's election manifesto had indicated that there would be both new domestic legislation, in the form of a national minimum wage and rights to trade union recognition, and agreement to sign up to the European Union (EU) employment directives previously the subject of an 'opt out' clause for the UK in the Maastricht Treaty. A key aspect of this changed political terrain has been a commitment, at least in government rhetoric, to improving 'employee voice' in public-sector employment, partly as a means of facilitating continued public management reforms (Farnham, Hondeghem and Horton 2005a). The UK public sector consists of those government, or tax-funded, organizations providing public services to the population – largely through central government, the National Health Service (NHS) and local government authorities.

In UK public services, the legal employers are state agencies, including the civil service, NHS trusts, local authorities and other public bodies such as the British Broadcasting Corporation (BBC). Employees are public servants working in these agencies or other public bodies under contracts of employment. These contracts are rooted in common law, supported by the same employment protection legislation as for private-sector workers. It is senior managers who represent public employers in negotiating, consulting and communicating with their staff or their representatives in public-service organizations. Public employees, in turn, are normally represented in their dealings with employers and senior managers by recognized unions, since trade union density is generally higher in the public sector than in the private sector (Millward, Bryson and Forth 2000, p. 96). Given this and the fact that the public sector has generally enjoyed the support of government for collective bargaining over a long period of time, various forms of employee voice have historically been much stronger in the public sector than in the private sector.

Employee voice is the means by which employers are informed of staff views, expectations and demands. Voice is obtained through systems of staff participation. Staff participation in public services can be analysed in terms of 'indirect staff participation' and 'direct staff participation'. Indirect staff participation is defined as those power-based arrangements either across organizations or within them that enable public employee representatives to take part in policy or managerial decision making processes affecting employees' daily working lives, such as on pay, terms, conditions, benefits and procedures of employment including grievances and disciplinary matters. The processes of indirect participation include collective bargaining and consultation. Direct staff participation, in contrast, consists of any management-driven initiative aimed at involving individual public employees or workgroups in the workplace. These can cover operational issues and are targeted at gaining the individual and personal contribution of public employees to organizational change, improving performance and public management reform (Farnham, et al. 2005a).

One of the main methods of direct staff participation used in the UK public sector is 'employee involvement' (EI). This is a 'low level' form of direct participation and stems from the needs for public organizations to improve performance and satisfy the needs of increasingly discerning public service 'customers'. EI is normally classified into two-way upward and downward communication practices and one-way downward communication practices. Two-way upward and downward communication encourages cooperation between managers and employees and legitimizes change. The techniques used may include employee attitude surveys, staff meetings, staff-management seminars, problem-solving groups and suggestion schemes. Downward communication is where managers provide either written or verbal information to employees (individually or collectively) to inform or 'educate' them on what is happening in their organizations. Examples include team briefings, bulletins, intranets, employee handbooks, letters to employees and notice boards (Farnham et al. 2005a).

The research reported in this chapter focuses on employee involvement in three major public services in the UK – the civil service, the NHS and local government. It seeks to answer three questions. First, what types of employee voice exist in the public services and how do these compare with private-sector practice? Second, how effective have these practices been in promoting employee voice within the public services? And third, what has been the effect of these policies in assisting public service reform agendas? We begin by placing recent developments in a historical context.

THE HISTORICAL CONTEXT OF EMPLOYEE INVOLVEMENT

The traditional approach to employee participation in the UK has been through voluntary agreements between employers and trades unions, rather than through statutory regulation as in most of Europe (Clegg 1976). From the period following the First World War, most UK public services adopted a system of joint national councils (JNCs), known as 'Whitley Councils' after the report of a committee in 1916, chaired by J.H. Whitley, Deputy Speaker of the House of Commons (Farnham 1979). The committee recommended that these joint bodies should meet frequently to enable disputes over wages, conditions of employment, efficiency and methods of settling differences between the parties to be resolved. It also considered that working people should have greater opportunity for participating in the discussion and adjustment of all those aspects of their employment conditions of most concern to them. While the original intention was that such JNCs should become the basis for private-sector industrial relations, it was actually in the civil service and local government that such arrangements became well established. As new public-sector organizations were created, the JNC became the model for these too.

This system of joint 'cooperation' between employers and trades unions in the public services remained in place for the whole of the post-Second World War period until the end of the 1970s. What challenged public-service 'Whitleyism' during the next two decades was the New Public Management that was introduced into the sector by successive Conservative administrations from 1979 till 1997. Under these administrations, the public utilities were privatized, some public services were broken up into agencies, trade union reform legislation was passed, the freedom to take lawful industrial action was narrowed and managers in the public services gained a new confidence in their 'right to manage'. Traditional, paternalist approaches to personnel management were superseded by new, performance-driven styles of people management that drew upon private-sector people management practices. These tended to weaken trade union power and influence, challenge accepted Whitley practices and strengthen individualism in the workplace (Farnham and Horton 1996). As a government White Paper put it (Employment Department 1992, p. 1): 'There is new recognition of the role and importance of the individual employee. Traditional patterns of industrial relations, based on collective bargaining and collective agreements seem increasingly inappropriate and are in decline'. It went on to state that there was 'a growing trend to individually negotiated packages which reflect the individual's personal skills, experience, efforts and performance'.

New patterns of employer-initiated information and communication practices began to appear in the private sector in the 1970s and 1980s. In large part, they were a response to the need for management to gain the commitment of their staff, raise productivity and quality of work and overcome resistance to change in an increasingly uncertain and volatile market environment. In particular they were influenced by new management practices that accompanied the influx of American and Japanese companies into the UK. They were also in response to weakened trade unions. Companies increasingly learned that committed and motivated staff are more productive and loyal than uncommitted ones, as well as being a major source of knowledge, skills and competencies. These approaches were central to both 'hard' and 'soft' models of Human Resources Management (HRM) (Storey 1989) and were introduced by managers in the belief that these were the key to gaining employee commitment. These forms of EI were mainly shop floor or office-based, direct rather than indirect and were task- and function-focused rather than at strategic levels. The aim was to involve workers in discussing work methods and organization in order to improve quality and productivity, rather than to give workers a voice in determining company policy, their work conditions or improving the quality of working life. These new concepts of EI, such as quality circles, were largely borrowed from abroad, where such practices had been seen as an integral part of the international success of Japanese companies in the 1970s (Juran 1989). Such EI practices were strongly promoted by the Confederation of British Industry after 1979 and found their way into the public sector during the 1980s, as the Conservative government attempted to mimic private-sector practices.

NEW LABOUR, NEW POLICY?

The election of a Labour Government in 1997 heralded a policy shift on employee voice. Labour was elected on a manifesto that included a pledge to improve the relationship between employers and employees, although it re-emphasized the Conservative Government's commitment to labour market flexibility and resisted the trades unions' demands to repeal or amend the legislation covering unions and industrial conflict, passed in the 1980s. There was, however, a commitment to end the 'opt out' from the Social Protocol of the Maastricht Treaty, which made it less easy for British employers to block EU initiatives on employment regulation. This commitment to restoring some balance to the relationship between capital and labour was manifested in the 'Fairness at Work White Paper' (DTI 1998), which outlined a number of new employment rights for both individuals and trades unions. In the foreword to the White Paper, the Prime Minister argued for the replacement of the 'notion of conflict between employers and employees with the promotion of partnership' (DTI 1998). The Departments for Trade and Industry and for Education and Employment also launched a joint guide to partnership at work (DTI/DfEE Undated). In the public sector, Labour's overall policy of reform was set out in the 1999 White Paper, 'Modernising Government' (Cabinet Office 1999). This laid down three main objectives: to ensure that policymaking was more integrated and strategic; to ensure public service users, not providers, were the focus by matching services more closely to people's lives; and to deliver public services that were high quality and efficient. Most importantly, the 1999 White Paper established a new approach to industrial relations in the public services. It stated that the Government would 'continue to work closely with the public sector trade unions to achieve our shared goals of committed, fair, efficient and effective public services' (Cabinet Office 1999, p. 2).

As Tailby and Winchester (2005) indicate, the concept of partnership working endorsed by the Labour Government had its origins in a number of developments. First, the decline of trade union power led the peak body for the trades unions, the Trades Union Congress (TUC), to seek out more productive relationships with employers as a means to protecting and improving union presence in the workplace. The TUC began campaigning for partnership principles from the early 1990s. Second, growing interest in the European social model – with its concept of 'social partners' – became increasingly attractive to union leaders and the Labour Party. In particular the use of works councils in many European countries, with their emphasis upon joint decision making, appealed as a contrast to the unremitting confrontational approach to employment relations of the British Conservative governments. Third, the concept developed out of the 'mutual gains enterprise' paradigm emerging from the USA (Kochan and Osterman 1994) and the 'high performance workplace' literature (Godard 2004). Employee involvement was seen as a key to improved productivity and commitment at work. Kochan and Osterman (1994, p. 145) argued that the active partnership of union representatives could be 'a powerful force for sustaining commitment to workplace innovations'.

HOW PREVALENT IS EMPLOYEE INVOLVEMENT?

Our first question was how prevalent are employee involvement practices within UK public services and our second was how successful are these in providing employee voice? In addition to drawing upon relevant secondary literature sources, in order to answer these two questions, we have used two data sets in this study: the Workplace Employee Relations Survey (WERS 1998) and our own postal survey of major public-service employers carried out in summer 2003. A series of WERS has been conducted in the UK with Central Government support at irregular intervals since 1980, and they provide data on various forms of employee voice in the workplace. These data include representation through recognized trade unions, consultative committees with union elected representatives, consultative committees with representatives not chosen by union members, regular management/staff meetings, briefing groups, problem-solving groups and non-union employee representatives (Millward et al. 2000). Two main dimensions of employee voice identified in WERS are indirect participation (through representative or collective voice) and direct participation (through individual voice). The WERS data also allow us to analyse separate employer and employee responses.

The WERS data used in this chapter are unpublished figures from the 1998 survey. The questions to employees do not mirror exactly those to employers, but certain questions can be used to measure employee views on consultation, communication and EI. We examine both the 1998 WERS employer and employee data in terms of public- and private-sector results and compare these data with our own, smaller survey of public-sector employers in the three main public services – the civil service, NHS and local government. A new WERS was conducted in 2004, but only the basic first findings were available at the time of writing this chapter in late 2005.

One problem with WERS is that, although one can compare public services and private sectors at aggregate level, the sample sizes are not large enough to make informed and reliable comparisons between different public services. For this reason we decided to expand on the WERS results by developing our own survey of just public-service employers. This second data set was collected through a postal survey of human resources managers in the civil service, NHS and local government. We sent the survey questionnaire during summer 2003 to a range of civil service departments and agencies, NHS trusts and local authorities of various types (county councils, unitary councils, district councils, etc.). In the main, we asked questions based on the WERS questionnaire so that some comparisons could be made, but we also added a number of our own questions.

Although the WERS was our starting point, there were differences in our methodology, and this needs to be taken account in discussing our findings. Our survey was a postal survey, whilst WERS was conducted through interviews in the workplace. The latter clearly reduced the percentage of non-respondents and assisted in clarifying the meaning of questions to get full and accurate responses. We also chose to survey individual organizations (e.g. government departments and agencies, NHS trusts and local authorities), rather than workplaces.

Due to time constraints we designed our sampling frame to achieve a sample of around a hundred respondent organizations (i.e. around 10 per cent of the total number of public service organizations). Names and addresses of respondents were taken from relevant directories for the services concerned. Selections were made on the basis of systematic sampling with a randomized start point. Sixty-five organizations replied. As in the WERS, we used a weighting variable (*Est_wt*) to equalize the response rate between the three public services surveyed to the aggregate response rate of 5.7 per cent. This was necessary to ensure that the respondents' profile resembled that of the population of interest.

Our research findings are selective and cover three main areas of employee voice and EI. These are: consultative committees (including partnership arrangements); two-way up and down communication (problem-solving groups and employee attitude groups); and one-way downward communication (team briefings and other methods of one-way communication). These are reported and analysed below.

CONSULTATIVE COMMITTEES

The WERS 1998 data indicated that 34 per cent of public-sector workplaces had committees of managers and employees primarily concerned with consultation, rather than negotiation. This compares with around 20 per cent of private-sector workplaces. Our survey found that over 98 per cent of public service organizations had such committees with the civil service and NHS registering 100 per cent (see Table 12.1). This is a very strong contrast to WERS and may be explained partly by the fact that our survey was of organizations, not of workplaces. Responses to our question on workplace committees confirmed a picture more like the WERS data, but still showed a greater presence of such committees (64 per cent).

When asked what issues such consultative committees discussed, WERS found that the most common issues in the public sector were future plans/trends, working practices and health and safety. In the private sector the most common issues were similar. In our survey we found that managing health and safety was the most important issue, followed by managing change, welfare and facilities, employment, future plans/trends and working practices. Few organizations discussed financial matters at these meetings. Government regulations were discussed much more in local government and the NHS than in central government, probably because these services are more subject to government audits on quality and external monitoring of service levels. Training and development was less likely to be an issue for consultation in local government, than in the NHS and central government.

Table 12.1 Consultative committees at organizational level and workplace level

	Organizational Level		Workplace Level	
Central Government	9/9	100.0%	8/9	88.9%
Local Government	28/29	96.6%	20/29	69.0%
NHS	31/31	100.0%	16/29	55.2%
Overall	68/69	98.6%	44/69	63.8%

Source: Greenwich Survey 2003.

We asked which categories of employees these consultative committees covered. WERS found that 51 per cent of public-sector workplaces covered all staff, compared to 58 per cent in the private sector. Our survey found that 40 per cent of central government organizations covered all staff, 50 per cent of NHS and 63 per cent of local government. According to WERS, in the public sector membership of such committees was much more likely to include managers, professionals, clerical and secretarial staffs than in the private, reflecting both the different occupational composition of the public sector (largely non-manual workers) and the higher likelihood that such staff are unionized.

We asked respondents to list all such committees present in their organization. There were a range of titles for such committees – e.g. local Whitley council, joint consultative committee, audit committee, health and safety committee, quality environmental committee, joint safety committee and partnership forum.

We also asked how employee representatives were appointed to these consultative committees. WERS indicated that in the public-sector representatives were much more likely to be appointed by unions than in the private. It also indicated that 34 per cent of public-sector workplaces had representatives elected by employees. Our survey indicated a lower figure

(25 per cent of organizations), but 84 per cent of respondents said that their employee representatives were 'chosen by unions/staff associations', compared to just 25 per cent in WERS (see Table 12.2). Unions, of course, may choose their representatives through elections.

We also asked if any employee representatives on these committees were also union representatives. Overall 78 per cent of public-sector workplaces answered positively to this question in WERS, compared to only 26 per cent of private-sector workplaces. Our survey gave a higher figure than WERS at 93.2 per cent of public service organizations. We also asked a question not included in WERS – whether representatives from contractors' staff are included in any of these consultative committees. Overall, some 11 per cent answered positively to this question. The inclusion of contractors' staff in such committees was most likely in central government (19 per cent), compared to 14 per cent in the NHS and 4 per cent in local government.

A key question was whether management saw such committees as useful. We asked how influential managers thought the committees were on management decision making. Our respondents were more cautious in their views, than those sampled in WERS. WERS showed that public-sector managers were much more likely to see these committees as 'very influential' than private-sector managers (51 per cent compared to 35 per cent). As Table 12.3 shows, in our survey only 19 per cent of respondents thought that their committees were 'very influential'. Some 65 per cent thought their committees were 'fairly influential', compared to 37 per cent in WERS. However, no local authorities thought that their committees were 'very influential' and 30 per cent thought they were 'not very influential'.

We also asked whether trade unions participated in decision making in respondents' organizations. Some 67 per cent of respondents answered positively. The highest proportion of positive answers was in central government (75 per cent) and the lowest in local government (57 per cent). We went on to ask whether there are trade union representatives on the major decision making bodies at three levels – organization, workplace and department/section. Table 12.4 below shows the results. At organization level the answer was 100 per cent, but the figures were much lower at workplace and departmental/section level.

Given the current vogue for 'partnership' forums we also asked whether organizations had a formal 'partnership agreement' with employees (although we did not define the concept). Overall, 41 per cent answered positively. Such arrangements were most common in the NHS (64 per cent), followed by central government (35 per cent) and lastly local government (17 per cent).

Table 12.2 Method of appointing employee representatives

	Elected by employees	Appointed by management	Chosen by union/ staff association	Volunteered	All involved/ invited	Other	Total
Central Government	3	3	7	2	-	-	9
Central Government %	30%	35%	74%	25%	-	-	100%
Local Government	8	5	22	2	-	1	28
Local Government %	27%	17%	77%	7%	0%	3%	97%
NHS	7	9	29	4	-	-	31
NHS %	22%	29%	93%	14%	0%	-	100%
Overall	17	17	58	9	-	1	69
Overall %	25%	24%	84%	12%	0%	1%	99%

Note: Overall figures may not equal simple column totals due to rounding

Source: Greenwich Survey 2003

Table 12.3 How influential is this committee over management decisions?

	Very	Fairly	Not very	Not at all	Totals
Central Government	2	6	2	0	9
Central Government %	20%	60%	20%	0%	100%
Local Government	0	19	9	0	29
Local Government %	0%	69%	31%	0%	100%
NHS	11	20	0	0	31
NHS %	35%	65%	0%	0%	100%
Overall	13	45	11	0	69
Overall %	19%	65%	16%	0%	100%

Source: Greenwich Survey 2003.

Table 12.4 Union participation in decision making

Level	Organization	Workplace	Department/ section	Total yes
Central Government	7	3	2	7
Central Government %	100%	47%	33%	100%
Local Government	16	6	5	16
Local Government %	100%	35%	29%	100%
NHS	27	9	11	27
NHS %	100%	33%	42%	100%
Overall	50	18	18	50
Overall %	100%	36%	37%	100%

Source: Greenwich Survey 2003.

TWO-WAY UP AND DOWN COMMUNICATION

A significant development in the 1980s and 1990s was the use of task-based EI practices to improve working methods and quality of service. The WERS survey found that such groups were more likely to be found in the public sector than the private (43 per cent compared to 30 per cent). In our survey we asked whether organizations had any problem-solving groups that discussed specific problems or aspects of work performance or quality (e.g. quality circles, problem-solving groups or continuous improvement groups). We found that 38 per cent of public-service organizations had such groups, less than the WERS figure. They were most common in the civil service (57 per cent) and less common in the NHS and local government (36 per cent and 32 per cent respectively). In central government, respondents informed us that there were departmental Whitley councils and sub-committees; in local government working groups and subject specific groups; and in the NHS monthly performance management meetings, clinical governance committees and patients' liaison committees. We also asked whether these committees were permanent or of finite life. The WERS data indicated that such groups were less likely to be permanent in the public sector than the private sector (46 per cent compared to 62 per cent). Our results suggested even less permanency. The groups were much less likely to be permanent in local government than in central government and the NHS.

We also asked our respondents how influential they thought such problem-solving groups were. They scored more highly than the consultative committees reported above, with some 93 per cent overall of those responding regarding them as either 'very effective' or 'fairly effective' (see Table 12.5). Managers in central government seemed most enthusiastic.

Table 12.5 Effectiveness of problem solving groups

	Very	Fairly	Not very	Not at all	Totals
Central Government	3	3	1	0	7
Central Government %	40%	46%	13%	0%	100%
Local Government	3	8	2	0	13
Local Government %	23%	62%	15%	0%	100%
NHS	7	13	0	0	20
NHS %	34%	67%	0%	0%	100%
Overall	12	24	3	0	39
Overall %	31%	62%	7%	0%	100%

Source: Greenwich Survey 2003.

Some employers also actively seek the views of their workers through staff attitude surveys. We asked organizations if they conducted such surveys and found that some 92 per cent claimed to do so (see Table 12.6). WERS found that the public sector was more likely to conduct attitude surveys than the private sector (54 per cent of workplaces compared to 34 per cent). In the NHS they are now required in all NHS Trusts by the Department of Health, hence the 100 per cent score for that service. Attitude surveys appeared to be least common in local government. In terms of making the results of such surveys available to employees, in the NHS 100 per cent of employers did so, but only 86 per cent of local authority respondents did so. WERS found that around 62 per cent of public-sector workplaces made the results available to staff, but our figure is much higher at 92 per cent. This may reflect again the fact that our survey was organization-based, rather than workplace-based. Clearly there may have been a commitment to this at organization level but not at workplace level. Our survey was also undertaken five years after WERS.

Table 12.6 Employee attitude surveys

	Number	**Total respondents**	**% Yes**
Central Government	9	9	95.2%
Local Government	24	29	83.3%
NHS	31	31	100.0%
Overall	64	70	92.4%

Source: Greenwich Survey 2003.

The WERS employee questionnaire asked a number of questions concerning employee voice in discussing workplace issues. Although there was not a great deal of difference between the public and private sectors within this data, overall the public sector was slightly better than the private in involving employees in workplace issues. The two issues where organizations were least likely to discuss matters with employees were, not surprisingly, redundancy and pay. The most likely was health and safety.

WERS also asked employees questions about how good managers are at communicating with them (see Table 12.7). Again, in general there was little difference in the responses from public- and private-sector employees, but the public sector still appeared to be slightly better than the private. The one area where the private sector had a higher score was in responding to suggestions from employees.

Table 12.7 How good are managers at communicating?

Question	Sector	Very good	Good	Neither	Poor	Very poor
How good are managers at keeping everyone up to date about proposed changes?	Public	10.9%	35.7%	26.5%	18.7%	8.1%
	Private	9.8%	32.7%	26.4%	21.0%	10.1%
How good are managers at providing everyone with a chance to comment on proposed changes?	Public	7.4%	27.8%	30.3%	23.3%	11.2%
	Private	6.3%	23.7%	29.6%	25.7%	14.7%
How good are managers at responding to suggestions from employees?	Public	6.0%	26.1%	34.8%	21.8%	11.3%
	Private	6.4%	27.1%	32.2%	21.9%	12.3%

Source: WERS Survey 1998.

ONE-WAY DOWNWARD COMMUNICATION

WERS found that 95 per cent of public-sector workplaces had a system for team briefings of their workforces, compared to 79 per cent of private-sector workplaces. Table 12.8 shows the responses to this question in our survey. Our overall figure of 97 per cent compares well with WERS, but local government was lower than the civil service and NHS.

Table 12.8 Is there a system for team briefings for any section of the workforce?

	Number	**Total Respondents**	**% Yes**
Central Government	9	9	100.0
Local Government	27	29	93.1
NHS	31	31	100.0
Overall	67	69	97.1

Source: Greenwich Survey 2003.

WERS indicated that team briefings in public-sector workplaces were more likely to be targeted at group, section and team level, than in the private sector. Our research (see Table 12.9) confirmed this overall pattern. It also showed that central government tended to have more briefings at team level and fewer at organization level. Local government also concentrated briefings more at group or team level whereas the NHS suggested the opposite pattern – the whole organization level was most important.

We also asked the proportion of time given to employees to ask questions or to offer their views at these meetings. WERS indicated that 63 per cent of the respondents allowed a quarter or more of the meeting time for employees' input, compared to 53 per cent in the private sector. Our data suggest this might be rather optimistic. We found that around 37 per cent of our sample allocated up to 10 per cent of the time, a further 37 per cent allocated 10-24 per cent of the time and only 26 per cent allocated a quarter of the meeting time to employees. The poorest response came from local government, where only 21 per cent gave a quarter of the time to workers.

Table 12.9 Who is the team briefing for?

	Group/team	Department	Whole workplace	Whole organization	Other group	Total respondents
Central Government	8	7	7	6	0	9
Central Government %	89%	78%	78%	67%	0%	-
Local Government	21	15	6	12	5	29
Local Government %	72%	52%	21%	41%	17%	-
NHS	13	11	4	24	0	31
NHS %	42%	35%	13%	77%	0%	-
Overall	43	33	17	42	5	69
Overall %	62%	48%	25%	61%	7%	-

Note: Our survey allowed respondents to answer more than one category, whereas WERS gave only one choice.

Source: Greenwich Survey 2003

226

Other popular methods of one-way downward employee communication included chain/cascade information systems, regular meetings in the workplace, newsletters, internet bulletins, etc. (see Table 12.10). We asked our respondents to identify which of these they used. The most common method was chain/cascade and internet bulletins. 'Other' methods that did not feature greatly included leaflets, focus groups, posters, briefings and one-to-one meetings between manager and staff member. When we asked organizations to what extent they felt these methods were effective, 66 per cent opted for 'fairly effective'. Central government was most enthusiastic with 40 per cent viewing these methods as 'very effective'. Some 28 per cent of local government respondents thought these methods were 'not very effective'.

There are a number of key areas where employees need information. We asked organizations to identify whether they provided information on a number of issues. This question registered some very high percentages. In general, central government seemed the best at providing key information to workers and local government the least. This information included the financial positions of departments (or organizations), performance against standards, staffing plans and changes in organizational strategy or structure.

We also analysed the WERS employee data on downward communication methods. There were four questions in the employee survey (see Table 12.11 below) which related to this issue. Here the views of public-sector workers were not that different to those in the private sector in terms of their evaluation of various communication methods. The main finding was that workplace newsletters and magazines appeared to be more common in the public than the private sector. In neither sector was e-mail used extensively.

DISCUSSION

As the data discussed above have demonstrated, employee voice practices appear to be more strongly entrenched in the UK public services than in the private sector. Moreover, despite the 18 years of Conservative government when policy shifted away from collective, indirect participative structures to more individualistic, direct, task-focused methods of employee voice, collective voice mechanisms remain strong in UK public services. This largely reflects the continuing resilience of trade union organization within the public sector generally compared to the private sector.

Based on the evidence provided here, the answer to our first research question about the types of employee voice found, is that in terms of indirect participation a range of consultative committees is now extant in UK public

Table 12.10 Methods of employee communication

	Regular meetings	Chain/cascade	Internet bulletin	Regular Newsletters	Other
Central Government	4	9	8	7	3
Central Government %	48%	95%	86%	71%	29%
Local Government	9	23	26	24	6
Local Government %	30%	80%	90%	83%	20%
NHS	9	29	29	29	4
NHS %	29%	93%	93%	93%	14%
Overall	22	61	63	60	13
Overall %	32%	88%	91%	86%	19%

Source: Greenwich Survey 2003

Table 12.11 Employee views on downward communication methods

Question	Sector	Very helpful	Helpful	Not very helpful	Not helpful at all	Not used here
How helpful do you find notice boards in keeping up-to-date about this workplace?	Public	13.5%	49.3%	24.5%	6.7%	5.9%
	Private	15.4%	50.4%	19.8%	5.1%	9.3%
How helpful do you find e-mail in keeping up-to-date about this workplace?	Public	7.9%	19.8%	10.5%	8.2%	53.3%
	Private	10.5%	18.4%	8.1%	5.7%	57.3%
How helpful do you find workplace newsletter or magazine in keeping up-to-date about this workplace?	Public	10.8%	49.3%	19.4%	5.5%	14.9%
	Private	9.8%	37.1%	16.3%	4.8%	32.0%
How helpful do you find meetings with managers in keeping up-to-date about this workplace?	Public	15.5%	47.0%	18.8%	8.0%	10.5%
	Private	15.0%	42.4%	17.4%	7.3%	17.7%

Source: WERS Survey 1998.

services. Within them, a large proportion of staff representatives are chosen by union/staff associations and a high proportion of these are also union representatives. Our survey showed that some two-thirds of these committees were 'fairly' influential bodies. However, in terms of direct participation, problem-solving groups were more commonly identified in WERS than in our study, but were deemed to be more influential than consultative committees, especially in central government. Also, like in WERS, our survey demonstrated high levels of team briefings in public services, as well as other one-way downward communication channels.

The answer to our second research question, concerning the success of these indirect and direct methods of employee voice, is that they have been generally positive (see also Farnham, Horton and White 2005b) although it is noteworthy that the WERS data indicate a differential in the perceptions of public service managers and workers about the success of such practices.

This links with the third research question on the extent that such employee voice practices have assisted the process of public-sector reform, given that much was expected from the manifesto commitments of the Labour Party in 1997. While the relationship between government and trades unions has continued to be precarious, as manifested by several high profile public-sector industrial disputes in the public services since 1997, both sides would acknowledge a step of change in the overall approach to employee involvement and consultation. This has been most evident in the NHS, where a completely new pay and grading system has been implemented using 'partnership' principles, and also in the civil service where new pay and management systems have been introduced through partnership too. In addition, a partnership approach was used in introducing a workload agreement for school teachers, using classroom teaching assistants to relieve teachers of some duties (DfES 2003). There have also been moves to improve employee involvement and participation in other parts of the public sector.

In March 2000, the Minister for the Civil Service signed a partnership agreement with the three civil service unions (Farnham, Horton and White 2003). The agreement set out how the parties would work together to achieve 'a positive and effective relationship between departments and agencies and their trade union representatives'. All those who signed the agreement, committed themselves to encourage 'partnership' and to work jointly to assist organizations achieve it. According to both civil service managers and trade union officers interviewed for this research, there is now better consultation on every aspect of policy and staff views are taken into account. A major example of this new relationship was the consultation with staff over the new Senior Civil Service (SCS) competency framework and pay and performance systems introduced in 2001. In this case every member of the SCS was consulted via the internet and invited to comment on the proposals (Horton 2005). In addition 1 000 of the 3 000 staff were consulted directly through focus groups and working parties.

The Cabinet Office works closely with the trade unions to keep reform continually under review and new policies on diversity, flexible working and equal pay have been agreed. At least seven departments have entered into such partnership agreements with their trade unions.

In the NHS the election of Labour in 1997 saw a major reappraisal of previous attempts to decentralize pay bargaining and employee involvement and consultation methods. In 1999 the Health Secretary announced a root and branch reform of the existing NHS pay and grading system – the so-called 'Agenda for Change' (Department of Health 1999a). This proposed new negotiating machinery which brought together a number of separate bargaining groups on to two linked pay spines; a new job-evaluated pay and grading structure; and harmonization of existing conditions of service. Government also announced a new commitment to employee involvement in its 'NHS Plan' document (Department of Health 2000a). This was followed by a separate 'HR in the NHS Plan' (Department of Health 2002) which aimed to make the NHS a 'model employer'. A study of 15 NHS Trusts in 1998 (Industrial Relations Services 1998) found that partnership was already in place in many Trusts. The main reasons cited for the introduction of partnership arrangements was recognition that increasing employee involvement and commitment was key to organizational change, improved performance and better staff relations. In 1998 the Health Secretary established a taskforce to see how frontline staff could be more involved in improving services. A report, published in 1999 (Department of Health 1999b), argued that frontline staff were best placed to make decisions about patient care and that staff involvement/employee voice were already working well in some areas. The report also said that partnership working was the only way to break away from the destructive 'win-lose' industrial relations, that had characterized the NHS in the past. The Taskforce came up with a list of recommendations for action and in 2000 Government announced that the Social Partnership Forum, composed of employers, unions and the NHS Executive, had developed an action plan for implementing partnership working (Department of Health 2000b).

Unpublished research by the local government employers' body on employee involvement and consultation identified a number of drivers encouraging such practices as partnership. These drivers were both internal and external but were entirely domestic in nature, not driven by European policy. In general, though, as our research indicates, moves towards greater employee voice mechanisms are less evident in local government, where central government has much less direct influence upon policies (each council being an autonomous employer) (Farnham et al. 2003).

As can be seen from the examples above, at institutional level there is a new commitment to better public service industrial relations and recognition that public service reform can only be achieved with the cooperation of staff and their trade unions. While there is no doubt that the partnership agreements being promoted throughout the public services have some linkage to the European concept of social partnership, the drivers for change in the UK public services are largely domestic. The recent EU Directive on information and consultation has been passed into UK law, but it will have limited effect on the public services, many of which are excluded from the law by the definition of an 'undertaking'.

Labour has been twice re-elected since 1997 on manifestos promising major investments in public services and substantial increases in public spending on health, education and public order and policing. While real action to improve public services did not begin until Labour's second term in 2002, there has been a clear view that the strength of public-sector trade unionism and the trust which employees have in their unions means that industrial relations' conflict is seen as a costly diversion from the task of reform. This does not mean that all public employers have embraced the new partnership style approach, and many line managers remain unconvinced of its value. On the employee side, while union national officers may see the value in improved relations with employers, many rank and file trade union members remain sceptical of the value and permanency of such agreements (Danford, Richardson, Stewart, Tailby and Upchurch 2004). The Government itself remains committed in its rhetoric to partnership and this was reinforced prior to the 2005 general election with the establishment of a Public Service Forum in September 2003. This provides a mechanism for Government to meet with the public-sector trade unions to discuss major employee relations issues which could escalate into industrial action, for example over reform of public service pensions. Following meetings of the Forum during 2005, agreement was reached between the parties on the principles of public service pension reform (DTI 2005). However, whether this consensus between government and public service unions continues when the details have to be agreed remains to be seen, especially after publication of the Turner report (Pensions Commission 2005) which recommends raising the state pension age in the UK.

REFERENCES

Cabinet Office (1999), *Modernising Government*, Cm 4310, London: Stationery Office.

Clegg, H.A. (1976), *The System of Industrial Relations in Great Britain*, Oxford: Blackwell, third edition.

Danford A., M. Richardson, P. Stewart, S. Tailby and M. Upchurch (2004), 'High performance work systems and workplace partnership', *New Technology, Work and Employment*, **19** (1), 14-29.

DfES (Department for Education and Skills) (2003), *Agreement on contractual and legal changes for school staff means radical new working conditions in schools*, DfES Press Release, 17 June.

Department of Health (1999a), *Agenda for Change: Modernising the NHS Pay System*, London: DoH.

Department of Health (1999b), *Report of the NHS Taskforce on Staff Involvement*, London: DoH.

Department of Health (2000a), *The NHS Plan*, London: DoH.

Department of Health (2000b), *Partnership in Action: The Action Plan to implement the Recommendations of the NHS Taskforce on Staff Involvement*, London: DoH/NHS Executive.

Department of Health (2002), *HR in the NHS Plan, Executive Summary: More Staff Working Differently*, London: DoH.

Department of Trade/Department of Education and Employment (Undated), *Partnerships with People: A Practical Guide*, London: DTI/DfEE.

DTI (Department of Trade and Industry) (1998), 'Fairness at Work', DTI White paper, Cm3968, London: Stationery Offic.e

DTI (Department of Trade and Industry) (2005), *Agreement reached on public sector pensions*, DTI Press Release, 18 October.

Employment Department (1992), *People, Jobs and Opportunity*, London: Stationery Office.

Farnham, D. (1979), 'Sixty years of Whitleyism', *Whitley Bulletin: Journal of the Civil Service National Whitley Council (Staff Side)*, **59** (1), 9.

Farnham, D., A. Hondeghem and S. Horton (2005a), *Staff Participation and Public Management Reform: Some International Comparisons*, Basingstoke: Palgrave Macmillan.

Farnham, D. and S. Horton (1996), *Managing People in the New Public Services*, London: Macmillan.

Farnham, D., S. Horton and G. White (2003), 'Organizational change and staff participation and involvement in Britain's public services', *International Journal of Public Sector Management*, **16** (6), 434-445.

Farnham, D., S. Horton and G. White (2005b), 'New directions in staff consultation and communication in the British civil service and prison service', *Review of Public Personnel Administration*, **25** (1), 69-81.

Godard, J. (2004), 'A critical assessment of the high-performance paradigm', *British Journal of Industrial Relations*, **42** (2), 349-378.

Horton, S. (2005), 'Participation and Involvement of Senior Staff in the Reform of the British Civil Service', *Review of Public Personnel Administration*, **25**, 56-68.

Industrial Relations Services (1998), 'All Together Now: Partnership in the NHS', Health Service Report, Spring, 2-12.

Juran, J. (1989), *Juran on Leadership for Quality*, New York: Free Press.

Kochan, T. and P. Osterman (1994), *The Mutual Gains Enterprise*, Boston: Harvard Business School Press.

Millward, N., A. Bryson and J. Forth (2000), *All Change at Work? British employment relations 1980-1998, as portrayed by the Workplace Industrial Relations Survey series*, London: Routledge.

Pensions Commission (2005), *Pensions: challenges and choices – final report*, London: Stationery Office.

Storey, J. (ed.) (1989), *New Perspectives on Human Resource Management*, London: Routledge.

Tailby, S. and D. Winchester (2005), 'Management and Trade Unions: Partnership at Work?', in S. Bach, Managing Human Resources, Oxford: Blackwell, fourth edition.

13. Concluding Analysis

Peter Leisink, Bram Steijn and Ulke Veersma

INTRODUCTION

The central question driving this book was formulated as: 'how does the process of European integration impact on industrial relations at the various levels, and who are the main actors in this process?' Following the answers provided by the individual chapters, we now aim to examine this question by putting it into the broader picture of an enlarged Europe that is experiencing severe pressure from globalization. We will have a closer look at the various national systems that exist under the umbrella of Europe, and the European Social Model that is part of it. We will first attempt to formulate an answer to the central question by examining three of the possible expectations with regard to Europeanization and national industrial relations, and then evaluate these by factoring in the actors involved. Indeed, as Knill and Lehmkuhl (2002) note, the diversity of the localized responses to the Europeanization process can only be understood by taking account of the active involvement of national actors with their respective interests and the resources they can mobilize.

Following an analysis of the impact of Europeanization on national industrial relations practices, we will turn specifically to public-sector industrial relations and the way in which these are changing under the sway of the public management reform ideas currently seen in Europe. Finally, the chapter will shed some light on the future of European industrial relations and the possible development of a social Europe involving an even broader spectrum of national and supranational actors than before the May 2004 expansion.

THE IMPACT OF THE PROCESS OF EUROPEAN INTEGRATION ON NATIONAL INDUSTRIAL RELATIONS

Among politicians and the general public, various expectations of the impact of the process of European integration can be found, that have their counterparts in the academic literature. Regarding the main issue of the European Social Model, that is the social policy and employment standards coupled with the actual involvement of industrial relations actors in determining these standards through collective bargaining and social dialogue, we distinguish three different expectations. First, the process of European integration will lead to convergence at the lowest common denominator – that is to common minimum standards such as those currently prevailing in the new EU Member States in Central and Eastern Europe (CEE). Second, the process of European integration sees a gradual upward harmonization towards the level of social standards currently prevailing in the EU-15 Member States. The third expectation is of a midway outcome, with a downgrading of standards in the EU-15 Member States and an upgrading of living and working conditions in the CEE Member States.

It can readily be seen that the first two hypotheses are mutual opposites. The first hypothesis suggests degraded social standards, and is in line with what the critics of the neo-liberal version of globalization predict to be the consequences of unregulated global competition, which they see European integration as representing (cf. Leisink 1999). The second version suggests a general upward harmonization of social standards. This is an expectation that fits with the general assumptions of a linear modernization process in which less developed countries will eventually catch up with the more advanced nations. The assumptions behind this view have recently been criticized extensively by Dimitrova (2004). The third hypothesis predicts a differentiated impact, with the EU-15 Member States facing a downgrading and the CEE Member States experiencing an upgrading of social standards. This can be seen as a sort of convergence to the middle or averaging out.

We should note that each of these hypotheses glosses over the large differences in socioeconomic aspects among the various EU-15 Member States as well as among the CEE Member States. For instance, one of the new Member States, Slovenia, in economic terms outperforms Portugal and Greece, two of the old Member States, in terms of Gross Domestic Product (GDP) per capita at the time of accession, whereas those CEE Member States at the bottom of the EU-25 list (Poland, Estonia, Lithuania and Latvia) have GDPs per capita between 30 and 40 per cent of the EU-25 average. One should not overlook the fact that the two new Member States – Slovenia and Hungary – included in this study represent the best performers (along with the Czech Republic) among the CEE Countries that acceded in May 2004. With this proviso in mind, how do we evaluate the expectations on the impact of the European integration process based on the analyses and information presented by the contributors to this book?

The expectation that the European integration process will have a negative impact is most clearly present in the chapter on Spain by Köhler and Gonzalez Begega. The anticipated reduction in Spain's share of the EU's cohesion funding is a direct result of EU enlargement. Another expected negative impact of European integration is of foreign multinational corporations (MNCs) relocating production from Spain to CEE Member States. However, overall, Köhler and Gonzalez Begega do not predict a downward impact on the old EU Member States from the enlargement process. As they point out, German MNCs will probably lead the investment activities in the CEE Member States and, as a result, the German economy is likely to benefit from further economic integration. Thus, according to Köhler and Gonzalez Begega, the process of European integration will have a differentiated impact on the old Member States, with some like Germany gaining, and others like Spain losing out. Competition with new Member States makes those EU-15 countries with a relatively low level of prosperity and lower wages probably more aware of their relative position – they now have to compete with new Member States profiting from the common market and offering even lower wage levels. In addition, the chapters by Neumann and by Stanojevic and Vehovar also demonstrate that the process of European integration has a differentiated impact among the new CEE States. While the transposition of the *acquis communautaire* has seen a formal and a practical deterioration in the protection of workers in Hungary when undertakings are transferred to new owners and in terms of working hours, the preparation for accession has not affected the prevailing social standards in Slovenia.

Slovenia went through a different development process, not only starting from a higher level of economic prosperity but also taking a different approach to transforming the economy. After Yugoslavia as a state collapsed, a gradual transformation process was adopted instead of the shock therapy approach taken in many other CEE economies. The trade unions that were here, as elsewhere, initially split between backing the 'old' and the 'new' elites very rapidly recaptured their position and articulated effectively the voice of the workers, as is shown by Stanojevic and Vehovar. Slovenia is, in this respect, an interesting example for other countries as the inclusive nature of the industrial relations system that subsequently developed has more in common with a balanced, co-ordinated market economy than with the neo-liberal alternative.

This differentiated effect of the process of European integration can be explained, as Knill and Lehmkuhl (2002) have suggested, by the roles of the specific industrial relations actors and the power they have. In Hungary, the unions are weak or at best fragmented, and collective bargaining institutions are lacking at the sectoral level. At the same time, neo-liberal governments and employers, particularly those in small and medium-sized enterprises, have not been interested in involving the unions. By contrast, in Slovenia, the unions have been able to preserve their strong position with collective bargaining institutions existing on several levels, while the centre-left governments which remained in power throughout the 1990s assisted by creating institutions for social dialogue. The comparison between old new Member States, like Spain, and CEE Member States, made by Köhler and Gonzalez Begaga, is interesting because it shows how the situation in a country may change with further European integration. Both the old and the new groups of new Member States could be characterized by a low level of institutionalized industrial relations systems. Although Spain and other southern European countries share the characteristics of less favourable employment conditions and a relative high level of unemployment, their position has changed profoundly since they joined the European Union. Looking to the future we can expect differences to appear between the new CEE Member States, as occurred with the old new Member States. Variations may be expected as the result of differences in the development of institutions, the development and strategies of trade unions and employers' organizations, and the stability of political regimes, and also as a result of the actions of MNCs and other economic actors.

The differential impact of the process of European integration, and of the actions taken by national actors from the individual Member States, can be seen as more complex than the one suggested by the third expectation formulated above. There is no general pattern of increased standards in CEE Member States and a downgrading of standards in the old Member States. As has been indicated above, there are instances where standards that provided protection to workers, such as those in Hungary that originated in the former state socialist era, in CEE states are being downgraded. There are also instances of upgrading social standards in old Member States.

The Directive on Information and Consultation, and the emergence of social partnerships in the UK at the company level may be viewed as examples of upgrading social standards in the old EU Member States. Stuart and Martinez Lucio discuss the emergence of such partnership-based practices in the late 1990s, and point out that these arose in anticipation of European directives and the values these represent. Although the Directive on Information and Consultation leaves considerable leeway for Member States to decide which type of arrangements they prefer, it is nevertheless the value placed on information, consultation and social dialogue that has to frame domestic initiatives. In the case of the UK, these values were supported by the trade unions – although they had earlier had their reservations concerning social dialogue – and by the Labour government that decided to sign up to the Social Protocol of the Treaty of Maastricht when it came to power in 1997. The partnership-based approach that grew out of this effectively opened the door for improved employment relations in the UK, but this does imply that improvement can automatically be expected to be a clear-cut outcome of any regulation for, as Stuart and Martinez Lucio observe, effective partnerships in work situations require the involvement of strong and independent unions.

Whereas Stuart and Martinez Lucio view social partnership from the perspective of European industrial relations practices, van der Maas adopts the opposite approach: looking at the various positions that trade unions can take with regard to European integration and the EMU. The first two, extreme, expectations outlined at the beginning of this chapter are both part of the discourse found among trade unions. The first sees European integration as a part of the neo-liberal version of globalization, a view which is likely to lead to trade unions protecting their members by resisting further integration and enlargement. The second, based on the view that Europeanization results in a general upward harmonization of social standards, would be beneficial for employees in most EU Member States and therefore seen by the trade unions as a good thing to be encouraged. The chapter shows that the position adopted by an individual trade union is first of all dependent on structural factors such as the impact of European integration on the sector in which the trade union organizes employees, but also on other factors such as the views of the union leadership and its internal structure and policy.

Europeanization should therefore not only be seen as adaptation to EU regulatory objectives, but also as the framing of the beliefs of domestic actors in a form of 'bottom-up' Europeanization. The UK offers a scenario in which the distinct policies of the various trade unions can be perceived as the outcomes of strategic choices as, firstly, trade unions in the UK are fairly autonomous organizations within the decentralized, loose conglomeration of the TUC, and, secondly, because the UK is a large EU Member State in which the inhabitants are generally critical of European integration – especially insofar as the ambitions of European federation are perceived as leading to further European integration. The latter especially makes it likely that trade unions will adopt a strong view on European integration – varying between Euro-optimism and Euro-pessimism. The UK illustrates most clearly that while elements of the European Social Model, at least in theory, hold out potentials, it is domestic actors, with their values and powers, that determine whether and how these are realized.

It is interesting to note, as Köhler and Gonzalez Begega do, that the anticipated impact of the enlargement process has spurred Spanish unions to take a greater interest in the opportunities offered by the European Works Councils (EWCs) concerning transnational worker cooperation and pan-European trade union strategies. In Spain, although the new competition with CEE Countries has not enhanced support for European integration, trade unions have become more involved with the EWCs as their fears about MNCs relocating operations have been realized. Only now have the actors appeared to realize the potential of transnational cooperation among workers. The first stage of implementing the EWCs designated considerable freedom to company-level structures for information exchange and consultation, and most closely resembled the most voluntary form of Europeanization described by Knill and Lehmkuhl as framing the beliefs of domestic actors. There is, however, good reason for perceiving EWCs as changing domestic opportunity structures. Whereas national experiences dominated, as the result of bottom-up developments, in the first phase of EWC implementation (Veersma 2002), changes have since taken place towards a Europeanization within MNCs, although a 'country of origin' effect is still visible (Marginson 2004, p. 470). As Köhler and Gonzalez Begega emphasize, the lesson from the case of EWCs in Spain is that, even when most of the MNCs are based in another country, the use of information and consultation rights may help employee representatives to learn from each other at the supranational level. Cooperation within EWCs can help to create a win-win situation.

Notwithstanding the EWCs as an example of a major innovation in the social policy of Europe there is – despite all the rhetoric of European policymakers – considerable evidence of Europeanization having negative effects on industrial relations and employment conditions. The ongoing process of economic globalization, which affects the powers of the unions, coupled with the dominant EU policy of stimulating the abolishment of national forms of regulation creates conditions in which the development of social policy in Europe is likely to stagnate. The abolishment of national regulatory arrangements, which are regarded as obstacles to a free market but which were institutional resources that unions could make use of, endangers most profoundly the position of trade unions. While there are examples of trade unions successfully resisting attempts to abolish or liberalize labour market regulations, as in the case of the dockworkers whose protests forced the European Commission in March 2006 to withdraw a directive on Ports Services which would have led to more competition in transshipment thereby threatening employment of dockworkers, other conflicts such as the one over conditions for Latvian construction workers in Sweden demonstrate the underlying weaknesses in the application of European labour legislation and, as a consequence, the precarious preservation of a European social model

(Woolfson and Somers 2006). The lack of Europeanization through institutional compliance, to use the terms of Knill and Lehmkuhl, and the dominance of negative integration through the abolishment of market regulations, makes the social dimension of the European Union extremely vulnerable.

We will return later to these contradictory developments and the future of the European social dimension when looking at the future for enlargement, integration and reform. We will first turn to changes in the public sector and the positions adopted by actors in this sector.

PUBLIC SECTOR REFORM: MORE THAN 'EUROPEANIZATION BY FRAMING DOMESTIC BELIEFS'?

In the introduction, we introduced the subject of 'public sector employment' as a topic that warrants special attention in a book on changing industrial relations in Europe. In this part of the conclusions we will draw on the four country chapters in Part II and go back to the questions we formulated in the introduction about public-sector industrial relations.

A first conclusion is that public sector reform is clearly seen as of paramount importance. In all the four countries, reforms have changed public-sector employment. In Part II of this book some of these changes are clearly delineated. In the UK, the Maastricht Treaty clearly played a role with the commitment of the Labour government to the Social Protocol implying an increase in employment regulations and a greater role for unions and individual workers – although this has probably had a greater impact in the private sector than in the public sector. In terms of Knill and Lehmkuhl (2002) this appears to be an example of 'Europeanization by framing domestic beliefs', in this case those of the dominant actors within the public sector. The role of the public-sector unions within collective bargaining was clearly eroded during the previous Conservative governments in the UK, but the coming to power of Labour appears to have stopped this process. Although reforming the public sector remained a major goal for the incoming Labour government, union involvement to support this process was clearly a component as the active pursuit of 'partnership arrangements' shows. A widely shared view in the UK seems to be – at least for now – that public service reform can only be achieved with the active cooperation of staff and their trade unions. As a consequence, the position of the unions within the system of industrial relations has recently become stronger, following years of substantial weakening during the long period of Conservative rule in the 1980s and 1990s.

The chapter on Germany is less optimistic about the future role of the unions. Indeed, the chapter suggests that Germany is no longer lagging with respect to public sector reforms as several reforms are now underway which are having clear effects on public-sector industrial relations. As in the German private sector, industrial relations in the public sector are becoming decentralized and fragmented. Privatizations have clearly contributed to this process as these have not only led to a decrease in public-sector employment, but also to a shift in power with the unions in a disadvantaged position because a large number of former public-sector manual workers have been moved into the private sector. These were the workers that used to be the backbone of public-sector union power as they were the first to use the strike weapon in the old days. Interestingly, the processes of decentralization have also led to fragmentation on the employers' side, which also puts a question mark over the traditional centralized structure of German collective bargaining.

The Belgium case differs again. Public sector reform is again high on the agenda but Belgian unions seem to have had a major influence on its execution. They appear to be in a strong position and are able to influence the direction of these reforms, not so much during the process of agenda setting but more so during the implementation phase that follows. Negatively expressed, it could be stated that they have a large amount of 'nuisance power' that is shaped by two important factors: a) the Belgian structure of 'social dialogue' which is still very hierarchical and centralized, and b) the rather detailed trade union statute in Belgium which lays down procedures in public service labour relations that give unions a relatively strong position during consultations and negotiations.

These differences between Germany and Belgium in the institutional structure and relative power of the unions again illustrate the point made by Knill and Lehmkuhl (2002) that differences among countries within Europe as regards converging or diverging processes are shaped and reinforced by the role domestic actors (in this case the government and unions) play and their relative power positions. The differences in the institutional structures in Belgium and Germany lead to different outcomes, even though both governments share views on the need for Public Management Reform.

France again provides a different picture. It appears as if the introduction of public reforms is a rather slow process here – which is very much in accordance with Bordogna's (2003) characterization of French public industrial relations reforms. Mériaux, the author of the chapter on France, refers to both the juridical system and to 'sociological rules' as impediments to the introduction and diffusion of such reforms. A major conclusion in this chapter is: 'Status by itself is not an obstacle to reform; it is much more the way in which it has been used by the civil service's "social partners" that has reinforced its potential for rigidity'. In other words, institutional features, and how social partners handle these, shape the way public reforms affect public-sector industrial relations in France.

What answers do these chapters offer to the questions we posed in the introduction? Although our answers cannot be definitive, we believe the chapters do shed some light on the questions. Our first question relates to the extent to which the traditional characteristics of the public sector are still visible. In the introduction, four characteristics seen as typical were outlined: a paternalistic style of government, standardized employment practices, collectivized industrial relations and public organizations as model employers. The country chapters provide some relevant material, especially with respect to the last three characteristics. The evidence seems to suggest that in most countries employment practices have become less standardized. This clearly concurs with the conclusion in the OECD study (2005) about 'modernizing government'. However, there are substantial variations among countries, with decentralization – implying less standardization – seemingly high in the UK, on the increase in Germany, but less developed in France and Belgium – although the delegation of HRM responsibilities is seen as fairly high in Belgium in the OECD study (2005, p. 170).

In all the countries examined, public-sector industrial relations are still strongly collectivized. Indeed, the movement towards 'partnership' seems to have given this a new impetus in the UK. Also, the power position of the public-sector unions seems to be still high in all four countries, although privatization has recently weakened the union position in Germany. Nevertheless, it appears that public-sector unions overall remain in a stronger position within the system of public-sector industrial relations than their private sector counterparts.

Are public employers still model employers? It is difficult to say, but one can note that, in the UK, employers and unions are actively seeking partnerships and that the employees' voice is louder in the public than in the private sector. In Belgium, the consultation and negotiation rights of public-sector unions are well regulated; in France, the status rights of the '*corps*' remain virtually unchallenged; and although public-sector unions in Germany are on the defensive, many of their traditional rights remain. Therefore we can concur with the conclusion of Boyne, Poole and Jenkins (1999, p. 417): it appears that public-sector employment relations still differ from those in the private sector, although it may well be that these differences are becoming less pronounced over time due to the continuing process of public sector reform.

Our second question refers to what these reforms imply for the positions of employers and unions within the public industrial relations system. Again, we can observe substantial differences among countries. Institutional differences (and hence path dependency) seem to play an important role in this respect. The Belgian and France cases illustrate this nicely. The structural characteristics of the Belgian public industrial relation system (highly centralized and highly regulated) make change difficult as unions have a lot of nuisance power (Leisink and Steijn (2005) drew a similar conclusion for the Netherlands). The same appears to be true for France, although other institutional characteristics (including the very existence of the '*corps*' in the first place) also make reforms difficult here. Traditionally, Germany has also tended to lag with respect to reform; and the once powerful position of the unions has undoubtedly contributed to this. Interestingly, however, the situation appears to be changing with the slow reforms of the past having altered the balance. Unions have lost significant power since the manual workers – their former power base – have been moved out of the public sector. At the same time, the UK seems to be going in a different direction. The unions lost a lot of power in the 1980s and 1990s, but the change to a Labour government seems to have reversed this trend somewhat. The current government is actively seeking cooperation with the unions, and so the influence of the latter is probably increasing. One may ask the question, however, whether this amounts to a structural change: if a UK government again decides to change the policy would the unions be in a position to challenge this or not?

The above discussion also provides answers to our third question (what are the differences among the countries under study?). The differences among the countries studied are huge, and are mainly determined by the existing institutional differences and the role of domestic actors. Although public-sector reforms are taking place in all countries, the contents of these reforms and their impacts on public-sector industrial relations differ widely. In other words, there is absolutely no sign of full convergence taking place. Our analysis confirms, in this respect, the conclusions of Bach, Bordogna, Della Rocca and Winchester (1999) and Bordogna (2003). To cite Bordogna (2003, p. 63):

> . . . differences between public and private sector employment practices and regulations within countries have been fading away in many (but not all) cases under cost-efficiency and quality-enhancement pressures, those across countries have been more resistant to change, deeply rooted as they are in country-specific legal and institutional traditions, which are less easily modifiable in the public than in the private sector.

The latter part of this conclusion is particularly relevant to the main theme of this book: it appears that the public sector is even more resistant to convergence than the private sector.

Bordogna relates these differences to legal and institutional traditions, which is also illustrated by our country chapters. The three distinct Europeanization mechanisms, as described by Knill and Lehmkuhl (2002), provide a more elaborate interpretation of this lack of convergence. In the first place, Europeanization by institutional compliance is, with respect to public sector reform (and also its potential effect on public-sector industrial relations), almost nonexistent. Although some EU directives – especially those that have led directly or indirectly to privatizations such as of postal and railway services – have directly addressed public institutions, the EU rarely addresses directly the legal and institutional structures of the public sector. The same appears to be true for the second mechanism distinguished – Europeanization by changing domestic opportunity structures – in terms of the impact on industrial relations. It appears that only the third mechanism distinguished – Europeanization by framing domestic beliefs – plays a significant role in terms of public-sector industrial relations reform. This is illustrated by the fact that the ideology behind the NPM reforms fits nicely with the neo-liberal ideology that is currently propelling the European integration process (not dissimilar to the UK in the Thatcher period discussed earlier). At the same time, however, domestic public actors have considerable freedom with respect to the implementation of these ideas. Mériaux' analysis of the situation in France fits well with this interpretation: reform of the public sector in France seems almost impossible not so much because of 'structural' elements within the French system but as a consequence of the perceptions and actions of relevant actors.

In other words, the divergence in public-sector industrial relations can at least partly be explained by the rather limited impact of Europeanization mechanisms on the public sector actors in the various countries. The outcome in individual countries is further shaped by the importance attached to the role of the domestic actors and their position in the power structure.

This brings us to the fourth question: what will these developments mean for the future of public-sector industrial relations, and will there be a convergence in the actual industrial relations systems of the various countries and between the public and private sectors? The preceding discussion has already given a partial answer to this question. Some convergence between the public and private sectors has certainly taken place – indeed in some countries the special status granted to public-sector employees has been weakened (Italy, the Netherlands). It is not clear, however, how far this process will progress. It is not even certain that all countries will move in the same direction. Currently, institutional differences appear to be obstructing further convergence among European countries. The fact that employment in the public sector in most countries is relatively free from market pressures and, as shown above, less prone to Europeanization mechanisms will probably contribute to this diversity remaining. 'Europe' will probably be the key in determining what will happen in the future. A strong process of European integration will influence public-sector employment and employment relations in the various countries since this will encourage Europeanization by institutional compliance, which is likely to give an impetus to further convergence of public-sector industrial relations. If, however, the European integration process comes to a standstill – thereby leaving 'Europeanization by framing domestic beliefs' as the only mechanism to promote further convergence – the current diversity found in public-sector industrial relations will undoubtedly continue for a long time to come.

OUTLOOK

The chapters contained in this book illustrate the diversity within the European Member States and the differential effects of the process of Europeanization on various Member States. While accepting that this is not a systematic comparative study, it is nevertheless evident that there is no uniform pattern of effects, not even within the group of old Member States on the one hand, or within the new Member States on the other. It is the recognition of this diversity that has prompted many concerns about the European social model (such as by Scharpf 2002; Vaughan-Whitehead 2003) and, indeed, recent events confirm the basis of such concerns about the sustainability of welfare state regimes.

In an early stage of the debate on the diversity among Member States, Scharpf (2002) perceived the differences among Member States not just as differences in economic development, but rather as an expression of differences in normative orientation and institutional structures. Thus, the point was made that it is very difficult to conceive of social standards that would be both substantively meaningful and economically viable throughout the EU and, moreover, that the very idea of social standards is contested because there are different normative assumptions regarding the state and concerning both collective and private responsibilities for providing social protection. The significance of these differences is related to what Scharpf labels 'constitutional asymmetry': the existence of European legislation on economic integration that constrains Member States' economic policies versus the absence of any equivalent legislation on social policies, as a consequence of which national diversities inevitably impede the adoption of European social policies.

This is the main argument that Scharpf (2002) uses in making a case for framework directives, with substantially differing directives for distinct groups of Member States. Subsidiarity, which has been the basis of European legislation for about a decade, would then be supplemented with an Open Method of Co-ordination approach for implementing such directives (see also the chapter by Vos in this book). One example of how this type of approach would work is that those Member States that share a similar system of pensions would be required to devise their own national action plans (thus giving due recognition to economic and political differences among Member States) that would ensure that their pension systems remain sustainable in the face of demographic trends (the common European policy goal) and learn from each other's policies. From the perspective of European governance this implies not only a potential improvement in the implementation of legislation – because there is less need for European-level comprehensive legislation – but also offers encouragement for policy learning and for serious policy commitments – at least between those Member States that share similarities in their pension systems.

This coincides with the view of European integration advanced by Rifkin (2004, p. 282) as a process which is not merely about the opening of borders, but rather about a regionalization of politics through establishing networks built upon nation states and aiming to accommodate national identities and the multiple identities of the post-modern persona within the forces of globalization.

Scharpf's analysis certainly deserves serious consideration, and the contributions to this book demonstrate that the social dimension needs to be supplemented by institutional arrangements that provide voice mechanisms for national industrial relations actors. More specifically, the 'articulation gap' (Marginson 2006) that presently exists because of the absence of sectoral-level bargaining institutions in the new Member States disempowers trade unions in many of the former CEE Member States such as Hungary (see Neumann's contribution). The relative powerlessness of the, at best, fragmented trade unions, and the absence of strong institutions in most CEE Member States, adds to the vulnerability of employees whose social protection is hardly enhanced by the implementation of labour legislation. Supplementing framework directives with institutional conditions that provide platforms for voice is also a recognition of the theoretical point made by Knill and Lehmkuhl (2002) that domestic actors at the national level will make use of their powers and resources to push through regulatory changes that are in their own interests.

While the creation of institutional conditions that enable voices to be heard does not remove the differences in power and normative orientations between domestic actors, there would be at least a platform for voices that might possibly impact on national policies. Another basic element of the European Social Model is the representation of collective interests by trade unions. A trade union, as an actor, may have a voice in not only addressing the employment conditions of employees, but also in addressing their further goals such as participation and power sharing. As national actors they continue to have a role in Europeanization. It is therefore worth looking again here at their playing fields and their perceptions of the opportunities and threats offered by European integration.

Trade unions have various options and may display various discourses. European integration and enlargement are taking place under conditions of strong global competition. The relationships between European integration, globalization, liberalization and the sovereignty of national actors are however, not all one-way. As van der Maas shows in his analysis, the positions of trade unions may differ markedly depending on the structural effects expected from European integration in the sectors where they have their members. If integration is predominantly viewed as part of an attempt to liberalize markets then it is perceived to have negative effects on employment conditions and therefore the trade unions can be expected to be hostile. If, on the other hand, integration amounts to the building of a Social Europe – with an emphasis on social protection and participation – then this would lead to better protection against global competition and the trade unions would therefore be in favour. Indeed, as Stuart and Martinez Lucio show, industrial relations have received an impetus from the various pieces of European legislation on information exchange and consultation involving employees – first at the level of the MNC and more recently also at the level of companies operating within a single Member State.

The debate in the UK reflects also the more structural differences in normative orientations and institutional structures (Scharpf 2002). The UK Labour government formed by a party with whom trade unions have traditionally been directly connected, has on many issues adopted a stance that is opposed to the position of, for example, the political left in France. Nevertheless, as mentioned earlier, the Labour government signed up to the Social Protocol of the Maastricht Treaty as soon as they came to power in 1997. This mixed position is probably also representative of the prevailing political stance in the UK with regard to European integration. On the one hand, the development of the social dimension is generally welcomed as it implies an improvement in certain employment conditions such as a minimum wage and social protection. Employment security, on the other hand, is not very high on the political agenda of the main political actors and here the Social Protocol may be viewed as too protective. A preference for voluntary relationships is still part of the national outlook as was particularly reflected in the position adopted by the Labour government with regard to the proposed directive on working hours. The provision to consult trade unions or employee representatives before agreeing a tailor-made arrangement between an employer and an employee was viewed as giving too much importance to collective employment agreements. Rather, in the view of the British government, individual employees should be free to come to an agreement outside the standardized regulations.

How enlargement may lead to new alliances within Europe is especially reflected in the political coalitions being forged between the UK government and the governments of various new Member States. A telling example is the Services Directive, which is now in its final preparatory stages, and which impacts on various, sometimes conflicting, national interests within the expanded Europe. The largest fear of what might happen when services can be delivered across borders is that domestic levels of employment conditions and wage levels will be undercut. When employment conditions can be in accordance with the employment conditions in the country of origin, i.e. from where the services are provided, this could endanger the level of employment conditions in the country where the services are delivered. Fear of the 'Polish plumber' has been driving the strong opposition to this Directive. In March 2006, the European Parliament adopted a number of revisions to the draft, including stipulating that the health and safety provisions of the host country should be observed. Also, some sectors are exempted from the obligation to accept the free delivery of services across Europe, including healthcare, temporary jobs agencies and child nurseries. The first version of the Directive, as proposed by former Commissioner Bolkestein, led to massive protests and demonstrations. The current version of the Directive – after revision by the European Parliament and the European Commission – will be the basis for the provision of services across borders within Europe and will outlaw the use of various kinds of permits to restrict free trade. The varying positions adopted in reviewing this revised Directive illustrate the various expectations of the effects of freeing up services on employment conditions. Germany and France were most strongly opposed, whereas the UK was rather sceptical about the limited reach of the directive. The more neo-liberal views that prevail in the UK emphasized the Directive's ability to increase economic activity with regard to the provision of services – whereas some of the continental countries tend to see competition as negatively impacting on the existing employment conditions. The outcome to this testing of the direction of the European Social Model depends on the actions of those involved with policymaking.

As becomes clear from this and other examples, the prevailing expectations within the various Member States are not only divided along political lines, but are also influenced by national orientations that are often deeply rooted in traditions of governance and the regulation regimes concerning employment. What is also clear is that an examination of the positions of the various national actors is now even more relevant since the European integration project is increasingly determined by multilevel policymaking than by uniform policies forcefully implemented through supranational bodies. Diversity was not only the reason for starting the European project; it is also the material that has to be built upon. Identities will become multi-layered rather than national identities being replaced by a supranational identity.

ENLARGEMENT, INTEGRATION AND REFORM

The title of this book refers to the New Europe as one that encompasses enlargement, integration and reform. Reform takes place within the national Member States, as the answer to intrinsic problems and in response to EMU and market pressures. Here we dealt specifically with public sector reform. Changes in the public sector are closely related to changes in the role of the welfare state and budget reforms. Actors within the national systems of industrial relations are confronted with attempts to increase flexibility, to reform social security and to privatize and liberalize markets. This striving takes place under the constellation of a globalizing economy and under the pressure created by severe internal problems within Europe. These include the welfare state being under serious pressure due to profound demographic changes and a high level of unemployment in many EU Member States. Furthermore, the voting down of the European Constitution by the French and the Dutch is generally viewed as reflecting a growing reluctance among citizens to accept a strong Europe and, especially, any further enlargement.

The debate on the social dimension of the European Union has been fuelled by the fear of social dumping in the old Member States and the migration of workers from Eastern to Western Europe. Labour mobility within the EU is another issue like the Services Directive that reflects considerable differences among countries in terms of normative orientations. The Polish plumber became the symbol of the resistance, particularly in France, to the Services Directive, whereas other, and not only the former CEE, countries showed strong support. The same applies to the opening up of the labour market for employees from the new EU Member States. While countries like Germany and Austria continue to keep their borders closed to immigrating employees from these Member States, others, like the

Netherlands, are partially beginning to open their borders, and the UK and Ireland did so right from the moment of enlargement in 2004. Trade unions and the government in the Netherlands are seeking, in an attempt to prevent current levels of employment conditions from falling, to maintain current wage levels, and to compel employers of immigrating workers to pay them the same rate. However, despite these ongoing concerns, a recent report by the European Commission shows that the effects of immigration have been limited, and in many cases largely positive for the respective economies. First of all, mobility has been not as high as was predicted. Secondly, countries that did not apply restrictions after May 2004 (UK, Ireland and Sweden) have experienced good economic growth, a fall in unemployment and a rise in employment. Some undesirable side effects have been found in some countries, such as higher levels of undeclared work and bogus self-employed status (Directorate Employment, Social Affairs and Equal Opportunities 2006).

Enlargement of Europe has clearly added to the diversity within Europe through the use of various forms of flexibility. Within Europe there was already a general divide between northern and southern Member States when looking at the types of flexibility employed, and this also impacted on the level of employment conditions. Whereas part-time employment may contribute to improved opportunities to combine paid work with leisure and care of others, temporary contracts often lead to uncertainty. Part-time work is more common in the northern Member States (Communal and Brewster 2004). Current developments with the enlargement into Eastern Europe show that employment patterns now vary even more across Europe. As Vaughan-Whitehead shows, many forms of flexibility are used, some of which may already have existed under the *ancienne regime* such as moonlighting under the old communist regime in Hungary. Following the transition towards a market economy, and with accession to the European Union, flexibility has increased in some of the new Member States. Some of the forms of flexibility now found contrast strongly with the old communist ways of a heavily protected labour market with low efficiency and hidden unemployment. Self-employment, moonlighting and multiple contracts are widespread in many CEE Member States. Most of these forms of flexibility pose a threat to social protection, and the resulting low wages encourage employees to take on more than one job or to work excessive overtime in order to receive an adequate income. In terms of long-term development, a choice may already have been made in favour of a neo-liberal policy as Vaughan-Whitehead concludes.

As recent developments in the 'old Europe', and especially in France, show, citizens are reluctant to accept an increase in labour market flexibility. The 2006 protests in France against the law concerning First Employment Contracts (known as the *CPE* in France) were the largest seen since 1968.

The new law, the French government claimed, would help to bring down the high level of youth employment by allowing the employer of a young newly-recruited employee to terminate the contract within two years, virtually without needing to give any reason. Although the government was initially unwilling to revise the law, it eventually gave in, encouraged by President Chirac, after pressure from street demonstrations in all the large cities in France and political pressure from trade unions. According to its own statement, the government with this new law was only aiming to prevent youngsters from, as they perceived it, becoming the victims of global pressure. With the policy, they aimed to achieve adaptability and flexibility in the employment system as a means of realizing an adaptive labour market.

From the above it seems clear that the debate on a social Europe has been considerably influenced by the enlargement of the European Union. Some of the chapters in this book show that diversity has increased – with regard to institutions and social standards and also with respect to labour market structures and performance. Vaughan-Whitehead points to the fact that the differences between the 'old' and the 'new' Europe have also impacted on debates on European integration itself. His chapter in this book can also be read as a statement – or a warning – about the future development of the labour market and the future of social Europe. Flexibility in the labour markets of Eastern European Member States initially reflected the transition stage of the economies in these countries. However, it remains to be seen if the current state of the labour market reflects a period of transition or if this will become a more structural model for many Eastern European countries. Furthermore, within the setting of the common market, and with the current drawing back of the process of European integration, this could also become a model for greater labour market flexibility in other European countries.

As was illustrated with the example of the proposed legislation on flexible contracting of youngsters in France, employers and governments in several European Member States are attempting to introduce greater flexibility into the workplace. There is, however, also evidence that those elements of the European social model that could help to overcome the current problems of unregulated, flexible labour markets in some countries should be preserved. Instruments that have proven their use, such as the introduction of a minimum wage – introduced in the UK less than a decade ago – could further help to prevent employees becoming socially excluded. Also, the introduction and wider use of collective contracts could help to establish and enforce a minimum level of employment conditions. This type of harmonization would also increase the quality of employment relations and stimulate a strategy of 'high road' development. Elements of the European social model, such as the participation of employees in decision-making within organizations and specific employer responsibilities towards their employees, are also needed as a further step in reforming European industrial relations.

The social dimension of Europe is, as has been emphasized in this analysis, partly dependent on the power relationships between national actors and the resources at their disposal. Europeanization is naturally also determined by the ongoing process of 'top-down European integration'. The current phase of European integration is characterized by various – to an extent contradictory – dynamics. The voting down of the European Constitution by the French and the Dutch electorates has been seen as signalling distrust in any further European integration. In France, the extensive protests against the Services Directive indicated also the strong concerns about regime competition and the threat to social security systems as potential outcomes of further liberalization. Conversely, other countries, and especially the UK and some from East Europe, have formed occasional coalitions to express their major concerns about European markets being overprotective, such that they impede further economic progress and increased prosperity. This is in support of the neo-liberal standpoint that heavily promotes the liberalization of markets and the privatization of services.

The process of European integration is ultimately dependent on these national preferences and decisions made among national actors at the European level. This leaves us with the question as to what this process has achieved in terms of social standards and employment conditions since the 1990s. As Vos shows in his chapter, the social dimension of European integration has gradually received greater recognition – not only as the outcome of economic progress and the resulting upgrading of social standards, but also as a preconditon for further European integration. This notion can be traced back through many of the policy documents issued by EU institutions. The Social Affairs Commissioner set this out in a report on desirable industrial relations published in 2000: 'respect for fundamental social rights in a frontier-free Europe; workers' rights to information and consultation on company operations; social dialogue as a mainstay of good governance and a means of involving citizens in the European venture' (cited in Sisson 2004). However, when looking at the type of regulations that have been developed at the European level, a marked change can be detected from 'hard' to 'soft' regulations. Open coordination methods are now applied such as, to use the terms of Knill and Lehmkuhl (2002), framing beliefs of domestic actors and, at best, changing domestic opportunity structures. Institutional compliance has become less relevant in the Europeanization of social policy.

The most ambitious part of European social policy has probably been the Lisbon Agenda, which reflected the changes in European policy towards integrating economic and employment policy aims. The agenda was agreed at the summit in Lisbon in 2000, while Portugal was holding the Presidency of the European Union. The most ambitious aim agreed at this summit was that the European Union would develop the most competitive economy in the world. This agenda would lead Europe towards a more inclusive and highly knowledge-intensive economy. The targets that were formulated under this overarching goal relate to labour market criteria, such as the proportion of the population in employment (70 per cent overall, including 60 per cent of women and 50 per cent of elderly people). The most innovative aspect of this policy is that the labour market and employment are perceived as competitive forces with the potential to lead to an increase in economic performance.

After six years it has, however, become clear that the overall aim was too ambitious and the heads of governments have decided to abandon this goal. This leaves the agenda rather open ended, and domestic actors are relied upon more than ever before. The lesson that should be learnt from this is perhaps that the Lisbon agenda presumed greater homogeneity and stability in the European labour market and in employment conditions than exists in reality. Looking to the future of European industrial relations, there is clear evidence supporting the development of a strong social dimension on the basis of diversity in national institutions and national orientations. The most relevant examples in this aspect of Europeanization are the experiences gained with EWCs and in developments within national information and consultation processes. As argued earlier, national subsidiairity and multilevelled policymaking are not intrinsically linked with laissez faire approaches. On the contrary, Europe could be a strong case for the development of networked policies (Rifkin 2004), and the first step towards this could be networking among economies with similar problems. This could lead to industrial relations actors learning about various policy solutions which could then be transferred among these countries (Scharpf 2002). Such an approach would likely further reinforce the processes of hybridizing industrial and employment relations across Europe, hybridization being the outcome of mutual interactions between persistent national institutions and orientations – within and between old EU Member States, old new Member States and new new Member States – and the confrontation of these with a slow but apparently continuing process of further European integration.

REFERENCES

Bach, S., L. Bordogna, G. Della Rocca and D. Winchester (eds) (1999), *Public service Employment Relations in Europe: Transformation, Modernization or Inertia?*, London and New York: Routledge.

Bordogna, L. (2003), 'The Reform of Public Sector Employment Relations in Industrialized Democracies', in J. Brock and D.B. Lipsky (eds), *Going Public: The Role of Labor-Management Relations in Delivering Quality Government Services*, Industrial Relations Research Association: University of Illinois, pp. 23-67.

Boyne, G., M. Poole and G. Jenkins (1999), 'Human Resource Management in the Public and Private Sectors: An Empirical Comparison', *Public Administration*, **77** (2), 407-420.

Communal, C. and C. Brewster (2004), 'HRM in Europe', in A.W. Harzing and J. van Ruysseveldt (eds), *International Human Resource Management*, London: Sage, second edition, pp. 167-194.

Dimitrova, D. (2004), 'Building Social Dialogue for Decent Work in Central and Eastern Europe', Paper presented at the IREC 2004 Conference, Utrecht: Utrecht School of Governance.

Directorate Employment, Social Affairs and Equal Opportunities (2006), 'Free movement of workers since the 2004 enlargement had a positive impact', http://europe.eu.int/comm/employment_social/emplweb/news/news_en.cfm?id=11 9, accessed on 1 May 2006.

European Journal of Industrial Relations (2005) – special issue, Peter Leisink (ed.) *Governance and European Industrial Relations*, **11** (3), November.

Knill, C. and D. Lehmkuhl (2002), 'The national impact of European Union regulatory policy: Three Europeanization mechanisms', *European Journal of Political Research*, 41, 255-280.

Leisink, P. (ed.) (1999), *Globalization and Labour Relations*, Cheltenham, UK and Northampton, MA, USA: Edward Elgar.

Leisink, P. and B. Steijn (2005), 'Public management reform and staff participation: the case of civil service modernisation in the Netherlands', in D. Farnham, S. Horton and A. van Hondeghem (eds), *Staff Participation and Management Reform: some international comparisons*, Palgrave: Houndmills, pp. 199-213.

Marginson, P. (2004), 'The Eurocompany and European works councils', in A.W Harzing and J. van Ruysseveldt (eds), *International Human Resource Management*, London: Sage, second edition, pp. 457-481.

Marginson, P. (2006), 'Between Europeanization and Regime Competition: Labour market regulation following EU enlargement', Warwick Papers in Industrial relations, 79, Coventry: IRRU.

OECD (2005), *Modernising Government: The way forward*, Paris: OECD.

Rifkin, J. (2004), *The European Dream: How Europe's vision of the Future is Quietly Eclipsing the American Dream*, Cambridge: Polity Press.

Scharpf, F. (2002), 'The European Social Model: Coping with the challenges of diversity', *Journal of Common Market Studies*, **40**, 645-670.

Sisson, K. (2004), 'Industrial relations in Europe: a multi-level system in the making?', in A.W Harzing and J. van Ruysseveldt (eds), *International Human Resource Management*, London: Sage, second edition, pp. 433-456.

Vaughan-Whitehead, D. (2003), *EU Enlargement versus Social Europe? The uncertain future of the European Social Model*, Cheltenham, UK and Northampton, MA, USA: Edward Elgar.

Veersma, U. (2002), 'The European Works Council: a Management Tool or a Carrier of Workers' Interests?, *International Employment Relations Review*, **2** (2), 1-16.
Woolfson, C. and J. Somers (2006), 'Labour Mobility in Construction: European Implications of the Laval un Partneri dispute with Swedish Labour', *European Journal of Industrial Relations*, **12** (1), 49-68.

Index